LINCOLN'S PREPARATION FOR GREATNESS

LINCOLN'S PREPARATION FOR GREATNESS

The Illinois Legislative Years

Paul Simon

UNIVERSITY OF ILLINOIS PRESS

URBANA AND CHICAGO

To my parents
who first told me about Lincoln
and
to my wife
whom I met when both of us served
in the Illinois House of Representatives
Lincoln's alma mater

Illini Books edition, 1971

© 1965 by the University of Oklahoma Press
Reprinted by permission of the University of Oklahoma Press
Manufactured in the United States of America
P 5 4 3 2

This book is printed on acid-free paper.

Library of Congress Cataloging-in-Publication Data

Simon, Paul, 1928-
    Lincoln's preparation for greatness : the Illinois legislative
years / Paul Simon.
        p.   cm.
    Includes index.
    ISBN 0-252-00203-2 (alk. paper)
    1. Lincoln, Abraham, 1809-1865—Political career before 1861.
2. Presidents—United States—Biography. 3. Illinois—Politics and
government—to 1865.   I. Title.
E457.35.S57   1989
327.773'092—dc20
[B]
                                                        89-4881
                                                           CIP

Digitally reprinted from the second paperback printing

Contents

Preface

THIS IS the story of Abraham Lincoln's service in his first elective office, the public office he held longer than any other.

I first became interested in the subject when I was elected to the Illinois House of Representatives in 1954. I went to the state library and asked for a book on Lincoln's four terms in the same Illinois House. They told me none existed. "Incredible," I thought. More than five thousand books about Lincoln, and none written in depth about this important phase. We have books about how the weather was decisive in Lincoln's life, one about messages Lincoln is said to have communicated from the grave about the United Nations and other current issues, and at least three alleging that the death of Lincoln was a Roman Catholic plot! With absurd material like that actually published, should not someone be willing to write the story of his first elective office?

Encouraging me were statements like the one in the William Barton biography published in 1925: "It is rather remarkable that we have so little information concerning Lincoln's activities as a member of the Legislature."[1] In 1936 the eminent biographer James G. Randall addressed the nation's historians on the question, "Has the Lincoln Theme Been Exhausted?"[2] He maintained that

[1] William Barton, *Life of Abraham Lincoln* (Indianapolis, Bobbs-Merrill, 1925), 206.
[2] James G. Randall, "Has the Lincoln Theme Been Exhausted?" *American Historical Review*, January, 1936.

the legislative years of Lincoln need study; surprisingly, no one followed through.

Because there has been so little study, not only is there a lack of information, but much of the published material in otherwise reliable sources is myth rather than fact. Chapter 4 deals with the greatest myth, and if any chapter is controversial, it is this one. If it is attacked, I shall remember Ida Tarbell's words: "A biographer who tries to break down a belittling legend meets with far less sympathy than he who strengthens or creates one."[3]

I owe a great deal to many who have assisted me—too many to acknowledge here. But a few should be mentioned.

Encouraging me at the start were Clyde Walton, then Illinois historian, and the distinguished Lincoln scholar, the late Mrs. Harry (Marion) Pratt.

At the Illinois State Historical Library, most helpful were Miss Margaret A. Flint, James Hickey, S. Ambrose Weatherbee, Mrs. Joyce Horney, James N. Adams, and Bernard Wax. At the Huntington Library in California, Allan Nevins, loaded with literary prizes and work, took time to encourage an amateur historian. At the Library of Congress, David Mearns and C. Percy Powell were particularly helpful. At the Chicago Historical Society, Paul M. Angle, who has contributed much to the world's knowledge of Lincoln, and Archie Motley were of assistance. At the Lincoln Library in Fort Wayne, Indiana, scholars Louis Warren and R. Gerald McMurty gave aid. At the Newberry Library in Chicago, Lawrence Towner was helpful. The staff of the Colby College Library, Waterville, Maine, helped with material for the Lovejoy chapter. I am indebted to the Missouri State Historical Society Library, the St. Louis Mercantile Library, the University of Chicago Library and over the state of Illinois to many librarians and historical societies who provided pieces of information embodied in the final product.

Others who have been generous to me have been Ralph G. Newman, the late John Allen, Theodore Cassady, Miss Mary Burtschi, Mrs. Gwen Grigsby, John Krenkel, and Senator Paul Douglas.

---

[3] Ida Tarbell, quoted by Benjamin Thomas, *Portrait for Posterity* (New Brunswick, N. J., Rutgers University Press, 1947), 193.

Willard King helped by showing that an amateur historian can produce a piece of solid scholarship as he did in *Lincoln's Manager David Davis* and by taking time from a busy schedule both to encourage and to give invaluable editorial help.

Also helpful in editorial work were Rev. Paul G. Birkmann and my father. My mother typed some of the final copy. My secretary, Mrs. Arno Ellis, a Mississippian by birth, has been patient with both Paul Simon and Abraham Lincoln for many years. Finally, my wife Jeanne has been helpful, encouraging, and patient. That last sentence sounds trite to the non-writer, but any married author knows its truth.

I have tried to do a thorough, scholarly piece of work that can be helpful to future Lincoln biographers, in addition to being of interest to Lincoln readers.

Ten years elapsed between my first inquiry and the completion of the manuscript. The University of Oklahoma Press published the original hard-cover edition, now sold out. When approached by the University of Illinois Press about a reprint edition, I was pleased at their interest and felt it appropriate that the book should be reissued in the Land of Lincoln.

When my daughter Sheila was two and a half years old, she was asked what her father does. She replied, "He works on Abraham Lincoln." Perhaps the opposite is more nearly true. Abraham Lincoln has worked on me—as I hope he always will on men everywhere.

PAUL SIMON

Troy, Illinois
February 12, 1971

LINCOLN'S PREPARATION FOR GREATNESS

Abbreviations

To avoid excessive repetition, the following abbreviations have been used in annotations:

CW *The Collected Works of Abraham Lincoln*, ed. by Roy P. Basler (New Brunswick, N. J., Rutgers University Press, 1953)

HJ *House Journal*

IHL Illinois State Historical Library

ISHSJ *Illinois State Historical Society Journal*

ISR *Illinois State Register*

LIll *Laws of Illinois*

RTL Robert Todd Lincoln Collection, Library of Congress

SgJ *Sangamo Journal*

1

Lincoln Loses But Learns

Every man is said to have his peculiar ambition. Whether it be true or not, I can say for one that I have no other so great as that of being truly esteemed by my fellow men, by rendering myself worthy of their esteem. How far I shall succeed in gratifying this ambition, is yet to be developed. I am young and unknown to many of you. I was born and have ever remained in the most humble walks of life. I have no wealthy or popular relations to recommend me. My case is thrown exclusively upon the independent voters of this county, and if elected they will have conferred a favor upon me, for which I shall be unremitting in my labors to compensate. But if the good people in their wisdom shall see fit to keep me in the background, I have been too familiar with disappointments to be very much chagrined.—A. Lincoln in *Sangamo Journal*, March 15, 1832.

WITH THESE WORDS a historic political career began. The above announcement of his candidacy for the office of representative in the Illinois General Assembly was signed simply "A. Lincoln."

This most recent addition to the growing list of candidates for the House of Representatives had just turned twenty-three. He was ambitious but not sure what he wanted to do for a living. Perhaps he would be a businessman. He considered becoming a blacksmith; anyone in that profession had steady work and was respected in his community. Certainly nobody would have guessed that he would ever rise to anything higher. A fifteen-year-old boy

3

saw him and later recalled: "He had on a ragged coat, an old drooping hat, and a pair of tattered jean pants, the half of one leg which was then off . . . a coarse pair of gaping shoes. . . . I do not believe the tailor ever lived who was skillful enough to make clothes fit Lincoln. He was the roughest and most irregular man in outline I ever saw. But no child was afraid of him and no woman would declare him to be ugly. Yet any description of his appearance you would write down would warrant the conclusion that he was anything but good looking. . . . The very skin of the man did not fit, for it appeared to be loose on his features."[1]

What made this young man want to run for office?

During his youth in Indiana, he had shown interest in reading newspapers and had at least a casual interest in politics. To the Thomas Lincoln home when Abe was a boy, some believe, "all the local politicians used to come . . . to discuss politics" with Lincoln's father.[2] Thomas Lincoln had Whig, or Clay, leanings. But there is nothing to indicate that Abe then had "set his hat" on a political career. At the little village of New Salem, his outlook broadened; here he had the opportunity to work his way by boat to New Orleans and back and to learn of the outside world. More important, in New Salem he met at least three men who influenced his career.

One was Bowling Green, justice of the peace for the area. A short man of about 250 or 300 pounds, he had a protruding stomach that earned him the nickname "Pot." Genial and fun-loving, Green liked the humor of Lincoln. The two became close friends. Green's court was not a model for judicial procedure, but Lincoln learned some law from Green, who had come by much of his legal lore by being tried himself (several times for being drunk and disorderly). A canal commissioner for the state, he had an interest in what was called "internal improvements." Lincoln's early years were marked by considerable financial difficulty, and Green may have suggested running for the state legislature as a

[1] Rufus Rockwell Wilson, *Lincoln Among His Friends* (Caldwell, Caxton Printers, 1942), 60–61, quoting Philip Clark.

[2] Louis A. Warren, "Lincoln's Early Political Backgrounds," *Illinois State Historical Society Journal* (hereafter cited as *ISHSJ*), January, 1931.

good way out. "Mr. Lincoln used to say that he owed more to Mr. Green for his advancement than to any other man," wrote a New Salem neighbor.[3] At Green's funeral, Lincoln acknowledged that Green had contributed much to him.

A second man who encouraged Lincoln in his political ambitions was Vermont-born Dr. John Allen, a graduate of Dartmouth. Allen had come to New Salem for reasons of health. "A thin cripple" with a clipped white beard, he suffered from consumption.[4] His intellectual gifts to the community were greater than his medical. Patients in that era were "purged, bled, blistered, puked, and salivated."[5] Dr. Allen brought many new ideas to the rugged little town. A strict Presbyterian, he started the first Sunday school in New Salem and formed the New Salem Debating Society, to which Lincoln belonged and which contributed much to his intellectual growth. A temperance man in a heavy-drinking town, Dr. Allen also brought with him New England antislavery ideas which did not appeal to the southern-born majority of New Salem's residents. Lincoln admired Dr. Allen and frequently visited with him. While there is no proof that the Doctor urged Lincoln to run for the state legislature, he at least helped prepare Lincoln for the decision and for the responsibilities of public office.

The third man who exerted an influence on Lincoln in New Salem was Mentor Graham, a thin-faced teacher. Six years older than Lincoln, Graham lived to be eighty-six and to see his New Salem fellow citizen achieve the highest office in the land.[6] Although Graham was not a good speller, he helped Lincoln with his English grammar, essay writing, and basic mathematics. Graham, somewhat talkative, encouraged Lincoln's reading habits. The New Salem teacher was "quite a dresser" and frequently wore fancy satin vests— very unusual in a small frontier village.[7] There was a warm feeling between the two, and Graham may have

[3] A. Y. Ellis to William Herndon, December 6, 1866, Library of Congress.

[4] Kunigunde Duncan and D. F. Nichols, *Mentor Graham, the Man Who Taught Lincoln* (Chicago, University of Chicago Press, 1944), 117.

[5] Benjamin F. Thomas, *Lincoln's New Salem* (New York, Knopf, 1954), 47.

[6] Hazel O. Bailey, "Mentor Graham, Lincoln's School Teacher," *Scholastic*, January 10, 1934.

[7] Edgar De Witt, "Education Pathfinders of Illinois," *ISHSJ*, April, 1931.

assisted Lincoln in writing the statement announcing his first candidacy for public office.

James Rutledge, president of the local debating club, is also reported to have encouraged Lincoln to run.

In the *Sangamo Journal* Lincoln announced his three-point platform: (1) An internal improvement system; (2) Control of interest rates; and (3) A system of education. His platform also had this almost indefinable fourth point:

With regard to existing laws, some alterations are thought to be necessary. Many respectable men have suggested that our estray laws—the law respecting the issuing of executions, the road law, and some others, are deficient in their present form, and require alterations. But considering the great probability that the framers of those laws were wiser than myself, I should prefer [not] meddling with them, unless they were first attacked by others, in which case I should feel it both a privilege and a duty to take that stand, which in my view, might tend most to the advancement of justice. ... Holding it a sound maxim, that it is better to be only sometimes right, than at all times wrong, so soon as I discover my opinions to be erroneous, I shall be ready to renounce them.[8]

It was somewhat natural for Lincoln to make "internal improvements" his first point and to dwell on it at length. On this subject he had firsthand knowledge, and he did not hesitate telling the voters about it.

From my peculiar circumstances, it is probable that for the last twelve months I have given as particular attention to the stage of the water in this river, as any other person in the country. In the month of March, 1831, in company with others, I commenced the building of a flat boat on the Sangamo, and finished and took her out in the course of the spring. Since that time, I have been concerned in the mill at New Salem. These circumstances are sufficient evidence, that I have not been very inattentive to the stages of the water. ... It appears that my calculation with regard to the navigation of the Sangamo, cannot be unfounded in reason. ... [The

[8] *The Collected Works of Abraham Lincoln*, ed. by Roy P. Basler (9 vols., New Brunswick, N. J., Rutgers University Press, 1953), I, 8. (Hereafter cited as *CW*.)

Sangamo] never can be practically useful to any great extent without being greatly improved.

Internal improvement projects had wide public support, particularly in Sangamon County. Only a few weeks before, area residents had learned that, for the first time, a steamboat was going to dock at Springfield. The *Sangamo Journal* editorialized: "We seriously believe that the Sangamo River, with some little improvement, can be made navigable for steamboats, for several months in the year."[9] The same issue told of Springfield citizens meeting "to take into consideration what means ought to be adopted to assist the arrival of Mr. Bogue with his steamboat opposite said town."

Nine days after Lincoln's announcement appeared, the steamboat *Talisman* arrived five miles north of Springfield. It was a big day for the people of this area. On the return trip Lincoln served part of the way as assistant pilot of the *Talisman*. Public jubilation over the appearance of the steamboat turned out to be premature. Although the *Talisman* was able to make it, the project was a complete loss financially. The man who had chartered the boat eventually disappeared, leaving behind a host of unpaid bills. But the *Sangamo Journal* continued to editorialize: "Springfield can no longer be considered an inland town. . . . It is to be hoped that the next legislature will afford some aid to making the river safe and pleasant in its navigation."[10]

Interest in internal improvements persisted. The same issue of the *Sangamo Journal* in which Lincoln's announcement of his candidacy appeared contained an "address of the Committee of St. Clair County to the people of Illinois" on internal improvements. Lincoln was not unaware of the power of the press, and the *Sangamo Journal* had as main platform "promoting a general system of Internal Improvements."[11] A reader of this newspaper probably expressed public sentiment when he wrote: "The important subject of Internal Improvement seems to absorb all others."[12]

Other Sangamon House candidates were just as strong for in-

9 February 16, 1832.   10 March 29, 1832.

11 November 10, 1831.   12 June 12, 1832.

ternal improvements. One noted that "there is no subject of more pervading interest."[13] If the Illinois farmers could sell their produce to the outside world—as they could with either rail or river transportation—this would mean a big rise in much-needed income. A new Illinois resident exaggerated to his New Hampshire mother: "Many a rich farmer lives in a house not half so good as your old hog's pen and not any larger."[14] Illinois citizens were clamoring for better transportation and a better standard of living.

The second point in Lincoln's platform, control of interest rates, also came from personal observation. He had seen a great deal of abuse. In 1831, Denton Offutt, for whom Lincoln worked in New Salem, borrowed $110 for sixty days and was forced to pay 60 per cent interest.[15] Interest rates of 15 to 20 per cent imposed on people of good reputation were common.

The third area in Lincoln's platform was education. Lincoln did not have the schooling he wanted, and he was somewhat sensitive about it. Lincoln went to school "by littles," as he said, and the total of these "littles" did not exceed one year. In his 1832 platform he said education is "the most important subject which we as a people can be engaged in. . . . I desire to see the time when education . . . shall become much more general than at present."

But an important event was to interrupt Lincoln's campaign.

The week before his announcement, a newspaper contained this item: "We have heard it stated, on what was deemed good authority, that 5 or 6,000 Sauk and Fox Indians, have recrossed the Mississippi and located themselves 30 miles above Rock Island, where they declare their determination to make corn the ensuing season. If this be true . . . a more summary process will be employed to rid our territory of these Indians than was used on former occasions."[16]

The Black Hawk War soon began. Lincoln was among those

[13] George Forquer, letter in *Sangamo Journal* (hereafter cited as *SgJ*), July 12, 1832.

[14] "Sketch of Charles James Fox Clarke with Letters to His Mother," *ISHSJ*, January, 1930.

[15] Harry E. Pratt, *The Personal Finances of Abraham Lincoln* (Springfield, Ill., Abraham Lincoln Association, 1943), 72.

[16] *SgJ*, March 8, 1832.

who served in it. He saw no actual combat and did not demonstrate military aptitude. The political importance of the Black Hawk War for Lincoln was that it brought him into contact with many of the men with whom he was to serve in the legislature in future years, including John T. Stuart of Springfield, a strikingly handsome Whig leader. Stuart encouraged Lincoln to continue his political interests and urged him to study law. Stuart was a cousin of Mary Todd, Lincoln's wife nine years later.

Before Lincoln's outfit disbanded, the men of his mess agreed to back his candidacy for the legislature. The vote total shows that their enthusiasm was diverted before the election took place. Nevertheless, their action indicates his growing popularity. One of the men later recalled that Lincoln "was acquainted with everybody."[17]

Lincoln was discharged after three months of service, two months as a private, one as a captain. He arrived in New Salem just two weeks before the election. He immediately started campaigning.

Elections at that time centered on men rather than parties. As one observer noted in later years:

> The contests in those days were of short duration, and were scarcely ever repeated on the same grounds or questions. There were no parties. . . . The contests were mostly personal, and for men. . . . There are those who are apt to believe that this mode of conducting elections is likely to result in the choice of the best materials for administering government. But experience did not prove the fact to be so.[18]

Lincoln's first known campaign speech was at a sale in Pappsville, a village eleven miles west of Springfield. Of this speech— and of others—there are reports by observers. These give verbatim accounts of what he said and tell how he interrupted his speech to stop a fight. Given many years later, these accounts may be largely the products of overactive imaginations.

[17] Paul Angle, ed., *Herndon's Life of Lincoln* (Cleveland and New York, World Publishing Co., 1949), 81, quoting William L. Wilson.
[18] Thomas Ford, *A History of Illinois* (Chicago, S. C. Griggs & Co., 1854), 55.

9

A reliable account does come from Stephen T. Logan, who became one of the outstanding lawyers of the state and Lincoln's partner for three and one-half years. It was the first time he had seen Lincoln. He described him as "a very tall and gawky and rough looking fellow then; his pantaloons didn't meet his shoes by six inches. But after he began speaking I became very much interested in him. He made a very sensible speech. It was the time when Benton was running his theory of a gold circulation. Lincoln was attacking Benton's theory and I thought did it very well. . . . The manner of Mr. Lincoln's speech then was very much the same as his speeches in after life. . . . I knew nothing then about his vocation or calling at New Salem. The impression that I had at the time was that he was a sort of loafer down there. . . . In the election of 1832 he made a very considerable impression upon me as well as upon other people."[19]

On August 6, 1832, the election was held, and Lincoln received 657 votes, running eighth in a field of thirteen. Four of the thirteen were elected, two being men who would figure prominently in his future—John T. Stuart and Peter Cartwright, the colorful Methodist minister who was his opponent for a seat in Congress fourteen years later.

In the New Salem precinct, Lincoln received 277 of the 300 votes cast—more votes than there were in the village of Chicago in the northern part of the state. Lincoln's New Salem support included both the rougher element, like the Clary Grove Boys, and the more serious-minded, like Dr. John Allen and Mentor Graham. Voting was by voice, the voter telling the judge and clerk which candidate he favored. This encouraged a strong vote for a "home town boy," since it was known for what candidates a person voted.

Voting on a partisan basis was discouraged by the holding of the election for state and local offices three months prior to the national election. Lincoln admired Clay, but he occasionally found himself defending the colorful and controversial Jackson. He had done nothing so far to alienate Jackson supporters. Dr. John Allen noted with pride that "in the New Salem precinct he [Lincoln]

[19] Thomas, *Lincoln's New Salem*, 86.

got one more vote than the Jackson and Adams candidates for Congress put together."[20]

Lincoln studied the election returns and noted that where he had campaigned he ran strong. It was a lesson he would not forget. He had tasted political life, and even though he had been defeated, he liked it. He would be a businessman, surveyor, and lawyer, but all these occupations would be secondary to his political activities. Years later Lincoln noted that this was "the only time I have been beaten by the people."[21]

The defeated candidate had to find a way of earning a living. The opportunity came quickly. He bought a half-interest in a store operated by R. Rowan Herndon and William P. Berry. It was the first of several unfortunate business ventures he made. He had purchased Herndon's half of the business. Berry, the son of a temperance-minded minister, was drinking. As Lincoln and Berry piled up their debts, Berry took to drinking more and more. In January, 1835, he died. Lincoln assumed the debts, approximately $1,100, a tremendous sum in those days—so large that Lincoln referred to it as the "national debt."[22]

His willingness to assume Berry's debts and to meet fully his own obligations is a tribute to his character. Thomas Lincoln had not given his son much in the way of an intellectually stimulating childhood, but he had trained him to be honest. Thomas Lincoln always had paid his debts, and his son followed that example.[23]

Lincoln's unhappy early experiences in finance made him more cautious in later years and helped him acquire a comfortable income. He learned by experience also in governmental matters. His early, irresponsible actions as a legislator would help in ruining the financial position of Illinois, but the lesson he learned proved helpful to him and the nation in later years.

Once the election was over, Lincoln began looking ahead to the next one. This is nowhere more evident than in the election on

[20] "Recollections of John Allen," Robert Todd Lincoln Collection, Library of Congress (hereafter cited as RTL).

[21] *CW*, III, 512.

[22] Pratt, *Personal Finances*, 12–15.

[23] *Ibid.*, 10; Bess V. Ehrmann, *The Missing Chapter in the Life of Abraham Lincoln* (Chicago, Walter M. Hill, 1938), 97.

September 20, 1832, in New Salem, in which four local men were seeking the post of constable. Lincoln served as one of the clerks at the election, but did not vote.[24] He did not want to offend any of his friends, all of whom had supported him in the election just six weeks earlier.

For the national election in November, he again served as clerk and cast his vote for Clay. Jackson carried both New Salem and Sangamon County.

Lincoln's appointment as postmaster of New Salem on May 8, 1833, helped his political development as well as his precarious financial situation. It was the first of two part-time appointments he received from the Democrats while he lived in New Salem.

Samuel Hill, the former postmaster, was unpopular, particularly with the women of the village, because he made them wait for their mail while he sold liquor and other goods.[25] He had other faults besides, and so residents circulated a petition in New Salem to take the job away from Hill and give it to Lincoln.

The mail came only twice a week, and then not much. But it gave Lincoln the opportunity to read the newspapers which came through the New Salem post office. These included two newspapers of substance: The *Louisville Journal*, which gave good coverage to national and regional affairs and liked Lincoln's favorite, Henry Clay, came regularly; the other, the *Intelligencer* from Washington, covered Congressional sessions thoroughly.

The post office job also gave Lincoln an opportunity to get better acquainted with more people in the area surrounding New Salem. The village itself had only twenty-five families—the high point in its population—and he frequently put letters in his hat, which covered his wiry black hair, and personally delivered the mail. It was a common sight around New Salem to see the long frame of Lincoln, supported by his large feet, walking through the countryside to take a letter for which he knew someone waited. In walking, he carried his head forward and inclined downward, and somehow this added to the melancholy which his New Salem neighbors

[24] Earl Schenck Miers, *Lincoln Day by Day* (2 vols., Washington, Lincoln Sesquicentennial Commission, 1960), I, 30.

[25] *Lincoln and New Salem* (Petersburg, Ill., Old Salem Lincoln League, 1918), 50.

sensed about the man. A strange combination of sadness and humor, they noted.

He supplemented his post office work with any odd jobs he could get—clerking in a store, splitting rails, husking corn, and helping with the wheat. A New Salem friend years later recalled: "He was the best hand at husking corn on the stalk I ever saw."[26] Almost everyone carried on agricultural work. A letter written in 1836 describes the agricultural situation: "Corn in a good season sells for 20 to 25 cents. The usual plan of the farmer is to feed his corn to fatten his hogs, which is better than selling it for 25 cents. . . . Wheat is often sown in the corn between the rows, which in my opinion is a very slovenly way, but it is very common. . . . Chickens are raised in abundance and sell for a dollar a dozen. . . . Butter is 8, 10, and 16 cents, according to its abundance. Through the summer it will command 8 cents and in the winter double this sum."[27] With better access to markets those prices would rise, Lincoln heard when he worked on farms.

In addition to visiting, Lincoln made it a practice to change his place of residence frequently, boarding with one family for a few weeks or months and then moving on to live with another. As a result, many families in the area had a feeling of closeness to the young postmaster. He almost became part of their large families.

His opportunity to improve his finances further came when he was appointed assistant to the county surveyor, John Calhoun (not to be confused with the U. S. senator of the same name). Lincoln stayed at the home of Mentor Graham for a few weeks to study mathematics and soon had his studies mastered sufficiently to do a competent job. Calhoun, a Democrat, later was to become a controversial figure on the national political scene, but his kindness Lincoln would never forget. Calhoun and Lincoln frequently talked politics, and Milton Hay, who studied law in Lincoln's office, credits Calhoun with being a major influence on Lincoln.[28] Lincoln was a good listener and Calhoun a well-informed talker.

[26] James Short, letter to William Herndon, July 7, 1865, Library of Congress.

[27] Richard H. Beach, "A Letter from Illinois Written in 1836," *ISHSJ*, October, 1910.

[28] Thomas, *Lincoln's New Salem*, 102.

Calhoun encouraged Lincoln to become a lawyer and gave Lincoln the opportunity to travel about the county and get acquainted with more people. This meant votes.

In New Salem, Lincoln was looked to more and more for leadership. His name appears frequently on legal papers and on petitions. When tragedy struck one of the residents, Lincoln wrote the following petition:

> To the County Commissioners Court for the County of Sangamon when met at their March term for the 1833:
> We the undersigned citizens of Sangamon County being personally acquainted with Benj. Elmore (who also is resident in said County—): and knowing him to be insane and wholly unable to earn a livelihood either by labor or any other employment—and to have no relatives who can be lawfully made chargeable for his maintenance; therefore we respectfully request that his case be taken into consideration by your honorable body—[29]

Not only did Lincoln draw up the petition, but he signed twenty-one of the twenty-six names on it. He also drew up a petition to the county commissioners "to view and locate a road from Musick's ferry on Salt Creek via New Salem to the county line in the direction of Jacksonville."[30] This subject was soon to concern him as a legislator.

On March 1, 1834, Lincoln served as secretary of a meeting chaired by Bowling Green and described as a "respectable meeting of the citizens of New Salem."[31] It called for the drafting of General James D. Henry as a candidate for governor. Henry, former sheriff of Sangamon County, was one of the heroes of the Black Hawk War. The draft movement was short-lived. General Henry—at that time in New Orleans—died four days after the New Salem meeting was held.

On March 8, 1834, the *Sangamo Journal* carried a notice that "John T. Stuart, Esq., is a candidate for the House of Representatives of this State." This notice started electioneering in Lincoln's first successful campaign.

[29] *CW*, I, 17–18.
[30] *Ibid.*, 21.
[31] *Ibid.*, 21–22.

2

Vandalia—A Fascinating New World

In 1776, the Indian war being about played out, this great good man was unanimously defeated as a candidate for the Legislature. His constituents loved him too much to let him leave them. To divert himself he set up a post-office in New Salem. Shortly after this, came the turning-point of his existence. He once more entered the political arena, was twice elected to the Legislature, fell into evil company, and became a lawyer! How many poor wretches, alas! have dated back their fall, and the triumph of the fiend over them to the time when they began to associate with bad company. —Portion of a humorous biographical sketch published in 1864 which Lincoln reportedly enjoyed.[1]

IF THE ANNOUNCEMENT of Stuart's candidacy did not hasten Lincoln's own announcement, a meeting about nine miles from New Salem held a few weeks later certainly did. At this meeting Lincoln's name was not placed among those favored for the legislative races. The meeting was held on April 5, and on April 19, Lincoln announced his candidacy in the *Sangamo Journal* in the same issue that carried the story of the Richland gathering.

In this campaign Lincoln issued no statement. His platform had gained him few votes, if any, in the previous campaign. He received votes where people knew him and where he made personal con-

---

[1] Carl Sandburg, *The Lincoln Collector* (New York, Harcourt, Brace, 1949), 39, quoting from "Only Authentic Life of Abraham Lincoln," published by *Comic Monthly* in 1864.

tacts. So this campaign became "more of a handshaking campaign."[2]

Another factor which may have influenced him not to issue a statement setting forth his views was that he was receiving support from both political parties, and he did not want to alienate either of them. Political parties were still not strong, but they were beginning to develop, and the Jackson supporters were dividing themselves into the "whole hog" Jackson people, who supported the cause fully, and the "milk and cider" Jackson adherents, who supporter him only part of the way. The Jackson supporters were increasingly referred to as Democrats; the Clay supporters and the other anti-Jackson partisans were more and more called Whigs. Lincoln by this time considered himself a Whig, but when he received an offer of support from the Democrats, he did not reject it.

The Democratic move was an attempt to defeat Stuart. The Democrats guessed—and correctly—that Stuart later would be running for Congress, and they wanted to beat him before he got that far. Shortly after the Democrats approached Lincoln, he attended a "shooting" at Clear Lake, just west of Springfield, to which all the candidates had been invited. People attending displayed their marksmanship, the best shot winning a beef—paid for by the candidates. When Lincoln saw Stuart, he told him about the offer he had received from the Democrats. Stuart told Lincoln to tell them that he would take their votes. Stuart later related: "I believe he did so. I and my friends, knowing their tactics, then concentrated our fight against one of their men—it was Quinton— and in this we beat Quinton and elected Lincoln and myself."[3] But Stuart ran last among the successful candidates, and Richard Quinton, the man he hoped to defeat, almost defeated him.

Talk that circulated about Lincoln helped him in the campaign. On the 1834 contest, one man commented: "I was a merchant in Springfield and had never seen him but had heard of his power upon the stump from the young men in that part of the county. They were proud of him and spoke of him in high terms."[4]

Lincoln continued to do surveying, he performed various odd

2 Angle, *Herndon's Lincoln*, 103.
3 Thomas, *Lincoln's New Salem*, 113–14.

jobs he could pick up, and he did a few things of a semi-legal nature for his friends in New Salem. While he was doing these jobs, he was campaigning and shaking hands. He would "cradle" wheat with a crew on his way to do a surveying job, and he would visit sales and barbecues and other gatherings of people.

During the election campaign, Stuart once again advised Lincoln to study law. After the election, Lincoln borrowed some books from Stuart and began to study for his new career. In what one writer describes as the battle of "Blacksmith vs. Blackstone," the law had won out.[5]

About a month before the election, Lincoln, as postmaster, wrote a letter to one of the influential residents of the New Salem area. The letter obviously was not written by a veteran officeseeker, but it cost few votes, if any. Lincoln wrote: "At your request I send you a receipt for the postage on your paper. I am somewhat surprised at your request. I will, however, comply with it. The law requires newspaper postage to be paid in advance, and now that I have waited a full year you choose to wound my feelings by insinuating that unless you get a receipt I will probably make you pay it again."[6] The receipt was enclosed.

On August 4, 1834, Lincoln won his first public office. Of the four candidates for state representative, Lincoln ran second, only fourteen votes behind the leader, John Dawson. Others elected to the Sangamon County House delegation were Stuart and William Carpenter. The votes ran: Dawson, 1,390; Lincoln, 1,376; Carpenter, 1,170; and Stuart, 1,164.

Dawson was Lincoln's senior by eighteen years and the father of ten children. A Whig, he had had one term of previous service in the legislature.

William Carpenter called himself a Democrat—but he was a Democrat whose party loyalty was so much in question that in 1836, when he tried to get the support of both parties, he ended with the support of neither.

---

[4] Notes of William Herndon from an interview with Joshua Speed, undated, Library of Congress.

[5] R. Gerald McMurty, "Centre College, John Todd Stuart and Abraham Lincoln," *Filson Club History Quarterly* (Louisville), April, 1959.

[6] *CW*, I, 25.

Lincoln voted for Joseph Duncan for governor, W. F. Elkin for state senator, and for Stuart, Carpenter, Dawson, and Neale for the House. At this time people considered it rude to vote for one-self. During Lincoln's service in the House, there actually was a contest for a House seat in which the loser contended, in the bill of particulars, that the victorious candidate had promised to vote for his opponent but had not done so.

Of those for whom Lincoln voted, all were elected except Elkin and Neale. Elkin, the father of fifteen children, was successful in the next election (1836) and became one of the Long Nine. But Lincoln did not waste his vote for Neale for the House. Thomas N. Neale, twice unsuccessful as a candidate for the legislature, succeeded Calhoun as the Sangamon County surveyor. A lawyer by background, Virginia-born Neale took note both of Lincoln's good work in surveying and of his vote and made Lincoln his assistant.

At the same election, voters were to state their preference for a new location for the state capital. New Salem cast 250 out of 256 votes for Springfield, but the state-wide voting gave first place to Alton, which received 8,157 votes; Vandalia, 7,730; Springfield, 7,035; Geographical Center, 790; Peoria, 423; and Jacksonville, 273. Hoping to defeat Alton and Vandalia, people in the northern areas obviously had concentrated their vote on Springfield, but without success. The law which called for the ballot read, "The place or point receiving the highest number of votes shall forever remain the seat of government for the State of Illinois." According to the law, Alton was entitled to be the capital, but those not favoring Alton held a majority both of the popular votes and in the legislature. "The vote was never canvassed, nor the matter referred to during either session of the Ninth Assembly."[7]

In late October, Lincoln again served as clerk for the Congressional election, as he had for nearly all elections while he lived in New Salem. He cast his vote for William L. May, who served two terms in Congress. May was a Democrat, and no particular attention seems to have been paid to Lincoln's voting for a Democrat. He had done this before and would do it again.

[7] Joseph C. Burtschi, *Documentary History of Vandalia, Ill.* (Vandalia Chamber of Commerce, 1954), 54–55.

May was a controversial candidate. One unsympathetic writer said of May, "A greater compound of meanness and stupidity was never mingled." He explained:

May was accused of having been guilty of burglary a few years since. This charge was published in a newspaper. He immediately wrote to some of his friends who were acquainted with the transaction, and published a reply from one of them, which stated that at the time of the trial, it was the general impression that he (May) did not enter the House in the night time with a design to commit murder, but for the sake of an illicit intercourse with some female there. This, Mr. May published as his defense, and called upon the people to overlook the follies of his youth![8]

Despite the increased work Lincoln had as surveyor, just nine days before he left for Vandalia and the legislative halls, the sheriff took his horse, saddle, bridle, and surveying instruments because of an unpaid bill totaling $211. James Short bought them back and returned them to Lincoln—a favor Lincoln remembered in later years when making federal appointments. He appointed Short, then in serious financial circumstances, to a position at a California Indian reservation at a salary of $1,800 a year.[9]

Less than a week before Lincoln was sworn in as a lawmaker in Vandalia, a group of Sangamon County citizens met to promote a common school system for the state. Lincoln, Stuart, Carpenter, and Dawson were among those present and were made delegates to a state-wide meeting on education to be held in Vandalia.

At six o'clock in the morning on a late November day, Lincoln and his three fellow House members from Sangamon boarded the stage at Springfield, rode through Macoupin County, and completed the seventy-five mile trip to Vandalia the next afternoon at four o'clock—a thirty-four-hour trip. It was November 29, 1834, when he arrived, a day Lincoln never forgot.

To Lincoln it opened a fascinating new world. Here he saw the best and worst of humanity—sometimes in the same person. Here he came into contact with the poor and the wealthy, men of educa-

[8] B. Willis of Quincy to Artemas Hale, December 26, 1834, Illinois State Historical Library, (hereafter cited as IHL).

[9] Thomas, *Lincoln's New Salem*, 110.

19

tion and men with even less schooling than he had, men who, like himself, did not drink, and others who went to extremes in drinking, rough talk, and gambling. Whether it was an evening lecture by a visiting professor from McKendree College or a "bull session" among some of the members, Lincoln listened and learned. The sixty-dollar suit he was wearing, paid for with part of the $200 he had borrowed from his New Salem friend, Coleman Smoot, probably made him one of the better-dressed men in the legislature, even though on someone else the suit would have looked better.

Vandalia was the second Illinois state capital, and when Lincoln arrived there, it had between eight and nine hundred people. The first capital, Kaskaskia, had experienced difficulties with floods, and there was a general feeling that the capital should be moved northward. In 1819 a place was selected where there was nothing but wilderness, and they called it Vandalia. It grew rapidly for a frontier town, and when the legislature and the courts were in session, it was the "social capital of the state."[10] However, its two-story brick capitol and other structures did not impress an eastern visitor, who wrote:

> With the appearance of Vandalia . . . I was somewhat disappointed. . . . In the capital of a state we always anticipate something, if not superior or equal, at least not inferior to neighboring towns of less note. . . . The streets are of liberal breadth—some of them not less than eighty feet from kerb to kerb [sic]. . . The public edifices are very inconsiderable, consisting of an ordinary structure of brick for legislative purposes; a similar building originally erected as a banking establishment, but now occupied by the offices of the state authorities; a Presbyterian church, with cupola and bell, besides a number of lesser buildings.[11]

Of the fifty-five House members, all but nineteen were there for the first time. Of the remainder, seventeen were in their second term, one in his third term, and one in his fourth term.[12]

[10] Pratt, *Personal Finances,* Notes.

[11] Burtschi, *History of Vandalia,* 95. Description by Edward Flagg of New York, published in 1838, about an 1836 trip to Vandalia.

[12] William E. Baringer, *Lincoln's Vandalia* (New Brunswick, N. J., Rutgers University Press, 1949), 48–49.

A large number of new members was common in a frontier state legislature. Lincoln had one big advantage over the other new legislators—his roommate in Vandalia, John T. Stuart, the leader of the Whig minority. Only two years older than Lincoln, Stuart was the son of a well-educated Presbyterian minister. Into Stuart's room came legislators interested in promoting or stopping legislation. Lincoln became involved in most of these conversations. He learned more about politics and government from them than he did on the floor of the House. Stuart, a man with secret plans and plots for the Whig cause, earned the name "Jerry Sly" from his fellow legislators.[13]

Lincoln was one of the minority of anti-administration men, or Whigs. The "administration" meant the federal administration, not the state. One political observer wrote to Washington friends, "The political character of the Legislature of Illinois may be properly estimated to be about 60 for the administration and 21 against it."[14] A young Morgan County attorney, Stephen A. Douglas (who then spelled his name "Douglass") wrote to his brother-in-law, "The Jackson Anti Bank ticket has succeeded by a large majority."[15]

A majority of House members were farmers; about one-fourth were lawyers. Representation reflected the early movement of the Illinois population from the south to the north. Some of the counties in the south had two, three, or four representatives, where the combined counties of Peoria, Jo Daviess, Putnam, La Salle, Cook, and Rock Island had but one representative. This territory later contained more than two-thirds of the population of the state. In theory, each representative reflected a district population of about one thousand.

In the chamber on the second floor of the capitol sat the twenty-six Senate members, while the House met in the large downstairs space. Among the members who were to seat themselves at the

13 Usher F. Linder, *Reminiscences of the Early Bench and Bar of Illinois* (Chicago, Legal News, 1879), 348.

14 William C. Greenup to Sen. E. K. Kane, December 20, 1834, Chicago Historical Society Library.

15 *Letters of Stephen A. Douglas*, ed. by Robert W. Johannsen (Urbana, University of Illinois Press, 1961), 9.

long tables—three members to a table—only one member was younger than the twenty-five-year-old Lincoln: Jesse Dubois, a twenty-three-year-old red-haired Whig, whom Lincoln described as "a slim, handsome young man, with . . . sky blue eyes, with the elegant manners of a Frenchman."[16]

Even by the standards of 1834, the surroundings for the law-makers were not elegant. A water pail and two or three tin cups took care of their drinking needs; several containers with sand were handy for the tobacco chewers and for blotting ink. With the exception of tall stands for candles for night work and a stove, the room was barren.

Illinois has changed tremendously since Lincoln's first session. A look at the index of the laws passed in 1834 shows Alton listed twice—once with eighteen subheadings—while neither Chicago nor Cook County is even mentioned in the index.[17]

During this session, Lincoln voted on major economic problems the state faced, and he voted for appropriations, including $2.50 to Marmaduke Vickery "for fixing the stoves for State House. . . . [to] J. T. Eccles, the sum of six dollars, for swearing in members of the House of Representatives. . . . [to] William Flora the sum of ten dollars, for carrying wood for the Engrossing Clerks of both Houses of this General Assembly. . . . [to] John Roberts, the sum of thirty-seven and a half cents."[18] No reason was given for the last item mentioned.

But regardless of the nature of the measure, Lincoln was usually occupied and in his seat doing his duty. Out of 124 recorded votes on bills, only seven found him absent. Out of fourteen recorded votes on procedural matters, only one did not include his vote. His total of eight absences compares with the average for the House of 13.84 absences per member.

When John Reynolds resigned as governor in 1834, a few weeks before his term ended, to take his newly won seat in Congress, William Lee D. Ewing, speaker of the Senate, became governor. He served in this position for only fifteen days, long enough to

---

[16] *CW*, VIII, 422.
[17] *Laws of Illinois* (hereafter cited as *LIll*), 1834–35, index.
[18] *Ibid.*, 3–6.

send a message to the legislature noting that during the biennium state receipts totaled $147,000 and payments $146,000. It shocked Governor Ewing, who in less than three years was to have a bitter clash with Lincoln, that "the aggregate expenditures . . . of this State, from the period of its creation (1818) to the 30th of September, 1834, amounts to nearly the sum of $664,000, a sum enormous in the aggregate."[19] Lincoln and his colleagues two years later made that sum look small indeed—and in the process imperiled the solvency of the state.

Ewing called for judicial reform and reapportionment of the state legislature, to bring a better representation of the state's population. Ironically, Lincoln opposed the reapportionment. Yet, had it not been for this reapportionment, Springfield would not have been selected as the new capital. Ewing, who suggested the reapportionment, was a strong supporter of Vandalia, but his advocacy of reapportionment assured the moving of the capital from Vandalia to the more populous northern portion of the state.

Ewing took note of the falling plaster and bricks in the ten-year-old, badly-delapidated capitol. He stated that it "is manifestly inconvenient for the transaction of public business."[20]

After the message from Ewing, the official canvass of the votes for governor took place. Joseph Duncan was declared the winner with 17,330 votes to 10,224 for William Kinney and 4,320 for Robert McLaughlin.

The two losers were prominent on the Illinois political scene. McLaughlin, a former state treasurer, was the uncle of Joseph Duncan, who won. Related by marriage to the first governor of Illinois, Shadrach Bond, McLaughlin owned one of the better frame homes in Vandalia, known as the "Governor's Mansion."

William Kinney, the man who ran second to Duncan, served as lieutenant governor from 1826 to 1830 and was one of the colorful proslavery leaders in early Illinois. One of his fellow Democrats, Governor Thomas Ford, noted that "Kinney was one of the old sort of Baptist preachers; his morality was not of that pinched up kind which prevented him from using all the common arts of a

---

[19] *House Journal* (hereafter cited as *HJ*), 1834–35, p. 13.
[20] *Ibid.*, 17.

candidate for office. It was said that he went forth electioneering with a Bible in one pocket and a bottle of whiskey in the other; and thus armed with 'the sword of the Lord and the spirit', he could preach to one set of men and drink with another, and thus make himself agreeable to all."[21]

Governor Joseph Duncan, who had twice served in Congress, was there at election time and became "the only Governor of Illinois elected without electioneering or the making of speeches."[22] Duncan was a military hero and a man of unquestioned courage and integrity whose main weakness was his aloofness from legislators and political leaders. Probably because of this, many of his sound ideas did not receive the public or political support they should have had.

Duncan, a Democrat who had strayed somewhat from the fold, in later years became a Whig. His attitude is illustrated in a letter written in defense of certain Congressional votes he had cast: "Many have complained that I have not sufficiently supported the [Democratic] party in my votes in Congress. To such I would say, I have investigated every subject upon which I have been called upon to act, with a sincere desire to obtain correct information. My votes have been governed by my best judgment and an ardent wish to promote the interest and honor of the country without regard to what either party supported or opposed."[23]

Another time he wrote: "That man who is so weak or so wicked as to vote under the influence of party feelings, or party discipline, will be compelled almost every day to abandon his principles if he has ever assumed any—the interests of his constituents—his own—honor—and his independence—and I envy them not the praise they may receive from any party."[24]

Shortly after Duncan was inaugurated, Stephen A. Douglas

---

[21] Ford, *History of Illinois*, 104–105.

[22] Elizabeth Duncan Putnam, "The Life and Services of Joseph Duncan, Governor of Illinois," *Transactions of the Illinois State Historical Society, 1919*.

[23] E. W. Blatchford, "Biographical Sketch of Hon. Joseph Duncan" (read before the Chicago Historical Society, December 5, 1905, manuscript at Newberry Library), p. 10.

[24] *Western Observer*, June 14, 1831.

wrote to his brother-in-law, Julius Granger: "Illinois still remains sound to the core, although she has got a Traitor for Governor."[25]

In the governor's message to the legislature, Duncan recommended that for the purpose of education "the $100,000 accumulated from the federal government land program should be used now, and not let to accumulate. Every consideration connected with the virtue, elevation and happiness of man . . . calls upon you to establish some permanent system of common schools, by which an education may be placed within the power [of] . . . every child in the State."[26] He also called for a college program.

The Governor asked for construction of the canal from Lake Michigan to the Illinois River, commonly called the Illinois and Michigan Canal: "In my judgment, experience has shown canals to be much more useful, and generally cheaper of construction than railroads. . . . Railroads are kept in repair at a very heavy expense and will last but about 15 years."[27]

When committee appointments were made, Lincoln was one of seven members named to serve on the Committee on Public Accounts and Expenditures. The next day, only four days after the session began, Lincoln gave notice that within a few days he would introduce a bill "to limit the jurisdiction of Justices of the Peace," a subject that interested him throughout his legislative work. This is somewhat surprising, since one of his strong backers and closest friends was New Salem Justice of the Peace Bowling Green. The bill stated "that hereafter Justices of the Peace shall not entertain jurisdiction of any civil cases whatever" with certain exceptions— they would have jurisdiction "in the precinct in which the defendant resides."[28] Suits before justices of the peace in remote parts of a county have plagued Illinois from its beginning. It may be that Lincoln's financial difficulties, which resulted in the loss of some of his personal property, made him sensitive in this area. If he could have appeared before a local justice of the peace who knew him, he could have explained his financial dilemma and

[25] *Letters of Stephen A. Douglas*, February 22, 1835, 12.
[26] *HJ*, 1834–35, pp. 25f.
[27] *Ibid.*
[28] *CW*, I, 28.

worked out something that was mutually agreeable. As it was, Lincoln was not happy with the justice he had received. His bill was much amended in the House and finally defeated in the Senate. The day before Lincoln introduced his bill, he helped defeat a measure to extend the jurisdiction of the justices of the peace.

By now Lincoln was in the thick of things. On the last day of the first week of sessions, Stuart introduced a bill written largely by Lincoln. Writing bills for others was an activity in which Lincoln increasingly engaged. It made friends for him among the other legislators who lacked his gift of language or legible handwriting, and it was good background for his work as a lawyer. A biographer who studied Lincoln as a lawyer acknowledges that "possibly the single most important factor in Lincoln's preparation for the law was the experience gained as a member of the General Assembly."[29]

When a bill came up to fine soldiers for delinquencies, Lincoln did not vote. He probably believed in the theory, but recalling his own limited military experience—as a disciplinary measure he was required to wear a wooden sword—he sympathized with the soldiers who were to be disciplined.

A few days later Lincoln made his first motion—to change the rules. Each bill had three readings, on separate days, and Lincoln moved to change the rules so that it would not be in order to offer amendments after the third reading. In this way, when a bill came up for final passage, a member could know what it contained and would not have to worry about changes by amendments. The House defeated Lincoln's motion, but today the rules of the Illinois House of Representatives are in accord with Lincoln's suggestion in 1834.

On December 15, Lincoln introduced his first bill that became law: "An act to authorize Samuel Musick to build a toll bridge across Salt Creek in Sangamon County."

Much of the time of the legislature was devoted to bills of this nature, to benefit Samuel Musick or some other individual. A business could not be incorporated without a special act of the legislature, which did not hesitate to set limits and assign re-

[29] John J. Duff, *A. Lincoln, Prairie Lawyer* (New York, Rinehart & Co., 1960), 28.

sponsibilities to the corporations. During Lincoln's years in the legislature, there were, among the bills he considered, proposals to incorporate the Spoon River Navigation Company, the St. Clair Silk Company, the Pekin Hotel Company, the Illinois Beet Sugar Manufacturing Company, the Alton Exporting Company, the Chicago Hydraulic Company (Lincoln voted against this one), and many others.

Private bills included bills to grant divorce. It was accepted procedure to get a divorce either through the courts or through the legislature. Lincoln opposed motions to take this responsibility away from the legislature. He introduced bills for divorce and supported other members who also used this privilege.

The bills on which Lincoln voted included many which would be considered unusual at a later date—a bill to require "clock-pedlars" to pay fifty dollars for a three months' license, a bill to encourage the killing of wolves, and a bill to change the name of Clayborn Bell to Clayborn Elder Bell.

As a member of the Committee on Public Accounts and Expenditures, Lincoln wrote the report on the state's contingent fund, a report which was delivered by John Hughes, the chairman. The report noted "that some charges which have been allowed are exorbitant—and have resulted in a useless expenditure of the public money."[30] But Lincoln's motion to consider this report was defeated.

Resolutions to Congress by Lincoln and his colleagues always began, "That our Senators be instructed and our Representatives in Congress be requested," because senators were chosen by the legislature, whereas members of the national House of Representatives were chosen by the people.

In addition to choosing United States senators, the state legislature chose judges and state's attorneys (the equivalent of district attorneys in most states) and other state officials. Many functions later regarded as executive or judicial rather than legislative were then assumed by the General Assembly. In voting for individuals in this first session, Lincoln favored Richard M. Young, who was inclined to be a Whig, for United States senator, against John M.

[30] *CW*, I, 31.

Robinson, a Democrat. Robinson was elected, although two years later Young replaced him. Lincoln voted for John Dement, a Democrat, in his unsuccessful bid for state treasurer. Lincoln voted for Ninian W. Edwards, his future brother-in-law and son of Ninian Edwards, the former governor, for attorney general. For state's attorney in the First District, Lincoln voted for John J. Hardin, a Whig and a later associate of his, and against a Democrat who became even more famous, Stephen A. Douglas. Douglas won. For state's attorney in the Fifth District, Lincoln voted for a strong Democrat, William A. Richardson, who won against the Whig candidate, Orville H. Browning, later a close friend of Lincoln's.

It is clear from Lincoln's voting pattern that, while party lines were developing, they had not crystallized. An observer in 1834 noted that "it is difficult to catch the hang of parties here, for although there is considerable party feeling there is very little party organization."[31]

Lincoln quickly learned this political lesson: Members of the opposition party he supported for various posts often did not return the favor. It was true then as later that on issues the lines were crossed, but on personalities to fill various posts, the lines were more sharply drawn.

One of the more unusual positions taken by Lincoln was that the legislature should meet on Christmas Day. Lincoln's religious views at this period of his life are still a matter of controversy. Since legislators were paid for Christmas Day, Lincoln possibly felt they should work. In any event, there were no sessions on Christmas Day.

Lincoln found himself in the minority in voting on thirty-four occasions—on ninety-six he sided with the majority—in this first session. In the light of history, one must approve many of those minority votes; for example, his negative vote on a proposal to make a public prosecutor liable for court costs of any case he did not win.

As the session progressed, Lincoln more frequently made mo-

---

[31] Letter of Dr. Finley of Jacksonville, May 27, 1834, quoted by Elizabeth Duncan Putnam, *Transactions of the Illinois State Historical Society*, 1919.

tions and received appointments to special committees. On January 7, the Council of Revision—made up of the governor and Supreme Court members, with power to veto or approve bills—announced approval of Lincoln's first bill, the one authorizing Samuel Musick to build a toll bridge.

A matter of major state-wide significance was the passing of the measure authorizing the creation of the long-talked-about Illinois and Michigan canal. It was to be financed through $500,000 in bonds secured by the land along the canal. Lincoln supported the measure. The points at issue were whether it should be a railroad or a canal, whether it should be sponsored by a private company or by the state. Most legislators agreed with the view of the *Chicago Democrat*: "Let the state have the control of our public works, and not speculating companies."[32]

Lincoln began to be known for his stories and humor. When the legislature had acted to fill the post of county surveyor of Schuyler County on a false report that the incumbent had died, Lincoln favored letting "matters remain as they were, so that if the old surveyor should hereafter conclude to die, there would be a new one ready made without troubling the legislature."[33] (This account in the *Sangamo Journal* may have been written by Lincoln himself. Most students agree that he frequently was the Vandalia correspondent for this newspaper.)

Remarks by Lincoln on the floor of the House were rare in this first session. In 1860, when Lincoln ran for President for the first time, a biography checked by him reported that, in this first session in Springfield, he "did not attempt to make a speech."[34]

National politics were an important part of the picture at Vandalia, and here Lincoln's political leanings became clearer. Resolutions regarding the national bank were frequent during Lincoln's legislative years, and because the vote on the resolutions was paragraph by paragraph, rather than on the resolution as a whole, the reader can follow Lincoln's thinking.

[32] December 3, 1834.

[33] January 17, 1835.

[34] John Locke Scripps, *Life of Abraham Lincoln* (Peoria, Jacobs, originally published in 1860, reprinted in 1931), 30.

A resolution presented by Jesse B. Thomas, Jr., of Madison County finds Lincoln supporting the idea of a national bank. But a paragraph condemning the action of the United States Senate for its "arbitrary and unjustifiable" treatment of President Jackson on the bank issue also received his support.

Lincoln voted against a paragraph calling for measures to force a payment of United States claims against France; that paragraph described the conduct of the French government as "ungenerous and unjust."[35]

Lincoln introduced a resolution calling on the federal government to return to Illinois 20 per cent of the money received by the federal government for lands in Illinois. Since the federal government owned most of the land in the state, if the state could get some of the money as the land was sold, it would represent a substantial source of income. The resolution was defeated.

Despite Governor Duncan's plea in behalf of education, remarkably little was accomplished. And despite Lincoln's statement in behalf of education in 1832, his record in this field can only be called fair. A bill was passed providing that the interest on the school, college, and seminary funds—rather than the funds themselves, as Governor Duncan had suggested—should be distributed on the basis of "the number of white persons under 20 years of age."[36] Lincoln voted for this measure as well as for a more liberal one which was defeated. But there is no clear pattern in his voting. His inconsistencies in the field of providing for a common education indicate that he had not developed definite ideas. He did serve on a special three-man committee to consider two education bills during this first session. What he may have contributed in that committee is not a matter of record, but he had to study some of the problems and this study may have helped him. In cases where education and humanitarian interests clearly combined, Lincoln's response was what one would expect. He supported, for example, the bill "providing for the education of orphan children," a measure that lost 32–19.

In the field of higher education, Lincoln's record is clearer and

[35] *HJ*, 1834–35, p. 216.
[36] *LIll*, 1834–35, pp. 22–24.

more consistent. He felt everything possible must be done to encourage the establishment and maintenance of colleges. Illinois was lagging behind neighboring states in establishing state universities and was doing little to encourage persons who would fill that void with private institutions. When the matter of incorporating the Jacksonville Female Academy (later MacMurray College) came up, Lincoln voted against an amendment making each of the trustees liable for all contracts and debts of the institution, but the amendment carried. In part this was a slap at the not too popular Governor Duncan, one of the trustees. Lincoln helped defeat a restriction to strike the word "Illinois" from "Illinois College" in the bill incorporating several colleges.[37]

During the final weeks of the session, the House relied on Lincoln increasingly for special committees. He was named to a total of twelve special committees during this first session, well above the average number assigned to a legislator.

Part of the minority which voted against having the legislature appoint state's attorneys, Lincoln agreed with the Council of Revision that this authority should belong to the governor.

Lincoln supported a measure to permit religious societies to organize without having to incorporate through legislation, he voted for an anti-gambling measure, and he supported a bill "for the benefit of Bank Debtors."[38]

Lincoln took more than casual interest in the following resolution: "The revenue paid into the State Treasury is not sufficient to defray the necessary expenses of the State Government; and, in as much as, the members of the legislature do not serve for a remuneration, but for the country's good; Therefore, Resolved . . . that the patriotic members of this General Assembly do not de-

[37] *HJ*, 1834–35, pp. 406–407. Because of a printer's error, this portion of the *Journal* appears in the final pages of the *Journal* for the 1835–36 session. The move to change the name of Illinois College at Jacksonville never has died completely, although now the students and alumni of the college are involved and not lawmakers. Some feel that the present name is confused too easily with the University of Illinois. At least one member of the Board of Trustees of Illinois College favors changing the name to Beecher College, in honor of the fighting first president of the school.

[38] *Ibid.*, 444.

mand pay for the present session of this legislature, until March 1836."[39] Deeply in debt, Lincoln voted against this resolution.

The state also had its financial difficulties. The treasurer's report showed a balance of $296.66![40] Among the items spent to bring the state treasury to this low point: ten dollars "to John Y. Sawyer for printing the governor's address in relation to cholera," and fifty cents "to E. Capps for transporting two muskets from Springfield to Vandalia."[41]

During the final days of the session, a memorial service was held for William McHenry, the elder statesman of the House. McHenry had attended the 1818 constitutional convention and was a member of the First General Assembly. A veteran of Indian Wars and rugged pioneer life, he had once killed a bear with a knife. His colleagues buried McHenry in Vandalia. Like some of his fellow legislators, he had his less illustrious side. At the time of his death, he was being sued by his wife for nonsupport; he had not seen her for two years.

Also during this session, a bill was passed establishing the State Bank of Illinois in Springfield. Lincoln was a supporter of this bill and later became a defender of the bank. Governor Ford later described this as "the beginning of all the bad legislation which followed in a few years."[42]

Before his first session ended on the evening of Friday, February 13, 1835, the day after Lincoln's twenty-sixth birthday, he had received $258 and could look to a new world that had been opened to him.[43] He had met the old political leaders and the leaders-to-be; he had met the lobbyists, good and bad; and he had participated in the social life of the state capital. His record was neither outstanding nor bad. Lincoln probably told himself that for a poorly educated New Salem resident he had done surprisingly well.

A New Salem neighbor recalled years later, "I always thought that Mr. Lincoln improved rapidly in mind and manners after his return from Vandalia and his first session in the legislature."[44]

[39] *Ibid.*, 386.
[40] *LIll*, 1834–35, p. 238.
[41] *Ibid.*, 241–46.
[42] Ford, *History of Illinois*, 170–71.
[43] Pratt, *Personal Finances*, 143.

One of Lincoln's best biographers, Benjamin Thomas, notes: "Much more important than his participation in legislative activities at this session were the acquaintances that he made. Here he saw wealth, education, breeding, charm—things relatively unknown to him. Indeed to Lincoln, with his hitherto limited contacts, narrow horizon, and in some respects provincial point of view, his first term in the legislature was a liberal education more valuable than anything he could learn from books."[45]

Before his first term had expired, Lincoln was called back for a special session of the legislature, but in the meantime he returned to New Salem to continue his post office duties and to undertake some study of law with books borrowed from Stuart.

About a month before the special session began, Lincoln wrote a letter to Governor Duncan urging him to name a Democrat, Levi Davis, auditor of public accounts. Lincoln said the appointment of Davis "would be entirely satisfactory to me, and, I doubt not, to most others who are the friends of quailification [*sic*] and merit."[46] Whatever influence Lincoln's letter may have had, a few days later Davis was appointed.

The frontier state of Illinois provided an ideal spot for an unpolished but ambitious young man to move ahead. The population was beginning to grow rapidly, and word spread in the East that Illinois had an unusually healthy climate. However, some of the newcomers to Illinois were not much impressed. One wrote:

> Take the inhabitants of Illinois "en masse" and I have a most thorough contempt for them. They are most indolent, inefficient, faithless race of beings I ever knew. You cannot bind them in any way so that they will feel under the slightest obligation to fulfill an engagement.[47]

But people kept coming, coming, coming. The 1835 census showed a population of 269,974 and 40 per cent of those had come

[44] A. Y. Ellis, letter to William Herndon, December 6, 1866, Library of Congress.
[45] Thomas, *Lincoln's New Salem*, 120–21.
[46] *CW*, I, 38.
[47] Letter of Miss Ellen Bigelow, written from Peoria, June 27, 1835, IHL.

in the last five years. Abraham Lincoln undoubtedly noted with considerable pride that he was helping to govern a growing state.

On December 7, 1835, in snow-covered Vandalia, the special session of the legislature began. Only forty-eight of the fifty-five House members were present that first day. The death of one of the members was announced: Major James D. McGahey, one of the youngest members, whose father at the same time served as a member of the Senate.[48]

The Speaker immediately reappointed Lincoln to the Committee on Public Accounts and Expenditures. During this special session he was named to five special committees, and for the first time he served as chairman, of two select committees, both on the same bill.

Governor Duncan's message to the special session called for reapportionment of the state's legislative districts, state backing for bonds for the Illinois and Michigan canal project, and sale of Illinois Bank stock. Duncan also urged "the most liberal support" of internal improvement projects, "leaving the construction of all such works, whenever it can be done consistently with the general interest, chiefly to individual enterprise." He pointed out that Pennsylvania had "an enormous debt" because the state had tried to handle improvements.[49]

On the opening day of the session, something new happened in Illinois—a political convention. Democrats in the state, under the leadership of young Stephen A. Douglas, held a state-wide convention in Vandalia to decide on support of candidates and issues. To no one's surprise, the convention gave Van Buren a ringing endorsement. This convention "scheme" was denounced as un-American by its opponents. Lincoln was among those who voted that it "ought not to be tolerated in a republican government"[50] and considered it "dangerous to the liberties of the people."[51] One

---

[48] The only time a father and son team was to serve together in the Illinois legislature, as far as I can determine, until 1959 when Rep. Edwin Dale of Champaign County joined his father, Rep. Sam Dale of Wayne County, as a member of the Illinois House of Representatives.

[49] *HJ*, 1835–36, pp. 8f.

[50] *Ibid.*, 27.

[51] *Ibid.*, 234.

Democratic newspaper delighted in the reaction of the Whigs and said the right answer to Whig criticism was, "Pooh—pish—pashaw."[52]

Lincoln was looking out for Sangamon County interests—and votes. He introduced a bill "to relocate a part of the state road, leading from Crows, in the county of Morgan, to Musick's Bridge in Sangamon County."[53] This became law. The bill called for commissioners setting up the road to "meet at the House of Peter Cartwright on the first Monday in March next" to work out the details.[54]

A bill drawn by Lincoln, in response to a petition, called for relocating "a part of the state road, leading from Springfield to Lewistown." It became law.[55]

When a bill was passed to incorporate the Sangamon Fire Insurance Company, the names of the incorporators were written in Lincoln's hand, although the rest of the bill was not.

On one bill Lincoln added an amendment in the House providing for the construction of an additional bridge over the Sangamon River. When the Senate refused to go along with his amendment, he was forced to drop it.

Lincoln asked for a committee to "inquire into the expediency of incorporating a company to construct a canal upon the valley of the Sangamon river."[56] He served as chairman of the two committees which considered the question, and it resulted in an act "to incorporate the Beardstown and Sangamon Canal Company." One paragraph of one amendment written by Lincoln made it possible for the state or counties to take over the canal after ten years, provided they paid the initial cost plus 12 per cent interest.[57] After passage of the bill and the end of the legislative session, Lincoln talked to a crowd at Petersburg and urged them to buy stock. Two weeks later he is recorded as having paid $1.00 down and owing $4.00 on stock. He thought enough of the project—

[52] *Chicago Democrat*, January 6, 1836.

[53] *HJ*, 1835–36, p. 33.

[54] *LIll*, 1835–36, pp. 193–94.

[55] *HJ*, 1835–36, p. 64.

[56] *Ibid.*, 33–34.

[57] *Ibid.*, 41.

which came to nothing—that two months after the close of the session, he bought forty-seven acres along the Sangamon River from the federal government at $1.25 an acre. This land was one mile from the eastern end of the proposed canal.

The first bill Lincoln introduced which had more than local interest was meant "for the Relief of Insolvent Debtors." It provided procedures for action in the event of the absence of the probate judge. The measure passed the House but died in committee in the Senate.[58]

The move to back the Illinois and Michigan Canal enterprise with the full financial support of the state took a great deal of time. Early in the proceedings, a move to kill the proposal failed by a 28–27 vote, Lincoln's vote for the bill being one of the decisive votes. The measure as passed authorized the governor to negotiate a loan "not exceeding $500,000."[59] An amendment by Lincoln giving the governor greater authority in the procedures of obtaining a loan and operating the canal was defeated.

The passage of the measure giving the support of the state to a bond issue for the canal was big news in Chicago. A spontaneous celebration was held in which "a discharged soldier has his arm carried away by the accidental explosion of a gun. Nine hundred and fifty dollars was subscribed on the spot for his relief. . . . At 12 o'clock . . . 56 guns were fired in honor of the Senators and Representatives who had voted for the final passage of the bill."[60]

At Vandalia, on the floor of the House of Representatives, that night there were "200 citizens rejoicing at the passage of the bill amidst wine, champaigne and with the utmost good feeling."[61]

The *Chicago American* was pleased with the result, and in its issue of January 16, 1836, carried an honor roll of members who had voted for the canal. Lincoln was among those listed. The following week the newspaper also gave much credit to Stuart for the passage of the measure.

On reapportionment, Lincoln supported amendments which

[58] *Ibid.*

[59] *LIll*, 1835–36, pp. 145–54.

[60] *Chicago Democrat*, January 20, 1836.

[61] Theophilus W. Smith, Vandalia, to Ed. S. Kimberly, Chicago, January 7, 1836, Chicago Historical Society Library.

would have kept the legislature a small body. Consistently, he supported measures requiring a large population for each House and each Senate member. The 1835 census showed a total state population of 269,974. Morgan County had the largest population—19,214. Sangamon County followed with 17,573. Cook County, which includes Chicago, had 9,826. Chicago itself had less than 500. The county with the smallest population figure was Jasper, with 415. A motion by Lincoln to have one senator for 8,500 citizens failed. The figure approved (7,000), Lincoln voted against. On final passage of reapportionment, he voted in the negative.

Banking was a major topic of the special session. An amendment by Lincoln stipulating certain information the Bank of Illinois (at Shawneetown) must report was defeated. The amendment provided in part that "if said corporation shall at any time neglect or refuse to submit its books, papers, and all and everything necessary to a full and fair examination of its affairs, to any person or persons appointed by the General Assembly, for the purpose of making such examination, the said corporation shall forfeit its charter."[62]

Lincoln opposed a measure to "provide for the application of the interest of the fund arising from the sale of the school lands" for school purposes.[63] There was committee criticism of the measure for failing to provide safeguards for the funds.

Consistent with his action in the regular session of the legislature, Lincoln again opposed the motion to adjourn the legislature over Christmas Day.

One Lincoln resolution was adopted that "the committee on Public Accounts and Expenditures be instructed to enquire into the expediency of authorizing the publishing of the State laws, of a general nature, in the public newspapers."[64] Nothing came of the resolution.

During the special session, word was received of the death of United States Senator E. K. Kane, then only forty-one years old and already considered a patriarch of Illinois politics. He had been

[62] *HJ*, 1835–36, pp. 124–25.
[63] *Ibid.*, 131–32.
[64] *Ibid.*, 158–59.

a United States senator for eleven years. Kane's unexpected death caused turmoil in Vandalia. It took twelve ballots to elect his successor, and during the course of the balloting Lincoln voted for three candidates: Richard Young (four ballots), Lieutenant Governor Alexander M. Jenkins (three ballots), and William L. D. Ewing (five ballots). The race finally narrowed to Ewing and the Speaker of the House, James Semple, a tall, bewhiskered, distinguished-looking legislator from Madison County. Both Ewing and Semple were Democrats, Ewing the more independent of the two. Ewing finally won out. Eight years later, Semple became a member of the United States Senate.

On news of Kane's death, the *Sangamo Journal* carried the following story from Vandalia, possibly written by Lincoln:

> Last evening's mail brought intelligence to this place of the death of Hon. E. K. Kane, one of our Senators in Congress. This news had the magic effect to produce much of feigned sorrow and heartfelt rejoicing. . . . Kane has long been a respected member of the most respectable body on earth, and, at last is dead, and his greatest political friends are glad of it, not that they loved him less, but that they loved his office more. Ever since the news reached here, the town has been in continual commotion.[65]

One Whig wrote home what was undoubtedly the sentiment of most Whigs: "It was a bitter pill for me to vote for Ewing. I [would have] voted for any other man till the contest was ascertained to [be] between Semple and Ewing."[66]

On three of the twelve ballots for senator, Lincoln did not vote for the same candidates for whom Stuart voted. Lincoln was never a rubber stamp, neither for his party nor for his close friend Stuart. He voted against Stuart and his party occasionally not only on matters of substance but even on minor matters. Once when Stuart moved to adjourn until ten o'clock the next morning, his motion was defeated 26–15, Lincoln among those voting against him.[67]

[65] January 2, 1836.

[66] Letter from John Henry to John Hardin, December 31, 1835, Chicago Historical Society Library.

[67] *HJ*, 1835–36, pp. 256–57.

A resolution which passed with Lincoln's support requested the federal government to grant Illinois 500,000 acres of land at $1.25 an acre—to be paid in ten years with no interest charged to Illinois. The proceeds of the land would go for internal improvements, the theory being that the investment would pay off sufficiently that in ten years Illinois could repay the federal government. This was part of the legislature's response to a growing public demand for internal improvements.

The first measure authorizing the incorporation of the Central Railroad passed during this session, and among the fifty-eight incorporators were many of the most prominent political leaders of the state. The act provided that "the said railroad shall be commenced in five years and completed within twenty years from the passage of this act."[68] Lincoln voted for it.

During the session, bills were passed incorporating seventeen different railroads. All the railroads authorized were to be privately financed. Nothing was ever heard from most of them. Among the railroads incorporated were the Rushville Railroad Company and the Waverly and the Grand Prairie Railroad Company—a fact that perhaps only an Illinois resident acquainted with these three small towns can appreciate.

The act for the Wabash and Mississippi Railroad included this provision: "In case any married woman, infant, idiot, or insane person . . . shall be interested in any such land or real estate, the circuit court or justice of the peace shall appoint some competent and suitable person . . . to act for, and in behalf of, such married woman, infant, insane person, [or] idiot."[69]

It has been true through the years that frequently bills of major importance receive much less attention than unimportant proposals. The act which caused a big furor during Lincoln's first term was known as the "Little Bull" bill. It passed as "an act to improve the breed of cattle."[70] Lincoln had the good fortune to oppose it. The bill stated that "no bull over one year old shall be permitted to run at large out of enclosure." It provided for a series

[68] *LIll*, 1835–36, p. 132.
[69] *Ibid.*, 41.
[70] *Ibid.*, 254–55.

of fines for violation, the fine money to be awarded to the owners of the "three best bulls, three best cows, and three best heifers" within a county. There was a storm of protest over this measure, people charging that it favored the wealthy farmer and discriminated against the small one. Public indignation was so great that at the next session of the legislature, eleven months later, one of the first measures passed was a bill to repeal the "Little Bull" bill—and the repeal was voted 81–4.

Private bills passed during this session included one divorcing "Richard H. McGoon and Elizabeth his wife . . . Joshua S. Shaw and Fanny Ann his wife . . . George Flower and Jane his wife."[71]

While Lincoln was in Vandalia, the *Sangamo Journal* carried a list of names of addressees of letters "which if not called for within three months will be sent to the General Post Office as dead letters."[72] Included on the list was "A. Lincoln." In April the list was again published—and Lincoln's name was no longer on it; he had picked up his mail.

After the special session, Lincoln headed back to New Salem. He had made $162 as a legislator and had shown more leadership in this second session than he had in the first. He had made more motions and generally felt more at ease and more self-confident than he had in that first session. His attendance record stood well above average. Seven times he missed voting on proposals involving bills, but he was recorded on 114. The average House member missed voting 13.41 times.

The attendance record of Lincoln and that of his colleagues in this second session did not differ markedly from that of his first session. One thing changed: On measures which involved the substance of bills, or their fate, in the first session Lincoln voted with the majority eighty-five times and with the minority thirty-two times. In this special session he voted with the majority sixty-four times and with the minority fifty times. In part this was due to the sharpening of party lines and Lincoln's role as a minority member, but it also indicated his greater self-confidence. He dared to take an unpopular stand; he knew how far he could go without greatly

[71] *Ibid.*, 259–60.
[72] January 9, 1836, and April 2, 1836.

offending his colleagues. This added year of service gave him a better understanding of the measures on which he voted. Lincoln was in the thick of legislative activity, and he enjoyed it.

During his first term in the House, Lincoln did not introduce legislation for the three-point platform he had first run on in 1832—Sangamon River navigation, restrictions on interest rates, and education.

Two months after he returned to New Salem, Lincoln announced his candidacy for re-election. These two months he had spent studying, surveying, and taking care of special needs of his constituents. During this period he petitioned the county commissioners to give Travice Elmore more money for keeping Benjamin Elmore, "an absolute mad man."[73]

The day before he announced his candidacy for re-election, Lincoln advertised in the *Sangamo Journal* under the heading "Strayed or Stolen," that he had lost "a large bay horse, star in his forehead . . . supposed to be eight years old." People who could assist in returning the horse would "be liberally paid for their trouble."[74] The horse was never found. But the loss of a horse could not discourage a young man about to embark on his second successful campaign for public office.

[73] *CW*, I, 47.
[74] March 26, 1836.

3

One of the Long Nine

Williams of Adams presents no very beautiful frontispiece—but is a man of fine talents and sound judgment. He is one of the main stays of the liberal party in the House—but opposed to the Improvement System. There are also many of excellent sense in this body but awkward and ungraceful in debate. Among this number Lincoln of Sangamon, Dougherty of Union, and Shields of Randolph are prominent.—*North Western Gazette and Galena Advertiser*, August 5, 1837.

ON MARCH 19, 1836, Abraham Lincoln was one of three men who announced their candidacies for the Illinois House of Representatives in the *Sangamo Journal*. Stuart announced for Congress in the same issue. In this campaign Stuart was unsuccessful, but his leaving the state legislative scene gave Lincoln an opportunity to exert some leadership.

Five days after Lincoln's announcement appeared, he had his name entered on the record of the Sangamon Circuit Court as a person of good moral character, the first step necessary to obtaining admission to the bar.

Lincoln continued to combine his campaigning with his surveying and his postal chores. On April 9, he advertised in the *Sangamo Journal* the names of sixty-four persons who had mail in the New Salem post office and warned that if they wanted their letters, they had better get them by July 1. But a month before this deadline, the post office in the dying town of New Salem closed. Lincoln got $19.48 for his final three months of service as New Salem post-master.

Before that time the campaign had become a warm one. When a "letter to the editor" in the leading Springfield newspaper suggested that candidates state their position on the issues, Lincoln responded:

> In your paper last Saturday, I see a communication over the signature of "Many Voters," in which the candidates who are announced in the Journal, are called upon to "show their hands." Agreed. Here's mine:
>
> I go for all sharing the privileges of the government, who assist in bearing its burthens. Consequently I go for admitting *all whites* to the right of suffrage, who pay taxes or bear arms, (by no means excluding females).
>
> If elected, I shall consider the whole people of Sangamon my constituents, as well those that oppose as those that support me.
>
> While acting as their representative, I shall be governed by what their will is; and upon all others, I shall do what my own judgment teaches me will best advance their interests. Whether elected or not, I go for distributing the proceeds of the sales of the public lands to the several states, to enable our state, in common with others, to dig canals and construct rail roads, without borrowing money and paying interest on it.
>
> If alive on the first Monday in November, I shall vote for Hugh L. White for President. Very respectfully, A. LINCOLN.[1]

One of the more unusual items in that letter is that the young bachelor candidate advocated women's suffrage, at that time a somewhat radical position to take.

His support of White for the presidency helped Lincoln in Whig circles and did him no harm politically in Sangamon County, which had no great fondness for White's opponent, "that fancy Easterner, Van Buren." Even though Jackson was popular, Jackson could not transfer his popularity to Van Buren in New Salem and Sangamon County, both overwhelmingly for White. Illinois went for Van Buren, although the Whig newspapers had predicted a White landslide in Illinois. The *Shawneetown Journal* of Gallatin

[1] *SgJ*, June 18, 1836.

County commented, "Van Buren men are as scarce in old Gallatin as White men are in Africa."[2]

A Springfield visitor came through New Salem with the all-too-common type of political tale, and Lincoln addressed the following letter to him:

> I am told that during my absence last week, you passed through this place, and stated publicly that you were in possession of a fact or facts, which if known to the public, would entirely destroy the prospects of N. W. Edwards and myself at the ensuing election; but that, through favor to us, you should forbear to divulge them.
>
> No one has needed favours more than I, and generally, few have been less unwilling to accept them; but in this case, favour to me, would be injustice to the public, and therefore, I must beg your pardon for declining it. That I once had the confidence of the people of Sangamon is sufficiently evident, and if I have since done any thing, either by design or misadventure, which, if known, would subject me to a forfeiture of that confidence, he that knows that thing, and conceals it, is a traitor to his country's interest.
>
> I find myself wholly unable to form any conjecture of what fact or facts, real or supposed, you spoke; but my opinion of your veracity, will not permit me, for a moment to doubt, that you at least believed what you said.
>
> I am flattered with the personal regard you manifested for me, but I do hope that, on more mature reflection, you will view the public interest as a paramount consideration and therefore, determine to let the worst come.
>
> I here assure you, that the candid statement of facts, on your part, however low it may sink me, shall never break the tie of personal friendship between us.
>
> I wish an answer to this, and you are at liberty to publish both if you choose.
>
> Verry Respectfully,
> A. LINCOLN.[3]

The letter did not appear in the newspaper, and there was no further communication between Colonel Allen and Lincoln during

---

[2] Quoted in the *North Western Gazette and Galena Advertiser*, June 13, 1835.
[3] *CW*, I, 48–49.

the campaign. Some Springfield residents considered Allen a "bag of wind."[4]

Campaigning took Lincoln to any small gathering of people who would listen. The farm of Isaac Spear and the Varsell farm, the cluster of homes known as Allentown and Mechanicsburg, were among the scenes of his activities. Sometimes he would walk more than five miles to appear at a gathering.

It is somewhat amazing that this rough frontier town of Springfield should produce a remarkably high level of political debate. The same town that passed an ordinance that "no swine shall be suffered to run at large in the town of Springfield" was able to produce some of the most articulate political debates held anywhere in the nation.[5]

The courthouse at Springfield was the scene of the most interesting political meeting during the campaign. Lincoln received the assignment to reply to a talk by John Calhoun, his former employer, and the *Sangamo Journal*—in language typical of the journalism of that day—noted in an article obviously weighted in Lincoln's favor that Lincoln "lifted the lid and exposed to the eye the wretched condition of some of the acts of the Van Buren party. A girl might be born and become a mother before the Van Buren men will forget Mr. Lincoln. From beginning to end Mr. Lincoln was frequently interupted by loud bursts of applause from a generous people."[6]

A letter writer to the Whig newspaper—possibly Lincoln himself—noted that the Van Buren ticket "as it now stands can in truth be called the PREACHER TICKET—there being no less than three preachers out of seven candidates, a pretty heavy load, I think."[7]

The one thing all candidates agreed on was the development of Illinois resources through a system of internal improvements. Job Fletcher, Whig candidate for the State Senate, favored that

[4] Angle, *Herndon's Lincoln*, 136.

[5] T. Walter Johnson, "Charles Reynolds Matheny, Pioneer Settler of Illinois," *ISHSJ*, December, 1940.

[6] *SgJ*, July 16, 1836.

[7] July 9, 1836.

issue, plus making Springfield the seat of government. He concluded his appeal to the voters in the *Sangamo Journal*:

> If you should prefer my opponent I shall submit to your decision with all the patience of
>
> JOB FLETCHER[8]

On the night before the election, the legislative candidates again gathered at the Springfield courthouse and election eve tempers were on display. Two of the candidates—hot-tempered Ninian W. Edwards and Dr. Jacob Early—almost came to blows. One of the other candidates noted years later: "Lincoln . . . took up the subject in dispute, and handled it fairly, and with such ability that everyone was astonished and pleased. So that difficulty ended there. Then, for the first time, developed by the excitement of the occasion, he spoke in that tenor intonation of voice that ultimately settled down into that clear, shrill monotone style of speaking that enabled his audience, however large, to hear distinctly the lowest sound of his voice."[9]

Shortly before the election, a handbill signed "Truth Teller," attacking Stuart and Lincoln, was circulated. Lincoln issued a handbill in reply to charges that he and Stuart opposed payment of a state loan. Lincoln pointed out where "this lying Truth Teller" could find the votes listed in the *House Journal* and that he was absolutely wrong. Lincoln concluded: "The author is a *liar* and a *scoundrel*, and . . . if he will avow the authorship to me, I promise to give his proboscis a good wringing."[10]

Election day was August 1. Lincoln voted for the Whigs, including Stuart for Congress. Stuart lost to William L. May by fewer than two thousand votes.

In the legislative race, Lincoln was the top vote-getter among the seventeen candidates. In New Salem he ran first and in Springfield third. The results for the district: Lincoln, 1,716; Elkin, 1,674; Edwards, 1,659; Dawson, 1,641; Stone, 1,438; Wilson,

---

[8] July 16, 1836.

[9] R. L. Wilson, letter to William Herndon, February 10, 1868, Herndon-Weik Collection, Library of Congress.

[10] *CW*, VIII, 429.

1,353, and McCormick, 1,306. Calhoun headed the Democrats with 1,277, and the other losers trailed him.

That election sent to Vandalia seven House members and two senators from Sangamon County—all six feet or more in height. When the nine tall men from Sangamon came to Vandalia, they were quickly tagged "the Long Nine," a phrase used by sailors to describe certain guns on a ship. Five were lawyers, three were farmers, and one was an innkeeper. Seven were from the South originally, two from the North.

At twenty-seven, Lincoln was the youngest of the group—two months younger than Edwards. The average age of the Long Nine was only thirty-five. The oldest of the seven House members of Sangamon's Long Nine was balding John Dawson, forty-five, a veteran legislator and regarded as one of the abler members of the House. The Indians had once captured him in battle. He had ten children. Second to Dawson in age was William F. Elkin, forty-four, father of thirteen children. Lincoln had supported him in his earlier unsuccessful race for the State Senate.

Handsome Ninian W. Edwards was the son of former Governor Ninian Edwards. In the opinion of his legislative colleagues, he took too much pride in this fact. Edwards had abilities, but as one of colleagues commented, he "had inherited from his father so much vanity and egotism that it made him offensive to most of his acquaintances. . . . Naturally and constitutionally an aristocrat . . . he hated democracy as the devil is said to hate holy water."[11]

Andrew McCormick, thirty-five, weighed almost three hundred pounds, which made him look older. He was a stonecutter and the father of ten children.

Daniel Stone became known for signing, with Lincoln, a protest against slavery. He was a college-educated lawyer, a native of Vermont, and a former Ohio legislator.

Robert L. Wilson, thirty-one, of the small village of Athens, was a one-term member of the legislature, the father of eight children, lawyer and teacher, and in later years the source for some Lincoln stories of doubtful authenticity.

Senate members of the Long Nine were Job Fletcher and Archer

[11] Linder, *Reminiscences*, 279–80.

G. Herndon. Fletcher, with a long nose and narrow face, was the father of seven children, a resident of Sangamon County since 1819, and the purchaser of the first window glass in Sangamon County. Herndon was a businessman, as unpredictable in business as in politics, and the father of William Herndon, who later became Lincoln's law partner.

In 1836 all the members of the Long Nine were Whigs or at least "Whiggish." Party lines were still not clearly marked.

On September 9, 1836, Lincoln was licensed to practice law in Illinois. He had been handling some smaller legal matters for almost two years. Less than a month after his admission to the bar, he filed his first lawsuit.

About two weeks before Lincoln left for Vandalia to begin his second term in the legislature, a mass meeting of Sangamon County citizens was held in Springfield to discuss a system of internal improvements and to urge the legislature to adopt it.

The "large and respectable meeting of citizens" sent to a state-wide meeting to be held in Vandalia the following leading citizens of both parties to promote internal improvements: John Stuart, John Calhoun, George Forquer, John Taylor, Jesse B. Thomas, Jr., and others.[12] The *Sangamo Journal* editorialized, "It is not a party measure, and all our citizens can cordially unite in one rigorous effort to secure the adoption of a system of Internal Improvements for the State, which is so much needed, so much desired, and so absolutely necessary to its prosperity."[13] The same issue carried a letter from a citizen urging action. "Public opinion should be concentrated and made to act upon the legislature. That body should never adjourn until a system is adopted. . . . We need not fear involving the State in debt."

This type of public pressure was going on all over the state. By comparison, the issue of moving the seat of government received relatively little attention. One writer noted that the public seemed "almost insane" in support of internal improvements. Adding fuel to the general enthusiasm for the growth of the state's economy

[12] *SgJ*, November 26, 1836.
[13] November 19, 1836.

was $4 million put into Illinois by the federal government in support of the Black Hawk War.

Lincoln had always favored a system of canals and roads and railroads for the state. In Vandalia he found that most of the other members of the Tenth General Assembly were of the same mind. One legislator wrote to the Galena newspaper, "This is doubtless a mammoth undertaking for a state like ours; yet I am in favor of it in almost every particular, and particularly the state doing the work."[14]

This session of the state legislature, which opened at Vandalia on December 5, 1836, was one of the most illustrious in the history of the United States. Yet this star-studded group brought financial ruin to the state of Illinois through a wholly unrealistic system of internal improvements. While the Illinois legislative record has not always been the finest, in Vandalia in 1836 and 1837 it reached an all-time low.

Those who composed this legislature were all born outside the state. They represented some of the finest families from many states, but the large majority were new members who had no legislative experience.

With the exception of the House of Burgesses of Virginia's colony, probably no legislative body has had so many future national and state leaders. While most of the men in the Virginia House of Burgesses were "comparatively wealthy," the Illinois lawmakers were rather poor. In Virginia, family ties were important in achieving membership, but not in Illinois; the educational level of the burgesses was "remarkably high," but in Illinois somewhat low; all members of the Virginia body had Anglican affiliation, while the Illinois assembly represented a great variety of religious affiliations.[15]

Among those who served in the Illinois legislature during this term were six future United States senators, three governors, a cabinet member, several generals, eight congressmen, two presi-

---

[14] Signed simply "W," *North Western Gazette and Galena Advertiser*, March 4, 1837.

[15] Jack P. Greene, "Foundations of Political Powers in the Virginia House of Burgesses, 1720–1776," *William and Mary Quarterly*, October, 1959.

dential candidates, and one President, who was to become one of the most revered of all our presidents.

The *Sangamo Journal* correctly noted that "the present legislature embraces, perhaps, more talent than any legislative body ever before assembled in Illinois." But too optimistically this newspaper added, "Much good may result to the state from their deliberations."[16]

The passing of a bill like the Internal Improvements Act reflects the mood of the times. The Prairie State was starting to grow, and nothing seemed too extravagant to meet the needs—and to lure a mushrooming population. The people wanted civilization and industry and culture. To get these, they needed higher prices for farm products, which better transportation and a larger population would bring.

Lincoln's record is one of all-out support.

The state-wide convention on internal improvements held in Vandalia during the first two days of the legislative session recommended to the legislature a system of canals and railroads which would cost an estimated $10 million, to be financed by state bonds. The supporters of this system asserted that it would "pay for itself." Other states were undertaking internal improvements projects, they argued, and Illinois must do the same if it was not to lag behind. Ten million dollars was a substantial sum in Illinois in 1836; the total tax base in Illinois at that time was estimated at only slightly more than five million dollars.

In his message to the legislature, Governor Duncan urged a system of internal improvements to be achieved by the state working co-operatively with private companies. He suggested that the state should provide one-third of the money needed.

The Governor's approach met with little enthusiasm among the members. Before the session ended, they had voted $10,250,000 in bonds, including $200,000 to be divided among counties that received neither a railroad nor a canal under the plan. The Governor's plan would have encouraged private enterprise to help bear the burden, but the legislators were afraid of monopoly.

No surveys had been made. No experts had been called in for

16 *SgJ*, January 6, 1837.

advice. But that mattered little. The public clamor for the project was overwhelming. "Let's elect representatives who will borrow money to make Internal Improvements," the *Illinois State Register* of Vandalia had said before the election, and the people had done just that.[17] Newspapers demanded it, and the people cried for it. There was excitement throughout the state about it. The farmers wanted access to better markets, the merchants wanted cheaper freight and more customers, and land speculators wanted more buyers. "All our land speculators in town property are on the alert night and day," a Jacksonville resident wrote, "to catch the first news from Vandalia so that they can profit by the changes which the legislature shall make in passing the great mammoth bill for Internal Improvements, or the rejection of the same."[18]

If there were legislators who had misgivings, most of them decided that it was better to be "wrong with the voters than right against them." When the measure was vetoed, it took little time for the legislature to override the veto—again with Lincoln's help. The House overrode the veto 53–20. One legislator, who voted against the measure, wrote to his wife: "Many are in high spirits at the passage of the Big Improvements Bill. Yet many others of the friends of the measure are very uneasy for the consequence."[19]

Vandalia went wild the night of the bill's passage. "The huzzas and acclamation of the people were unprecedented," the *Sangamo Journal* reported. "All Vandalia was illuminated. Bonfires were built, and fire balls were thrown in every direction."[20] The newspaper also noted, "The names of those who have been conspicuous in bringing forward and sustaining this law will go down in the future as great benefactors."[21] Several newspapers called it the beginning of "a new era."[22] In Alton, the Reverend John M. Peck

---

17 *Illinois State Register and People's Advocate of Vandalia* (hereafter cited as *ISR*), July 29, 1836.

18 Thomas Melendy, letter to John Hardin, January 29, 1837, Chicago Historical Society Library.

19 John Hardin, February 26, 1837, Chicago Historical Society Library.

20 *SgJ*, March 4, 1837.

21 *Ibid.*

22 The Springfield and Galena newspapers used this exact phrase. Others said the same thing, if not in the same phrase.

announced he was going to publish a periodical devoted to internal improvements. Most Illinois citizens seemed confident they had taken a big step forward.

Two legislators from White County filed a protest in the *House Journal* after passage of the bill—a protest that was prophetic: "The undersigned look on with amazement and wonder, utterly at a loss to conceive what blessing, what advantage . . . is to be attained by plunging the state in debt, the interest on which will amount to more than ten times its present revenue. . . . The act provided for the construction of many immense works, in a great degree unconnected. . . . The successful works of Pennsylvania and New York afford no fair example or precedent to us; there they connect . . . cities of vast wealth, business, and population; while the works proposed by this act seem to the undersigned to be a bold attempt to create cities, and attract population and wealth."[23]

To add to the financial weakness of the bill, the legislature provided that construction on the various railroads and canals was to be commenced simultaneously at each end and at major points along the way.

The net result of the whole project was a mammoth debt for the state. The state was dotted with bridges from nowhere to nowhere, with partially dug canals, with roads with no meaningful beginning or ending. Of all the projects, only the Illinois and Michigan Canal (a separate bill and an additional debt) ever achieved success.

Four years after the passage of the measure, Illinois had a debt of $15,000,000, and Illinois bonds were selling for fifteen cents on the dollar. In 1842, for example, interest charges for the bonds amounted to almost $800,000, while the total state revenue for that year was $98,546.14. The state debt kept climbing. By 1853 the debt had reached almost $17,000,000. Not until 1857 was the state able to pay even the interest on the bonds. Not until 1882 were the bonds finally paid—forty-five years after passage of the measure and seventeen years after Lincoln's death.

Meantime, the legislature in which Lincoln served refused to authorize private corporations to build where there might be "com-

23 *HJ*, 1836–37, pp. 680–83.

52

petition" with the state. The result was that neither the state nor private concerns met the need. While other states experienced rapid population growth, some settlers avoided Illinois because of the Gargantuan debt the taxpayers had.

All in all, it was a most unhappy chapter in Illinois history—and those responsible for it became the leaders of the nation. Governor Ford called them "the spared monuments of popular wrath" for passing "the most senseless and disastrous policy which ever crippled the energies of a growing country."[24]

Other things occupied the time of Abraham Lincoln in Vandalia besides internal improvements.

For one thing, he had his own "internal improvement" to worry about; he was sick for more than a week. But this did not keep him from attending sessions. A visitor to Vandalia, David Davis, wrote, "There has been considerable sickness among the members."[25] An 1836 issue of the *Constantine Republican* of Michigan observed, "An editor in Illinois excuses himself for not getting out his paper in season, because the ague had shaken all his teeth loose, and compelled him to use both hands to hold his trousers on. Excuse enough."[26]

His sickness, said Lincoln, together "with other things I cannot account for, have conspired and have gotten my spirits so low, that I feel I would rather be any place in the world than here. I really cannot endure the thought of staying here ten weeks."[27]

But things moved too quickly for him to stay in this mood. Reapportionment and the extremely unpopular "Little Bull" bill of the previous session brought sixty-six new members into this House of Representatives so that, after one term, Lincoln found himself a veteran legislator with seniority over the majority of House members.

Accounts vary concerning the relative strength of the Whigs and the Democrats. It was about even in the Senate, but the Democrats outnumbered the Whigs almost two to one in the House.

24 Ford, *History of Illinois*, 186–87.

25 Letter, January 19, 1836, in Willard King Collection, Chicago Historical Society Library.

26 Quoted in the *North Western Gazette and Galena Advertiser*, August 20, 1836.

27 *CW*, I, 54–55.

When the session opened, there was a three-way race for House speaker. Lincoln's vote on four ballots went to one of the losing candidates, Newton Cloud of Morgan County, a farmer and Methodist preacher—and a Democrat. James Semple, the speaker for the previous session, won.

The clerk of the House was voted in on Lincoln's motion, an indication of Lincoln's increasing activity in the House.

When Governor Duncan addressed the legislature, he covered a great many subjects and took some strong slaps at internal improvements. Lincoln called his talk "an inflamitory political Message."[28] After more than a century, Duncan's talk stands up considerably better than Lincoln's comment on it.

Speaking in a state which even today has one of the more patronage-oriented systems of state employment, Governor Duncan denounced removing "men from office for an independent expression of opinion, or an honorable opposition. . . . When the public officer is appointed for his support of the party in power, he knows that this retention in office does not depend so much upon his qualifications and fidelity as on the zeal and ability he displays at elections in supporting his party."[29]

Lincoln was placed on the important Finance Committee and also on the Penitentiary Committee. He was one of a minority of thirty-four members appointed to two standing committees; the majority were appointed to only one.

Nine days after the session commenced, a United States senator had to be elected. There were five candidates. Lincoln voted on all three ballots for Archibald Williams of Quincy, tall and homely. Some thought he looked like Lincoln. A former member of the State Senate, he and Lincoln had become close friends. At this time he was a Democrat, but not a "whole hog" Democrat; he showed some "Whiggish" leanings. Williams lost to Richard Young, who in the 1835 session had received Lincoln's vote for the United States Senate on four ballots.

Newspapers in the state, almost all openly partisan, either gave unstinting praise to the senatorial candidates or denounced them. The Galena newspaper, for instance, stated, "The Van Buren can-

[28] *Ibid.*, 54. [29] *HJ*, 1836–37, p. 21.

didates for the U. S. Senate . . . are all, without exception, office-hunters and men whose sole study and aim is to be with the majority—without fixed principles as politicians."[30] This denunciation included Richard Young, the winner. Young threw a champagne party for the legislators and friends to celebrate. By the time he paid for drinks, food, broken dishes, and other damage, he had a bill of $600, a substantial sum in 1836. At this particular affair two of the better-known legislators—Douglas and Shields—ended up doing a dance on the tables and breaking a great many dishes and bottles in the process.

Legislators in Vandalia consumed more than their fair share of liquor. Advertisements in the Vandalia newspaper prove that the small community had an amazingly large selection of alcoholic beverages for sale. Benjamin Godfrey, the state's leading business-man, wrote from Vandalia:

> I have reached this place This Day and so far as I have been able to discover there is no person so much needed here as our mutual friend Mr. T. Turner [Turner was the leading Illinois temperance speaker of that day.] If you see him I would advise you to Recommend his being at this place before the adjernment of The Legislature which will not be for about 5 or Six weeks from this. This is now a terrible place. Greate Room for Reforme. Yours in hast.
>
> B. Godfrey
>
> P.S. I feel convincted that profest Christians neglect or do not pay that attention to the Elections That they should do and that it is high time that they should Give this subject more of their mind.[31]

Lobbyists had parties, and so did legislators successful with their bills. When Springfield was selected as the seat of government, the Sangamon "Nine" had a party for their colleagues. Ninian W. Edwards picked up the bill for $223.50, which included payment for eighty-one bottles of champagne, thirty-two pounds of almonds, fourteen pounds of raisins, cigars, oysters, and apples, "eatable," breakage, and "sundries."[32]

[30] *North Western Gazette and Galena Advertiser*, December 17, 1836.

[31] Letter to Theron Baldwin, January 5, 1837, IHL.

[32] Walter B. Stevens, *A Reporter's Lincoln* (St. Louis, Missouri Historical Society, 1916), 74. Tells of an interview with the son of Ninian W. Edwards, who showed Stevens the receipt.

Social activities were limited somewhat by the small number of women. A few legislators had their wives in Vandalia, but most did not. One visitor reported to the girl he hoped to marry, "Some few young ladies in attendance, looking out for husbands."[33]

Lincoln did not drink. He ate only sparingly. He liked honey on bread, popcorn, peaches, apples, "and fruits generally. He ate apples peculiarly—he clasped his finger-forefinger, and his thumb around the Equatorial part of the apple—the stem end being toward his mouth."[34]

He preferred an informal meeting with fellow legislators in a hotel room to a social affair. At this time he probably stayed at the Globe Hotel, sometimes called Lemuel Lee's Tavern.[35] It was only a short walk from his hotel to the musty and crude-looking capitol building.

A politically sensitive matter was a petition by a group of Sangamon County residents to break from Sangamon County and form a new county. Lincoln headed the special committee on the matter—the first time in this session that he was made chairman of a committee. When Lincoln moved to have the contents of the petitions for and against the new county printed in the *House Journal*, his motion failed.

This matter, said Usher Linder of Coles County, affected only Sangamon County. Linder told the House: "If they want the report, let them print it out of their own pockets. They are rich enough God knows: they hold the bag, like Judas; and with as little merit as he."[36] The phrase about Springfield holding the bag was a reference to the State Bank.

Public opinion was divided in Sangamon County, and this put the Sangamon legislators in an awkward position. In Sangamon County there were charges that some of the petitions were forged.

[33] David Davis, letter, Willard King Collection, Chicago Historical Society Library. The Davis letter is dated January 19, 1835, but King notes correctly that the date should be 1836.

[34] *A Letter from William H. Herndon* to Isaac N. Arnold (privately printed, 1937), IHL.

[35] Burtschi, *History of Vandalia*, 79. According to Mrs. Travis, granddaughter of Lemuel Lee.

[36] *ISR*, January 12, 1837.

Newspapers devoted a great deal more space to this proposal to divide the county than toward bringing the state capital to Springfield. A mass meeting in Springfield opposed dividing the county.

The new county was to include New Salem and part of Morgan County, which caused some of the Morgan County legislators to oppose the measure. When Lincoln reported for the committee, the House resolved, despite Lincoln's opposition, to change the name of the new county from "Marshall" to "Van Buren." (Eventually it became "Menard County.") The controversial measure went to a new committee composed of two of Lincoln's Sangamon colleagues and Douglas of Morgan County. When again no solution could be found, on Lincoln's motion—which Douglas opposed—the matter went to a committee of five members, with Lincoln chairman and Douglas a member. The committee agreed not to form a new county, but the House passed the measure anyway. The Senate finally killed it.

Lincoln had no strong feelings in the matter, but wanted to avoid any political damage to himself and to win a more crucial battle for Sangamon County—the relocation of the state capital. In Vandalia the legislature was meeting in a crude structure. Hastily built, the old capitol was in a shape "that precluded all possibility of repair."[37] These inadequate facilities helped put the legislature in a mood to move the seat of government.

Early in the session, the *Illinois State Register* of Vandalia reported:

> Very little business has been done in either the Senate or House of Representatives thus far, as will be manifest from the journal published. The cause of this is the unfinished situation of the State House. The plastering is new and damp, and it became necessary to the comfort and health of the members to have additional stoves put up. The workmen have been engaged with unwearied industry in finishing the rooms and putting up the stoves.[38]

On the motion of Gideon Minor of Edgar County, a committee of seven House members was appointed "to enquire into and report

[37] "Report of Joint Select Committee on Public Buildings," *HJ*, 1836–37, p. 480.
[38] December 15, 1836.

57

to this House, whether any legislative active [*sic*] ought to be had
. . . with regard to the removal and relocation of the seat of Government of this State."[39] The different areas interested in securing
the capital had their representatives on the committee. Dan Stone
represented Sangamon.

For more than a month there was relative quiet on the capital
measure in the House; then the Senate reported to the House a bill
sponsored by Senator Orville H. Browning of Adams County calling for permanently locating the seat of the state government. The
matter would be settled, according to the Senate bill, by a vote of
the legislators. Lincoln first became involved in struggles over
amendments to this Senate bill.

An amendment written by Lincoln was introduced by Alexander
P. Dunbar of Coles County, not a supporter of Springfield until
the final two ballots. Lincoln either may not have wanted to introduce his own amendment, or—since he often wrote bills and
amendments for his fellow legislators—he may have written the
amendment for Dunbar. The amendment provided that the city
selected as capital must donate $50,000 and two acres of land for
the new state buildings. It carried 53–26. The amendment in effect
eliminated the small towns in the state.

By a 39–38 vote, the bill to vote on a new capital was then laid
on the table "until July 4th." If a measure is tabled by a substantial vote, it is dead. But when the vote is close, it is usually
not difficult to get the bill off the table. A record was taken on the
39–38 vote, so that it was not difficult to contact legislators for a
change of votes. The next day Benjamin Enloe of Johnson County,
a Springfield supporter, moved to reconsider the vote to table, and
his motion carried 42–40. The motion to table lost 37–46. After
two more amendment proposals, Lincoln moved to table the measure for two days. After three days, the House got to the measure
again and defeated amendments that would have killed it. The
bill advanced to passage stage by a 48–34 vote. Lincoln moved to
amend the bill by adding, "The General Assembly reserves the
right to repeal this act at any time hereafter."[40] This amendment
carried 43–41. This was probably an attempt to make the measure

[39] *HJ*, 1836–37, pp. 155–56.   [40] *Ibid.*, 702.

a little more acceptable to its opponents. The phrase itself is meaningless, as Lincoln knew; the legislature has a right to change any law whether it is so specified or not. The measure calling for a vote passed 46–37. A few days later the bill was approved by the group having veto power, the Council of Revision (the governor and the Supreme Court).

Harry R. Pratt, a reliable student of this period, believes that John T. Stuart came down to Vandalia "to guide the move to make Springfield the state capital," although Stuart was no longer a House member.[41]

The folks back home were urging the various legislators to select their particular town as the seat of government. Typical is this letter in support of Jacksonville as the site: "I hope that our delegation will be unanimous in this matter and use all the influence they each possess . . . to have it brought here."[42] There was general agreement that the capital would move north, and Springfield seemed more acceptable than any other location, but it could run only second, in any citizen's mind, to his own home community. When Vandalia became the capital in 1820, a clause in the law provided that it could again be moved after twenty years. Actually, the legislature had the power to move it at any time, but the twenty-year clause made Vandalia seem temporary and obtaining the seat of government became fair game for any community.

Justice Lockwood of the Illinois Supreme Court described the situation:

> The law requires that both houses shall meet together on Thursday next & vote for a place to be the future seat of government— Our Springfield friends are in high spirits that their town will be successful—I think Jacksonville stands no chance—& the probability is in favor of Springfield—It is however possible that no place will be selected & in that event it will remain here, until further legislative action.[43]

[41] From some notes of Harry E. Pratt given the author by Mrs. Pratt.

[42] T. O. Duncan to John Hardin, December 29, 1836, Chicago Historical Society Library.

[43] Baringer, *Lincoln's Vandalia*, 109. Quoted from a letter of Samuel Lockwood to Mary V. Nash, February 26, 1837, copy, The Abraham Lincoln Association.

On the last day of February, the voting for the capital site took place. More than twenty Illinois communities received votes on at least one ballot.

On the first ballot, Springfield had thirty-five votes; Vandalia, sixteen; Alton, fifteen; Jacksonville, fourteen; and the rest scattered. Some of the towns which received ballots for the site of the state capital are no longer in existence.

On the second ballot, the vote was:

Springfield	43
Alton	15
Vandalia	15
Peoria	8
Jacksonville	15
Illiopolis	10
Bloomington	2
Carrollton	3
Shelbyville	2
Albion	1
Equality	1
Geographical Center	2
Caladonia	1

On the third ballot, Springfield moved ahead to fifty-three votes. Vandalia had sixteen; Alton, fourteen; Peoria eleven; Jacksonville, ten; and the rest scattered. One senator cast a vote for Purgatory, a town in Lawrence County.

The fourth and final ballot brought Springfield up to seventy-three votes, enough to win, while the next highest was Vandalia with sixteen votes. Springfield was declared the winner, with the understanding that her citizens would have to raise $50,000 to help finance the costs involved. It was a big day for the Sangamon delegation and Abraham Lincoln, who had been one of their leaders.

Major issues like moving the capital and internal improvements were not the only concerns of Lincoln. He introduced a resolution "that the Door-Keeper of this House be now requested to state publicly to this body whether in his opinion, an Assistant Door-Keeper is necessary"; the motion was defeated.[44] Lincoln sup-

44 *HJ*, 1836–37, p. 86.

ported a bill to make the offices of county clerk and county treasurer elective. He voted against allowing the citizens of Vandalia to have the legislative hall in the evening for a celebration in honor of the anniversary of the victory at New Orleans. He opposed a move to demand from the governor a list of all convicts pardoned, for what crimes they had been convicted, and why they had been pardoned. He voted against the bill "to encourage the killing of wolves, giving fifty cents for a wolf scalp with the ears thereon."[45] He voted against incorporating the Peoria Hotel Company, but supported a bill to "incorporate the Illinois beet-sugar, silk, and vegetable oil manufacturing company."[46]

The wolf-bounty bill elicited a humorous exchange on the House floor. William Lane of Greene County said a wolf scalp was not worth fifty cents. Peter Green of Clay County replied, by describing in detail the destruction done by the wolves. Lane then stated that he opposed the bill which "the gentleman from Clay had been advocating . . . because my county is densely populated with human beings and his with wolves. . . . I have not the honor of representing so many prairie wolves upon this floor." Lane predicted that the railroads running through Clay County under the Internal Improvements Bill would make so much noise that they would frighten the wolves away. The wolves will "seek refuge in Greene [County], where the friends of the mammoth bill have taken special care that the puffing of steam engines shall not annoy them, as it is almost the only county unprovided with one or more railroads, and the consequence will be, Sir, that my constituents will be able to make money by wolf scalps. Under these considerations, I am almost tempted to take the bounty and vote for the bill."[47]

Lane had voted for almost all amendments expanding the Internal Improvements Act, but finally voted against its passage. Within two months newspapers reported, "The Representative from Greene and Calhoun Counties has been detected in passing under his present assumed name since his arrival in the State. He

45 *Ibid.*, 384–85.
46 *Ibid.*, 598.
47 *ISR*, February 10, 1837.

was recognized by three young men from Virginia, who disclosed the fact of his having absconded for the alleged crime of forging Pension papers, leaving a family, and that his real name is Mitchell. He was elected last year . . . and acquired the confidence and good opinion of his associates. He has now left the country."[48]

When it came to legislative voting for people to fill positions, party lines were becoming more apparent. In addition to his vote for United States senator already mentioned in this chapter, Lincoln supported Augustus C. French, a colleague in the House and a Democrat, for state's attorney in the Fourth District. For auditor, Lincoln again supported his Democratic friend, Levi Davis. For treasurer, he voted for a Democratic state senator and former House member, John D. Whiteside of Monroe County. For attorney general, Lincoln voted for Democrat Benjamin Bond, state senator and brother of the first governor, Shadrach Bond. In the vote for public printer, Lincoln was one of five to vote for William Hodge, editor of the Vandalia *Free Press* and *Illinois Way*. When the House and Senate met on the final day of the session to vote for a judge for Chicago, Lincoln served as the teller for the House.

When any position was to be filled, legislative members had a distinct advantage since their colleagues elected men to fill the posts. This was sometimes abused. The *Alton Spectator* commented, "All have seen the evils resulting from another source, which should be prohibited by the constitution: and that is the eligibility of members to office the filling of which devolves upon the legislature; while they are eligible they will be constantly intriguing for these offices, too often to the neglect and detriment of public business."[49]

When a petition came to Lincoln about the Beardstown and Sangamon Canal, he referred it to the Committee on Petitions. Later, when Hardin made a motion to amend the Internal Improvements Act to have the state buy $100,000 worth of stock in the Beardstown and Sangamon Canal Company, Lincoln voted for the motion, which failed. This issue Lincoln understood for he had helped guide a boat on the Sangamo River, and as the

[48] *SgJ*, April 29, 1837.
[49] Quoted in the *SgJ*, February 4, 1837.

Sangamo Journal had pointed out, "At no place on the route will excavation be required to a greater depth than eleven feet."[50]

Banking legislation occupied much time this session. Not only were there financial and partisan political interests involved, but sectional interests, and House control versus Senate control complicated matters even more. Lincoln's lack of financial background did not stop him from taking an active part.

When smooth-talking Usher Linder—soon to be elected attorney general—introduced a resolution to investigate the State Bank of Illinois located at Springfield, Lincoln headed the defense of the Springfield establishment.

"It is not without a considerable degree of apprehension that I venture to cross the track of the gentleman from Coles," Lincoln stated in a speech recorded by the *Vandalia Free Press*.

> I do not believe I could muster a sufficienty of courage to come in contact with that gentleman, were it not for the fact that he, some days since, most graciously condescended to assure us that he would never be found wasting ammunition on small game. . . . In one faculty, at least, there can be no dispute of the gentleman's superiority over me, and most other men; and that is the faculty of entangling a subject, so that neither himself, or any other man, can find head or tail to it . . . More than one half of his opening speech has been made upon subjects about which there is not one word said in his resolution. . . .
>
> Much of what he had said has been with a view to make the impression that [the Bank] was unconstitutional in its inception. . . . The fact that the individuals composing our Supreme Court have, in an official capacity, decided in favor of the constitutionality of the Bank, would, in my mind, seem a sufficient answer to this. . . . No one can doubt that the examination proposed by this resolution must cost the State some ten or twelve thousand dollars; and all this to settle a question in which the people have no interest, and about which they care nothing. These capitalists generally act harmoniously, and in concert, to fleece the people, and now, that they have got into a quarrel with themselves, we are called upon to appropriate money to settle the quarrel. . . . If the Bank be inflicting injury upon the people, why is it, that not a single petition

[50] September 24, 1836.

is presented to this body on the subject? . . . The truth is, no such oppression exists. If it did, our table would groan with memorials and petitions, and we would not be permitted to rest day or night, till we had put it down. . . . Let [the people] call for an investigation and I shall ever stand ready to respond to the call. But they have made no such call. . . . This movement is exclusively the work of politicians; a set of men who have interests aside from the interests of the people, and who, to say the most of them, are, taken as a mass, at least one long step removed from honest men. I say this with the greater freedom because, being a politician myself, none can regard it as personal. . . . Cases might occur when an examination might be proper; but I do not believe any such case has yet occurred."[51]

Despite his eloquent speech, Lincoln lost 55–21. It was his first published speech. The *Sangamo Journal* commented: "Mr. Lincoln's remarks are quite to the point. Our friend carries the true Kentucky rifle, and when he fires seldom fails of sending the shot home." But the newspaper felt little bitterness toward Linder because the same issue comments editorially that Linder "will make a good attorney general."[52] This comment is surprising since only a few weeks earlier the same newspaper had taken note of two speeches Linder had made and described them as "little else than dirty appeals to party feeling, in which he attempted to skin his opponents; and in turn, for which, he got himself very handsomely skinned."[53]

Motives for the attack on the Springfield bank were several. Democrats were attacking a Whig institution. Originally, the idea to have a State Bank was proposed by the Democrats, but when the Whigs elected a majority of the board, the "leading Democrats of the state did not hesitate to say . . . that the charter was unconstitutional."[54] Opponents were also attempting to stop the flow of money to the Springfield bank and help the other banks.

[51] Reprinted in *SgJ*, January 28, 1837.

[52] *Ibid.*

[53] *Ibid.*, December 31, 1836.

[54] George W. Smith, *A History of Southern Illinois*, (2 vols., Chicago, Lewis, 1912), 197.

A similar Senate resolution "to examine into the condition and financial concerns of the State Bank of Illinois," located at Springfield—in reality a resolution for a full-scale investigation—passed with Lincoln against it. The banks at Shawneetown and Springfield were investigated as a result of the Senate resolution, but the investigations resulted in no re-examination of state policy and had no positive results. One non-legislative observer wrote to his wife that the investigations were "all a foolish project which can answer no good purpose."[55]

Lincoln voted at first to kill the bill extending the charter of the Kaskaskia bank, one of the competitors of the Springfield bank. However, when final passage of the bill came up, he voted for it. Lincoln favored the circulation of bank notes "of a less denomination than five dollars."[56] Later in the session, the Springfield delegation achieved a victory for their bank when the state was authorized to buy $100,000 worth of additional stock.

In school matters Lincoln's record again was not clear. He steered a middle road between the all-out supporters of education and the opponents of state aid to education. When an amendment to the Internal Improvements Act was proposed by the chairman of the Education Committee to provide $25,000 of the first internal improvements income to each county for common schools, the amendment was defeated 57–22. Lincoln opposed the measure. When a bill came up "distributing the School Funds of this State among the counties" for purposes of education, a move to kill the bill lost 61–9, Lincoln being one of the nine. The measure provided a system of distributing funds for schools and encouraging townships to set up common schools.

Lincoln favored an amendment to the school bill which would have called for the counties and townships to lend the money they received "at not less than ten per cent nor more than twelve per cent," the income to go to schools. Lincoln apparently felt that in this way the schools could operate on the interest and no taxation would be necessary. He favored striking out sections of the bill setting up procedures for distribution and care of the money, and

55 William Wilson to his wife, January 21, 1837, IHL.
56 *HJ*, 1836–37, pp. 536, 540.

providing that in each township every teacher should receive the same rate of compensation. The school bill finally passed 67–9, with Lincoln one of the nine voting against it.

Lincoln supported an amendment to the act incorporating the city of Alton which gave the town trustees the power to levy a personal property tax for school purposes. An amendment in one of the final days of the session calling for full use of the school funds to establish schools throughout the state was defeated 41–24, Lincoln opposing the measure. A favorable Lincoln vote for education was recorded in connection with the bill to incorporate the Quincy Academy. The bill was amended by adding, "The right to alter, change, amend or repeal this act is hereby reserved to subsequent Legislatures." The amendment carried 54–17. Lincoln was one of those who voted against the amendment.

During the session in Vandalia, two of the members died, and in each instance Lincoln joined his colleagues in wearing a black crepe band on his left sleeve for thirty days. He liked his colleagues, and they liked him. He felt more and more at home on the floor of the House, and as the session—now his third—progressed, he was more ready to offer amendments and procedural motions. Sometimes he won, sometimes he lost, but he was in the center of things.

Lincoln reported for the Committee on Finance on the financial condition of the state. He told of an estimated income of $57,895.15 and estimated expenditures of $55,151.97, a figure given the Committee on Finance by the Committee on Public Accounts and Expenditures. This figure allowed "much too small a sum" for a contingent fund, according to Lincoln, and he estimated a deficit of $12,256.82.[57] Note that while Lincoln was not the chairman of the Committee on Finance, he was a prominent member of it. This also shows his awareness of the financial condition of the state when he voted for the system of internal improvements.

A proposal for a constitutional convention to draft a new state constitution for the somewhat outdated one of 1818 carried in the House, 55–29. Lincoln voted against it. He may have feared bringing up the slavery issue again.

[57] *Ibid.*, 603–604.

Down to the next-to-final day of the session, resolutions concerned with national politics continued to come before the House.
Lincoln and the Whig minority were regularly defeated by the
Democrats. Contrary to later rules in the Illinois General Assembly, at this session members were required to vote when present.
The day before adjournment, one legislator asked to be excused
from voting on a bill. This caused an uproar. His request was
turned down.

On Saturday, March 4, 1837, Lincoln's most hectic and eventful
legislative session came to a close. On that day Lincoln received
a check for $312. In December he had received a check for $100,
making his total pay for the session $412; forty-four dollars of that
amount was for travel, the legislators receiving $4.00 for each day
of session and $4.00 for each twenty miles of travel. Monday the
legislature met pursuant to their resolution, but only a few were
there to transact the final routine business.

The following Tuesday or Wednesday Lincoln arrived in New
Salem to spend his last month in that village.

The day after Springfield was selected as the new seat of government, Lincoln had his name entered on the records of the
Illinois Supreme Court as an attorney. It was a step toward a
livelihood during the years to come—something to keep bread
on the table while he remained active in politics.

Lincoln did not receive large fees as a lawyer, but they totaled
in excess of $1,500 each of his first twelve years—an adequate
income in the 1830's and 1840's. By the end of his twelfth year
of practice, he was lending money at interest.[58]

About a month after the session in Vandalia ended, Lincoln
moved to Springfield from the dying town of New Salem and began
practice with Stuart. The small office was in "No. 4 Hoffman's
Row Upstairs."[59] Lincoln took the place of a young lawyer, Henry
Dummer, who moved to Beardstown to practice law. Dummer
recalled: "He was the most uncouth-looking young man I ever saw.
He seemed to have but little to say; seemed to feel timid, with a
tinge of sadness visible in the countenance, but when he did talk all

[58] Pratt, *Personal Finances*, viii.
[59] *SgJ*, April 15, 1837.

this disappeared for the time and he demonstrated that he was both strong and acute."[60]

The office was not pretentious, but for 1837 it was not bad. An old wood stove and a rough wooden table dominated the scene. About twenty-five legal books on the not-so-fancy shelves constituted one of the best law libraries in that area of the state. Once in a while Lincoln slept on "a lounge" in the corner, using the old buffalo hide in the office as a blanket.

Starting a law practice and living in a new city did not excite Lincoln. Less than a month after moving, he wrote that "living in Springfield is rather a dull business."[61] It was about this time that Daniel Webster visited the town and displayed his oratorical abilities. Lincoln and Webster may have met at this time.

A concern of Lincoln's was that the citizens of Springfield had pledged the $50,000 the law required of them in order to get the capital. Dr. Anson G. Henry, one of the men appointed to supervise the construction of the state house, went to Vandalia to see the auditor about financial arrangements, carrying with him a note of introduction from Lincoln.

The *Illinois Republican*, Springfield's Democratic newspaper, charged that Dr. Henry, a Whig leader, was "squandering disadvantageously" the money used for capitol construction. A mass meeting of citizens was held on the matter, and Lincoln wrote out a report calling for a bipartisan committee of seven members to investigate the matter. The committee's verdict: Dr. Henry was doing a good job.

Newspapers in Lincoln's day were outspoken. The *Illinois Republican* had run a series of articles, possibly written by Stephen A. Douglas, attacking Dr. Henry. Douglas was an influential friend of the *Republican* and occasionally contributed anonymous articles. The Henry article provoked a near riot and an actual violent attack on the offices of the *Republican*, with Douglas defending the office.

Lincoln and Douglas were both active in helping the editors take positions and sometimes in writing the material themselves.

[60] Angle, *Herndon's Lincoln*, 145n. Statement by Dummer to Herndon.
[61] *CW*, I, 78.

The men they associated with in the newspapers were plain-talking editors. The *Sangamo Journal* editor referred to another editor as "a cabbage head." The Galena editor denounced Shawneetown's editor as "one destitute of every moral or political principle." Lincoln's friend who edited the *Sangamo Journal* called the *Carrollton Times* editor "a lowbred, foul-mouthed fellow," and about his rival editor in Springfield had this comment: "It cannot be denied that in free countries . . . the most abusive Journals have generally the widest circulation." The *Illinois Republican* replied, "We suppose the editor wrote the above to show [that] his *extreme decency* is the reason why nobody reads his paper."

Physical violence often resulted because of the abuse of the press. In one issue, for example, the *Sangamo Journal* reported, "In the warmth of passion Col. Elkin took a course which his friends and the community regret—but of which the article in the *Republican* was the sole and only cause. . . . We need not enter into details: the result was that the editor of the *Republican*, according to an account in that paper, was sufficiently punished for the unjustifiable attack upon Col. Elkin, and the latter was stabbed by the editor's brother, and one or two others."[62]

When candidates favored by the newspapers lost, there was not the usual editorial of congratulations to the winners. The *Galena Gazette and Advertiser*, for example, backed Lincoln's partner Stuart for Congress rather than William May. When May won, it reacted, "Is it possible that this curse to the State is again to be saddled upon us for two more years?"[63]

Lincoln's relationship to the newspapers may not have been as close as that of Douglas, but it was close enough to both help him and hurt him politically—and close enough for him almost to lose his life before he laid aside his role of state representative.

The panic of 1837 cast gloom on the nation's economic picture and brought Illinois to the brink of disaster with the state's wild-eyed schemes for expansion. Governor Duncan called a special session of the legislature for July 10, 1837.

On the opening day Lincoln was absent, but he was there the next day to hear Governor Duncan deliver his message to the

[62] July 1, 1837.
[63] August 13, 1836.

legislature and urge the repeal of the Internal Improvement Act. "In the midst of disasters which have already fallen on the commercial world, and which are still threatening us on all sides, a favorable opportunity occurs to escape from the perils of that system of Internal Improvements . . . so fraught with evil."[64]

Duncan's sound advice was not heeded by the legislature, and Lincoln was among those who disagreed with the Governor. A few new faces among the legislators and the disappearance from the scene of a few veterans like Douglas did not aid the Governor's cause. Instead of repealing the measure, the Senate passed a bill increasing the scope of internal improvements, with Lincoln voting for it. On the final day of the session, the House Committee on Internal Improvements filed a lengthy report explaining why the governor's recommendation for repeal should not be followed.

"Here ends, we hope forever, the opposition to our noble system of Improvement," commented the *Illinois State Register* of July 15.

A new member in the Sangamon delegation during this special session was Edward D. Baker, elected to succeed Dan Stone, who had resigned to become a judge. A London-born Whig, Baker was a lawyer and a political orator. A year younger than Lincoln, Baker stood five feet, eight inches tall. As an orator, Baker was without peer. One contemporary recalled:

> If he only spoke for five minutes to the court on some point of law, the crowded court room was all attention. But if in a murder case he spoke for hours, his audience was thrilled to the verge of collapse. Two-thirds of a century has passed, but I can see that straight, lithe, graceful, blond youth as he swayed his audience, jurors, the bar and even the judge upon the bench.[65]

In the election held on July 1 to fill the Stone vacancy, Baker opposed John Calhoun. Lincoln did not vote, possibly because he was in agreement with Baker and his Whig policies, but he did not want to vote against Calhoun, to whom he was grateful. Besides,

[64] *HJ*, July, 1837, p. 13.

[65] William T. Davidson, "Famous Men I Have Known in the Military Tract," *Illinois State Historical Society Transactions*, 1908.

Baker favored division of Sangamon County whereas Calhoun opposed it. Lincoln avoided taking a stand on the matter by not voting.

In the course of the special session, Baker introduced an amendment to the State Bank Bill. This amendment asked the committee to "inquire whether any members of the House are indebted to the Bank; and if so, whether they can vote with propriety upon any bill relating to the termination of the existence of the bank."[66] The amendment was rejected 52–31, but Lincoln supported it.

A bill making stockholders and officers of the State Bank responsible for all debts of the bank passed, with Lincoln against it. On matters other than interest, he favored giving bank officers wide discretion. The banks were in trouble in Illinois, and Lincoln and some of the other legislators were eager to help them, but there was disagreement about the methods to be employed. The state had a vital interest; more than one million dollars in state funds was tied up in the bank.

A compromise on banking legislation was finally worked out. By combining some of Lincoln's ideas with some contributed by James Shields, the banks in the state were saved. This compromise was quite an accomplishment since sentiment in the state was against them. David Davis wrote, "There are a great many radicals . . . as well as desperate men, a great share of whom by some fortuitous circumstances, are members of the Legislature, and the cry at present, from one end of the state to the other, is, down with the Bank."[67]

On the third day of the session, Lincoln gave notice to the House that he would introduce a bill "to authorize Rhoda Hart and others to sell and convey certain real estate." The bill authorized a widow to sell property held by her late husband, but the measure lost. The children could make the decision when they reached legal age, the legislature felt.

Lincoln served as chairman of a committee to look into the possibility of building a road from Beardstown to Petersburg. He then wrote the bill and introduced it. It passed with little difficulty.

[66] *HJ*, July 18, 1837, pp. 85–86.
[67] David Davis to William P. Walker, July 1, 1837, IHL.

Archer G. Herndon, Sangamon's senator, introduced a bill which Lincoln had drafted, which extended the corporate powers of the officials of Springfield. When it came to the House, Lincoln was made chairman of the committee to consider it. It passed.

During this special session, Lincoln assumed increasing responsibilities. The legislature met less than two weeks, yet Lincoln served on five special committees and as chairman of three of them.

He introduced a bill (which passed) calling for relocation of part of a state road "leading from William Crow's in Morgan County to Musick's Bridge in Sangamon County."

In looking after Springfield's interests, Lincoln led the fight against a bill introduced by Vandalia's Representative W. L. D. Ewing, which called for the repeal of the act moving the state capital to Springfield. The Galena newspaper commented, "A bill has been introduced for repealing the law of last session, establishing the Seat of Government at Springfield. This frightens the members from Sangamon exceedingly—although I believe there is little ground for alarm. Vandalia is a pleasant place enough; but there are other pleasant places nearer the geographical centre of the State."[68] Ewing lost badly in this move, and Lincoln served on a committee to draw up some kind of compromise. Lincoln then amended the bill to the effect that no work could proceed until Springfield residents paid on the $50,000 they had pledged. The House accepted the amended bill, but the measure died in the Senate.

"Conflict of interest" reared its head during this special session. The House passed—with Lincoln's vote of approval—a measure stating that members of the legislature could not hold office under the Board of Public Works (internal improvements) or the Board of Canal Commissioners (Illinois and Michigan Canal). Lincoln favored making an exception of engineers, but the House rejected the idea. Edward Smith, the Democratic representative from Wabash County, was an engineer whom Lincoln regarded highly.

As a member of the Penitentiary Committee, Lincoln took an interest in the report of Warden B. S. Enloe that at the state penitentiary at Alton there were "muskets 374, bayonets 243, screw

[68] *North Western Gazette and Galena Advertiser*, July 29, 1837.

drivers 357, wipers 110, ball screws 35, bullet moulds 296, yaugers 312, chargers 51, handvices 31, swords 13, pistols 6."[69]

During this special session there were thirty-five roll calls, and Lincoln missed only one of them. On Saturday, July 22, 1837, the House adjourned, and Lincoln collected a check for ninety-six dollars for services and travel after eleven days of sessions. The time was long enough to give Lincoln his most prominent role to date in the legislative halls.

When Lincoln returned to Springfield, he resumed a fight in the newspapers over property held by a political opponent. Shortly after he had been admitted to the bar, Lincoln was approached by a widow who asserted that her late husband's attorney, General James Adams, had tricked her out of property. Lincoln took the case and apparently believed—rightly or wrongly—that the property was taken on the basis of a forged document.

Adams, not the noblest of men, had left Oswego County, New York, for Illinois, with a charge of forgery against him. There were other aspects of his record to show that Lincoln's suspicions about him may have been well grounded, although Adams was a popular man in Springfield and Sangamon County.

Lincoln and the other attorneys in the case agreed to take the widow's plea to court for half of the property involved if they should win, and for nothing if they should lose. The case might have been settled in court, but Adams became a candidate for probate judge against Lincoln's friend Dr. A. G. Henry. Lincoln and others soon began writing letters to the Whig newspaper, the *Sangamo Journal*, and Adams replied in the Democratic newspaper, the *Illinois Republican*.

Whatever the truth of the charges, there is a serious question about the propriety of trying a case in the newspapers. The public reaction was not what Lincoln had hoped. Adams won the election overwhelmingly. Places where Lincoln could be assumed to have some influence went just as top-heavy for Adams as did Democratic territory. New Salem, for example, gave Adams a majority of almost five to one. The public felt that Adams had been un-

[69] *HJ*, July, 1837, pp. 141–42.

fairly criticized. It marked the first time in three years that the Whigs had been defeated in Sangamon County.

The fighting with letters in the newspapers continued long after the election, held less than two weeks after the close of the special session. When Lincoln returned from Vandalia, he was embroiled in it. An unsigned handbill against Adams, distributed two days before the election, went into detail on Lincoln's side of the charges against Adams and ended, "I do not subscribe my name, but I hereby authorize the editor of the Journal to give it to anyone that may call for it."[70] After the election, the editor of the *Sangamo Journal* revealed that the author was Lincoln. The letters continued until, in his final reply to Adams, Lincoln concluded: "Farewell, General. I will see you again at court, if not before—when and where we will settle the question whether you or the widow shall have the land."[71] They did not see each other in court; the case was never brought to trial.

In his letters Adams referred to Lincoln and the other Sangamon County Whig leaders as a "junto," and this term stuck with Lincoln for many years afterward.

Despite the fact that there were eleven practicing lawyers in the small frontier town of Springfield, with a population of fifteen hundred, Lincoln and Stuart were kept busy in the practice of law. But the two took time from their practice to promote the Whig cause in general and the candidacy of Stuart for Congress in particular.

Civic activities—including helping to raise part of the $50,000 required from Springfield residents for the new capitol—also took some of Lincoln's time.

The *Chicago Democrat* charged that Springfield was likely to lose the capital "forever" because of its failure to come up with the pledged $50,000. The *Sangamo Journal* replied: "The raising of the money . . . has been attended with some difficulty. . . . The greatest portion of the money has been raised—and we have strong confidence that arrangements will be made to secure the balance

[70] *CW*, I, 93.
[71] *SgJ*, October 28, 1837.

thc present week. . . . We mean to fulfill our obligation."[72] A few months later Lincoln was one of 101 Springfield residents who signed the note at the State Bank for $17,000, which was due the state as part of the $50,000 pledged.

Lincoln celebrated his twenty-ninth birthday by voting for candidates for justice of the peace and constable. His candidate for justice of the peace lost, but his candidate for constable won. Twelve days later, the *Sangamo Journal* announced that Lincoln was again a candidate for the legislature.

[72] November 11, 1837.

4

"Lincoln the Log Roller"

The Long Nine did not ask much for their section in the way of Internal Improvements, but they never lost an opportunity to make a vote for the removal of the capital to Springfield. It is only surprising that, with such opportunities, they did not accomplish more.

JOHN CARROLL POWER, 1876[1]

IF THE READER likes "mysteries," this chapter may hold special interest. It deals with a historical "fact" in the life of Lincoln that investigation shows to be entirely different from the traditional stories.

Most biographers of Lincoln refer to his legislative years briefly, if at all. The usual comment concerns his leading the Long Nine through some logrolling on the Internal Improvements Act and in getting the capital located in Springfield. This was possible, these sources say, because, under Lincoln's leadership, the nine Sangamon County legislators—seven House members and two senators—voted as a unit on all things, and were willing to vote for or against anything if it aided their ultimate goal, making Springfield the capital.

States a respected Illinois historian, "The Springfield delegation in the legislative session of 1837, the famous 'Long Nine'—headed by Abraham Lincoln, traded their votes on the Internal Improve-

[1] John Carroll Power, *History of the Early Settlers of Sangamon County* (Springfield, Edwin A. Wilson and Co., 1876), 46.

76

ments System for the location of the capital at Springfield."[2] The best of the one-volume Lincoln biographies agrees: "Solidly behind [Lincoln] stood the Long Nine . . . with predetermined purpose to remove the seat of government to Springfield. . . . The situation became ideal for logrolling, and Lincoln and his colleagues from Sangamon made the most of it to promote their own design, promising support . . . in return for pledges of votes for Springfield. . . . Supporters for Vandalia and Alton attempted to counteract Lincoln's designs by similar tactics, but they lacked the power of the Long Nine, who, acting as a unit under Lincoln's leadership, could exert tremendous pressure."[3]

Others echo the same refrain: "The Long Nine were united for securing [the capital], and nothing could turn one of them from their purpose. They were ready to yield anything else, but when any other point was yielded, it secured votes for Springfield."[4] "Lincoln has taken his place as one of the wisest and cagiest political practitioners ever to come down the Illinois pike. In this matter of the relocation of the state capital . . . acting as unit under Lincoln, the Long Nine outmaneuvered the opposition at every stage of the contest."[5] "The 'Long Nine' . . . Lincoln led through a perfect maze of trading, swapping, and promising, all looking toward one goal—securing the state capital for Springfield."[6] "The Long Nine . . . went to Vandalia determined to move the capital to Springfield. They were ready to swap votes with any delegations which were not striving for the capital, but that wanted other concessions for their own localities."[7] "Lincoln led the 'Long Nine' in finding the votes in the legislature to pass a bill moving the capital of the state from Vandalia to Springfield. . . . A few members voted for the bill because they liked Lincoln, but most of the votes came through trade, deals, 'logrolling.'"[8] "The situation was ideal for

[2] Theodore Calvin Pease, *The Story of Illinois* (University of Chicago Press, 1949), 125.

[3] Benjamin Thomas, *Abraham Lincoln* (New York, Knopf, 1952), 55f.

[4] Power, *Settlers of Sangamon*, 46.   [5] Duff, *Prairie Lawyer*, 30.

[6] Blaine Brooks Garnon, *Lincoln in the Political Circus* (Chicago, Black Cat Press, 1936), 62.

[7] Barton, *Life of Lincoln*, 2–5.

[8] Carl Sandburg, *The Prairie Years* (2 vols., New York, Harcourt, Brace & World, Inc., 1926), 194.

well planned logrolling, and the Long Nine set about it."[9] "The Sangamon delegation, testifies one of Lincoln's colleagues, voted on every proposition in exchange for promises of support in the fight over the removal of the capital. . . . Alton was given three railroads to get her powerful support. No pledge, no threat, no manner of manipulation was overlooked."[10]

Many similar quotations could be cited, but dissenting voices are few. One is a statement by General T. H. Henderson, whose father served in the legislature with Lincoln in two succeeding sessions. The son is commenting on his father's opinions about a session prior to the father's actual service. The indirect origin of this statement makes it suspect.

More seriously must be taken what Lincoln's fellow legislator, Usher F. Linder, wrote: "The seat of government was removed by law, to Springfield and it has been hinted that the 'nine' traded a little to accomplish this result, but I vouch for nothing of the kind."[11] Written thirty-nine years after the 1837 session—after Lincoln had become a national hero—by itself it could not stand, although it is of more than casual interest. Peter Green of Clay County, one of Lincoln's colleagues in the House, not particularly close to Lincoln, but a supporter of Vandalia's claim, denied that a trade had been made "of votes for the capital at Springfield for votes for a system of Internal Improvements."[12] More serious disagreement comes, not from a Lincoln scholar, but from a book on the Illinois internal improvements by John H. Krenkel, professor of history at Arizona State University. He states that he finds no substance to the charges leveled against Lincoln and the Long Nine.[13] One of the good early Lincoln biographies judges that the logrolling case made against Lincoln "is by no means clear."[14]

[9] Baringer, *Lincoln's Vandalia*, 91.

[10] Albert Beveridge, *Abraham Lincoln, 1809–1858* (2 vols., New York, Houghton, Mifflin, 1925), 198.

[11] Linder, *Reminiscences*, 62.

[12] Theodore C. Pease, *The Frontier State* (2 vols., Chicago, McClurg, 1919), 205.

[13] John H. Krenkel, *Illinois Internal Improvements* (Cedar Rapids, Torch Press, 1958), 47.

[14] John G. Nicolay and John Hay, *Abraham Lincoln: A History* (10 vols., New York, Century, 1890), 198.

Where do the accusers get their information?

1. At the special session following the selection of Springfield as the new capital, Vandalia made a last, desperate effort to repeal the act selecting Springfield. For this special session of July, 1837, the highly respected General W. Lee D. Ewing, a former governor and United States senator, was elected to represent Vandalia in the House in place of John Dement. Ewing and Lincoln clashed on this capital removal bill. During the debate, Ewing addressed the Sangamon delegation about Lincoln and with anger asked, "Gentlemen, have you no other champion than this coarse and vulgar fellow to bring into the lists against me? Do you suppose I will condescend to break a lance with your low and obscure colleague?"[15] A duel seemed imminent, but wiser counsel prevailed. During the debate Ewing charged, "The arrogance of Springfield, its presumption in claiming the seat of government, was not to be endured . . . the law had been passed by chicanery and trickery . . . The Springfield delegation had sold out to the Internal Improvements men, and had promised their support to every measure that would gain them a vote."[16] This first source, then, is that of a political enemy; sometimes such a source can be relied upon, sometimes not.

2. Another source also comes from a political enemy, but it is a more substantial one— Governor Thomas Ford. In Ford's fascinating and frank history, he wrote:

> Amongst [the Long Nine] were some dexterous jugglers and managers in politics, whose whole object was to obtain the seat of government for Springfield. This delegation, from the beginning of the session, threw itself as a unit in support of, or in opposition to, every local measure of interest, but never without a bargain for votes in return on the seat of government question. . . . By such means "the long nine" rolled along like a snow-ball, gathering accessions of strength . . . which they managed to take almost as a unit in favor on the Internal Improvements System, in return for which the active supporters of that system were to vote for Springfield to be the seat of government. . . . By giving the seat of government to Springfield was the whole state bought up and bribed, to

15 Linder, *Reminiscences*, 63.
16 *Ibid.*, 62.

approve the most senseless and disastrous policy which ever crippled the energies of a growing country.[17]

3. The third source is the witness of a partisan, Robert L. Wilson, who was one of the Long Nine. Twenty-nine years after his service in the legislature, he wrote a letter to William H. Herndon in which he said, "The [Sangamon] delegation, acting during the whole session upon all questions as a unit, gave them a strength and influence that enabled them to carry through their measures and give efficient aid to their friends."[18] Nothing in this letter indicates that anything dishonest or dishonorable was done; in fact, just the opposite is implied.

There are two other sources, but they are suspect. Stephen T. Logan was interviewed by Herndon and then Herndon wrote down what he remembered. The interview took place in 1875, thirty-nine years after the original event. Logan is quoted as saying:

> He [Lincoln] was at the head of the project to remove the seat of government here; it was entirely entrusted to him to manage. The members . . . all looked to Lincoln as the head. I was in Vandalia that winter and had a talk with Lincoln there. I remember that I took him to task for voting for the Internal Improvement scheme. He seemed to acquiesce in the correctness of my views as I presented them to him, but he said he couldn't help himself—he had to vote for it in order to secure the removal here of the seat of government.[19]

Four things make this item suspect: (1) The interview took place thirty-nine years after the event, when Logan's memory must have been dim; (2) Herndon transcribed the interview later and further errors likely slipped in; (3) Herndon did not hesitate to change interviews to make them fit his preconceived theories; and (4) Logan's writings contain not so much as a hint of a "deal" between internal improvements and the seat of government.

Another dubious source is this one: On February 21, 1839, the

[17] Ford, *History of Illinois*, 186–87.

[18] Robert L. Wilson to William Herndon, Herndon-Weik Collection, Library of Congress.

[19] *Abraham Lincoln Association Bulletin*, November 1, 1928.

Vandalia *Free Press* quoted Lincoln as stating on the floor that he had to be for internal improvements because he had exchanged internal improvements votes for seat of government votes. No other newspaper printed such a statement. It was probably the attempt of a poor loser to find a scapegoat for defeat.

What are the facts?

In his final term in the House, Lincoln himself by implication denied those charges. One of the members, Lewis W. Ross, complained about the high cost of poor food and lodging in Springfield. He charged that when the legislature voted to come to Springfield, they had been promised better accommodations. The *Sangamo Journal* sums up Lincoln's reply:

> He [Lincoln] wished to reply to the gentleman from Fulton who had stated that better accomodations were promised as an inducement for the removal of the seat of government to this place, that so far as himself and the representatives from this county were concerned, such was not the fact; nor did he believe [the capital] was removed from such miserable motives. There was not a member of that Legislature, that would confess that he was influenced by such unworthy considerations. It was from the fact that the great body of population being North, that a more central location was desired, and *this it could not be doubted was the governing consideration with the Legislature.*[20] (Italics not in original)

While perhaps no promises of this kind were made, there was at least some talk about much improved living standards in Springfield. One resident recalled, "The most potent argument used against Vandalia, was they would feed the Illinois statesmen nothing but venison, quail, wild duck and prairie chicken. While in Springfield they would get hog meat."[21]

A study of the record shows that at least some gross exaggerations about trades have been accepted. There was less logrolling than most accounts indicate, the Sangamon delegation did not vote as a unit during the entire session, and Lincoln, though a leader, was not the star performer that biographies have made him.

[20] January 29, 1841.
[21] Caroline Owsley Brown, "Springfield Society Before the Civil War," *ISHSJ*, April, 1922.

Where did Robert Wilson, himself one of the Long Nine, get his information? Remember he wrote his letter almost thirty years after the actual happenings. Memory can play a man tricks. He mentions, for instance, Lincoln's serving on the Committee of Internal Improvements—which Lincoln did not. There are many such factual errors in Wilson's letter, perhaps because Wilson's attendance record was bad. Out of forty-four key votes, he was not recorded on thirteen, an attendance record so bad it was exceeded by only one other House member.

As to Governor Ford's criticism, it was that of a political opponent of Lincoln and the other Whigs, but also that of a man who kept silent when he could have spoken out vigorously against the system he claimed to have opposed. Judges at that time did not hesitate to voice an opinion. He became a critic after the system failed. Besides, the person closest to Ford, his brother-in-law George Forquer, who had provided funds for Ford's education, had him named judge and was in some ways both a brother and father to Ford. Forquer was one of the leaders in the internal improvements movement, and there is no reason to believe that in 1836–37 Ford did not share his brother-in-law's opinions.

Members voted for the removal of the seat of government for a variety of reasons. Some were tired of the rugged frontier life of Vandalia, and Springfield was known to be a little more refined; many saw the state's population shifting northward and felt the capital—never permanently located at Vandalia—should be permanently located more to the north. One legislator, Jesse Dubois, recalled later, "He [Lincoln] made Webb and me vote for the removal, though we belonged to the southern end of the State. We defended our vote before our constituents by saying that necessity would ultimately force the seat of government to a central position. But in reality we gave the vote to Lincoln because we liked him, because we wanted to oblige our friends."[22]

Lincoln biographers stress one more reason, allegedly the most important for their position—vote trading on internal improvements by a united Long Nine which followed Lincoln's lead.

But, does the House Journal show that the Long Nine voted

[22] Nicolay and Hay, *Lincoln*, I, 138.

as a unit throughout the session as the two chief sources, Ford and Wilson, state?

An examination of the record in the House alone blasts that theory quickly. There were twenty-five roll calls on issues where logrolling was clearly possible, excluding the nineteen additional roll calls on internal improvements and the capital relocation. On these twenty-five roll calls, the seven Sangamon House members all voted alike on five measures. On another five measures there were no conflicting votes, but one or more of their delegation was absent and not voting, which in at least some cases indicates no tremendous interest and "no deal." In the case of the motion to kill the bill extending the bank charter of Kaskaskia, for example, three of the seven Sangamon members did not vote; obviously there was no trade with such a vote. It is of much greater significance that on fifteen of the twenty-five roll calls there was division within the Sangamon delegation. This is particularly meaningful when it is considered that all seven were Whigs and could be expected to show cohesion. Therefore, Wilson's statement that the Sangamon delegation acted "during the session upon all questions as a unit" is wrong. As a matter of fact, there was surprisingly little unanimity within the Sangamon delegation.

Was public support lacking so that trades were necessary?

Public sentiment was overwhelmingly for internal improvements, so that Illinois did not need any capital relocation bill to force approval, any more than did any other state.

When former Governor John Reynolds returned to Illinois from Congress, he "found the people perfectly insane on the subject of improvements."[23] A biographer of Adams County legislator, James Ralston, said that Ralston "would have been ostracized by his party and by the community he represented" had he opposed internal improvements.[24] Even Ewing, one of those who made the "trade" charge against Lincoln, in 1834 had urged internal improvements in a message to the legislature.

Legislators who helped pass the measure were exceedingly proud

[23] John Reynolds, *My Own Times* (Chicago Historical Society, 1879), 324.

[24] John F. Snyder, *Selected Writings*, ed. by Clyde C. Walton (Springfield, Illinois State Historical Society, 1962), 119.

of their action, and one report said that you could always recognize a legislator in a crowd by his automatic repetition of the phrases, "Thirteen hundred—fellow citizens!—and fifty miles of railroad."[25]

A tremendous celebration was held in Vandalia the night the Internal Improvements Act was passed. "All was joy!" reported the Vandalia *State Register*.[26] In the House that night there were sixty-one lights to honor the sixty-one members who voted for the bill, and in the Senate chamber twenty-five lights for as many supporters.

"It will be the means of advancing the prosperity and future greatness of our state, as much as the birth of Washington did that of the United States," declared the *Alton Telegraph*.[27] Elijah P. Lovejoy reported in his *Alton Observer*, "The Great Internal Improvement Bill has passed the Legislature. . . . We cannot avoid congratulating our readers upon this auspicious result."[28]

David Prickett wrote to his brother, Colonel Isaac Prickett, that "the Internal Improvements System so far as I can learn is popular in the North."[29] The *Chicago American* was for it, but had some doubts that it would pass, because the legislature did not have enough vision; perhaps it appears "too mammoth for our Legislature."[30]

The system was so popular that the *Western Voice and Internal Improvement Journal* in its first issue noted, "The future prosperity and greatness of Illinois under the prosecution and after the completion of her system of improvements is not dimmed by doubts and apprehension."[31] In its second issue, the journal noted that public opinion on internal improvements was so strong that opponents of the system would be well advised not to seek state-wide office.

Cyrus Edwards of Alton, a member of the Senate and youngest

[25] Nicolay and Hay, *Lincoln*, I, 158–59.
[26] February 24, 1837.
[27] March 8, 1837.
[28] March 2, 1837.
[29] Letter of March 12, 1837, Chicago Historical Society Library.
[30] March 4, 1837.
[31] December 23, 1837.

brother of the early Illinois Governor Ninian Edwards, was seeking the governorship. From the outset he made it clear where he stood, so that the *Alton Spectator* could write, "We publish his letter with much pleasure and are happy to learn that he was one of the supporters of the bill."[32] Later, the same paper called Governor Duncan's request to repeal the Internal Improvements Act "dictatorial."[33]

Even an out of state observer wrote, "These gigantic works would startle the citizens of the East; but any judicious person, in examining the nature and extent of this great State, would say that they evidence great energy and sagacity. . . . Produce of the soil will be doubled in value . . . while every article of necessity or luxury procured from abroad will come at diminished cost."[34]

A Michigan man referred to Illinois internal improvements as "established and in successful operation. . . . Their state credit is unimpaired, and their plans and projects have been creditably sustained."[35]

Strong public opinion like this moved one observer to state, "The Internal Improvement scheme would have been adopted by the Legislature in some form in any event, whether the state capital were moved or not."[36]

Astute and well-educated David Davis felt for a while that internal improvements could be a success. By 1840 he had given up hope and commented, "Each party in the State is endeavoring amid the universal odium of 'the System' to throw the responsibility on the other, when in truth and fact, no party is responsible. The members of the Legislature as Individuals, differing in politics are responsible for it."[37] Davis knew what was going on, but there

[32] March 17, 1837.

[33] July 21, 1837.

[34] David Henshaw, *Letters on the Internal Improvements and Commerce of the West* (Boston, Dutton and Wentworth, 1839), 25. (Originally published in the Boston *Morning Post*.)

[35] "Honestus: A Brief Examination of the Projected System of Internal Improvements Now in Progress in This State" (Detroit, March 22, 1839), 5–6. Copy at the University of Chicago Library.

[36] Joseph Wallace, *Past and Present of the City of Springfield* (Chicago, Clark Publishing Co., 1904), 11–12.

[37] David Davis to unnamed relatives, January 19, 1840, IHL.

is no mention in all of his correspondence of purchasing the transfer to Springfield with internal improvements votes.

A historian of the times wrote, "Internal Improvements was agitated by all classes with increasing interest until it became the absorbing subject of thought and discussion to the exclusion of all other public matters. The people saw, with envy, at the close of 1835, that Massachusetts had 140 miles of railroads in successful operation; Pennsylvania had 218 miles of railroads, and was digging 914 miles of canals; and several other states were busily building railroads, canals and other public works. . . . They could see no reason why Illinois should be permitted to lag behind. . . . Before the next general election the matter of Internal Improvements took absolute possession of the people's minds, perverting the common sense and blinding the judgment of the most staid and conservative of them. . . . A majority of the people wildly advocated the immediate construction of a network of railroads and canals all over the State regardless of cost."[38]

If there had been a deal on internal improvements and the seat of government, Alton and Vandalia would have been expected to be bitter in their opposition to internal improvements, since both had led Springfield in the 1834 state-wide voting for a permanent seat of government.

One Vandalia newspaper was cool to the idea, but made no charge of a deal. The other newspaper of Vandalia was wildly enthusiastic: "We entertain no doubts as to the expediency of the measure. . . . We cannot but congratulate the people on the passage of this important law."[39] Earlier, it had urged the House to study "whether it would not be expedient to extend the system and embrace in it some other works, in addition to those reported upon."[40] A few weeks after the passage of the bill, the same Vandalia newspaper reported, "We have no doubt the passage of the bill has already increased the value of land in the State more than 100 per cent, and every day is adding to its value."[41]

[38] John F. Snyder, *Adam W. Snyder and His Period in Illinois History* (Virginia, Ill., Needham, 1906), 198–200.

[39] *Weekly State Register and People's Advocate*, February 24, 1837.

[40] *Ibid.*, January 12, 1837.

[41] *Ibid.*, March 6, 1837.

It is worth repeating here that Lincoln always had favored this type of legislation, calling for it in his first unsuccessful race for the legislature in 1832. This interest continued even after he was no longer in the legislature.

During the 1834 and 1836 campaigns, there was much more discussion in the Springfield newspaper about internal improvements than moving the seat of government. This was true even after the legislature was in session in 1836 and 1837. When the session was more than half over, Ninian W. Edwards wrote to the *Sangamo Journal* that there were "several important bills now pending before the Legislature."[42] He mentioned internal improvements, school funds, and the revenue measure, but not moving the seat of government. Springfield regarded internal improvements as much more important than becoming the capital.

John Dawson's pledge to support measures "calculated to develop the resources of the State" was typical of the candidacies in Sangamon County.[43] Edwards, in his statement of candidacy, stated he favored "a liberal system of Internal Improvements."[44] Feeling in Sangamon County strongly favored the projects, as did most of the state. Throughout the state, legislators made it the main issue. Except for the Van Buren and White candidacies for President, nothing stirred up so much interest. Even in the Galena area, which could benefit relatively little from the big project, two legislators were elected who took a strong stand for it, while the candidate who ignored this issue came in a poor fourth. Galena newspapers prior to the election—from July 9, 1836 to July 23, 1838—reveal that internal improvements was the big issue.

The *Belleville Gazette*'s praise of the passage of internal improvements as a "great and praiseworthy act" summed up the thinking in Illinois.[45]

Even the Democratic *State Register* of Vandalia was considerably more interested in internal improvements than in remaining the seat of government. This was due partly to its awareness that

42 July 2, 1836.
43 *SgJ*, April 9, 1836.
44 *Ibid.*, January 28, 1837.
45 Quoted in *Alton Telegraph*, March 29, 1837.

sooner or later the capital would move northward anyway, partly to its assessing internal improvements as much more important to the city. This Vandalia newspaper expressed its mood after the Internal Improvements Act passed: "All must see the propriety of the plan which the Legislature have [*sic*] adopted."[46] The editor was active in politics and would have been aware—at least through rumors—of any deal being made by the Sangamon delegation. Obviously he had heard of none, for more than a week after Springfield was chosen as the seat of government, he wrote about internal improvements, "If the present Legislature had done no more, they would have deserved the thanks of the People for the passage of this law."[47] Then he added this significant sentence: "It owes its existence to the strength and firmness of the Van Buren party." Since Lincoln and his colleagues were Whigs, not Van Buren men, the editor clearly was not giving the Sangamonites credit for the passage of the measure.

Adding much to the public clamor for internal improvements was the fact that although the legislature authorized private railroad lines in 1835–36, the private companies could not raise the money to build the lines. Seemingly the only way to get these facilities was through state action.

In addition, speculation ran wild. Douglas wrote to his brother-in-law, Julius Granger, "Every man that is industrious and economical gets rich, at any kind of business. . . . Fortunes can be made easily."[48] No goal seemed too high for the new state to attain, no feat too great for its citizens to accomplish.

What about the voting on the Internal Improvements Act? Did Lincoln and his colleagues support additional projects in trade for votes for Springfield?

Even when the internal improvements bill was vetoed by the Council of Revision, only nineteen of the House members had the courage or the foresight to vote against the measure. If there was a trade, the House of Representatives must not have been aware of it because eleven of the nineteen House members voting against the Internal Improvements Act voted for Springfield on at least one

---

[46] *ISR*, February 24, 1837. [47] *Ibid.*, March 6, 1837.
[48] *Letters of Stephen A. Douglas*, November 14, 1834, 11.

ballot. One of the House members who voted for Springfield on all four ballots was E. B. Webb of White County, who had earlier filed a biting but prophetic protest against the passage of the Internal Improvements Act.

Lincoln voted for all the amendments increasing the extent of the act, but there is no indication that he voted anything but his personal convictions. Of the eight amendments on which there are recorded roll calls, the seven Sangamon members voted as a unit on only two. On the other six amendments there were both negative and affirmative votes. Of the two issues on which they voted together, one was in support of an amendment by John Hardin of Morgan County, who voted for Jacksonville as the state capital on all four ballots. A majority of the Sangamon members voted for the two amendments by Franklin Witt of Greene County, but Witt voted for Carrollton twice as the capital site, for Springfield once on the third ballot, and then finally for Grafton. If there was some kind of trade, Witt either knew nothing about it, or broke his word—something rare within the ranks of the legislature. Of the sponsors of the Internal Improvements Act amendments on which votes can be traced, only one voted for Springfield on all four ballots—John Logan of Jackson County, who received the votes of five of the seven Sangamon County members on his amendment. *A check of the records shows that Springfield received proportionately fewer votes from sponsors of amendments to the Internal Improvements Act than it did from other members of the House.* If there was logrolling for Springfield before passage of the Internal Improvements Act, it was either miserably handled or it was virtually nonexistent. The latter seems the logical conclusion. Efforts to raise or lower the stature of Abraham Lincoln by making him look like a shrewd and calculating manipulator on the basis of this measure are ill-founded.

A study of the Senate record is less interesting because Lincoln is not so directly involved, but it shows substantially the same thing as the *House Journal.* Of the fifteen Senate members who opposed the Internal Improvements Act, eight voted for Springfield.

The Senate sponsor of the amendment for additional funds for counties without building projects voted for Alton, not Springfield.

The Senate sponsor of the bill which made possible the vote for a new state capital, Senator Orville H. Browning of Quincy, was an opponent of the internal improvements project, a fact overlooked by those who have repeated the "trade" charges. As a Browning biographer notes: "Browning belonged to a stubborn faction that fought the bill [internal improvements] during its entire course through the Legislature."[49] It is altogether out of character for Browning to take part in a trade which would have achieved passage of a bill he strongly opposed. In a speech on the floor of the Senate in 1840, Browning said of internal improvements, "From the very first moment the bill made its appearance in the Senate, I have been doing battle against it, and I thank God, that, in whatever else I may have erred, I have not to atone for the sin of having voted for one solitary measure connected with the whole system."[50] There is no reason to doubt him; and if Browning was not part of this "massive trade," it did not take place. On another occasion Browning said "he had never made trades on this [internal improvements] or any other subject."[51]

Those who have advanced the Springfield–internal improvements trade also have ignored the role of Governor Duncan in all of this. A strong and bitter opponent of the internal improvements measure and a man of unquestioned integrity, Governor Duncan would have favored a veto of the selection of Springfield, and the bill making it possible, if such obvious trading were taking place. This is particularly true since his home town of Jacksonville was being considered. But Duncan neither asked the Council of Revision for a veto nor issued one of the blistering messages for which he was known.

Governor Duncan also could have supported a veto on the basis of the 1834 vote for the seat of government, even though that vote had been indecisive. The 1834 vote between Alton, Vandalia, and Springfield was so close that few considered it conclusive even though the law said it would be. While 33,231 voters cast their

[49] Maurice Baxter, *Orville H. Browning* (Bloomington, Indiana University Press, 1957), 21.

[50] *SgJ*, January 17, 1840.

[51] *Ibid.*, January 28, 1840.

ballots on the issue, in some counties there were hardly any votes cast, and 8,984 voters around the state refused to vote on the issue. In Cook County, for example, 529 votes were cast in the race for governor, but only 52 votes on the seat of government question. In Putnam County, only four voters chose to vote on the issue. All of this clouded the matter to such an extent that the 1834 vote on the seat of government was never canvassed. There was general agreement among the large majority of political leaders that the capital would eventually be moved, but where and when was still a matter of dispute.

A little-publicized meeting had been held in Rushville on January 4, 1834, Daniel Stone presiding, at which many of the northern political leaders agreed that Springfield should be the capital. This accounts for the large Springfield vote.

There are many indications that the move to Springfield was not an unpopular move nor a move which required a great deal of bartering.

Newspapers from points as far apart as Shawneetown, in the extreme southern part of the state, to Chicago in the north, praised the choice of Springfield. Vandalia was in the southern third of the state, and the center of population was moving northward. Springfield is located within a few miles of the geographical center of the state. Many locations were turned down, but there was surprisingly little disapproval of Springfield. The *Shawneetown Journal* at the far southern part of the state noted that Springfield "not only from its central position, but from its situation in the heart of the richest part of Illinois . . . will suit the entire approbation of the people of the State."[52] The *Chicago Advertiser* termed the selection "judicious," and the *Chicago Democrat* noted, "No other town could have satisfied a greater portion of our citizens."[53] The *Jacksonville Patriot* observed that "the people are, on the whole, satisfied with the selection of Springfield as the seat of government."[54] David Davis wrote to a friend, "I find that the loca-

[52] Quoted in *Historical Encyclopedia of Illinois and History of Sangamon County,* ed. by Newton Bateman and Paul Selby (2 vols. in 3, Chicago, Munsell, 1912), II, 649.

[53] *Ibid.*

[54] Quoted in *SgJ,* July 15, 1837.

91

tion of the Seat of Government at Springfield is considered permanent."[55]

What about the charge that Alton was given three railroads in exchange for the support of Springfield?

It should be mentioned, first of all, that Alton was the logical terminal point for railroad traffic. Even private lines seeking legislative approval planned to terminate their facilities at Alton, the city which seemed destined to dwarf its neighbor across the river, St. Louis.

Yet even if this were not true, the most cursory glance at the *House Journal* shows that there was no such trade. Springfield got but one vote out of the Madison County (Alton) delegation—from John Hogan on the fourth ballot when it was clear that Alton was out of the picture. Hogan possibly did this out of his personal liking for Lincoln and some of the other Sangamon delegation. Certainly a fourth ballot vote by one of Madison County's three legislators was not exchanged for three railroad lines.

Do the Sangamon County legislators' votes for officials indicate a pattern of logrolling on internal improvements?

The most obvious opportunity for trading was at the opening of the session. There were three candidates for speaker of the House. The voting went to four ballots, and a block of seven votes in a ninety-one-member House represented real power. Members of the Sangamon House delegation voted for Cloud and Dement. In the capital matter, Cloud voted for Jacksonville on all four ballots, and Dement voted for Vandalia on all four ballots. Again there is no pattern of deal-making.

In the two ballots it took to elect an attorney general, the majority of the Sangamon delegation voted for State Senator Benjamin Bond, but Bond voted for Vandalia on the first three ballots and for Alton on the fourth. Usher Linder received one vote on each ballot from one of Lincoln's Springfield colleagues, but Linder resigned from the House before the capital location vote was taken.

In the balloting for state auditor, the Sangamon crew voted for Levi Davis, a Democrat who was not a member of the legislature. One of those whom Davis defeated was John Dougherty, a House

[55] David Davis to William P. Walker, July 1, 1837, IHL.

member who voted for Springfield on all four ballots. If there was a deal, Dougherty got the short end of it! It is more logical to assume that there was no deal on this vote.

There were three contestants for state treasurer: State Senator John G. Whiteside, Representative John Dement, and Representative Richard G. Murphy. Five of the seven Sangamon votes went to Whiteside, one went to Dement, and one was not cast. The only person not to get a Sangamon vote was Murphy. But on the capital location balloting, Whiteside voted for Alton all four times, Dement voted for Vandalia all four times, and Murphy voted for Springfield three out of four ballots. Again, here was a situation ripe for a trade, and no trade book place.

One of the sought-after jobs was that of warden of the state penitentiary. There were four candidates, but the race was chiefly between William Otwell, a nonmember, and Representative Benjamin S. Enloe. This voting went to three ballots. The majority of the Sangamon House members (by a five-to-one margin) supported Otwell on all three ballots. Yet when it came to the capital voting, Enloe supported Springfield on all four ballots.

The only case supporters of the logrolling theory can find in the selection of officials is in the race for state's attorney of the Fourth District when Representative Augustus C. French of Edgar County was selected over a nonmember with the votes of five of the seven Sangamonites. French voted for Decatur once, Illiopolis once, and then Springfield twice. But even in this case, the fact that he voted for other cities on the first two ballots gives evidence that there was no trade.

Certainly the overall record of voting for officials does not substantiate the charge of logrolling.

What about the measures on which Lincoln changed his position? Do they indicate a trade?

It is difficult to know with certainty when there was a change in position. The record indicates Lincoln rarely changed his position, and even in cases where this appears to be the case, it is possible that an amendment to a bill satisfied his original objection. In those few cases where there is an apparent reversal of his vote, there is no evidence of trading. The measure that best lent itself to a trade was the bill extending the charter of the Kaskaskia bank. Here he first voted to kill the bill, then finally voted for its passage. The two legislators from the Kaskaskia area were James Shields and Samuel Thompson. Shields voted for Kaskaskia as the seat of government on the first ballot and for Alton on the last three. Thompson voted for Alton on the first two and for Springfield on the last two. It seems unlikely that there was a reversal of position for a third and fourth ballot vote by one of two legislators.

Was there talk of a trade or bribery at that time?

There was—but not about a trade of the seat of government for internal improvements.

The "bribe" which haunted Springfield for several years was the $50,000 commitment to get the seat of government. This had been part of the original measure to move the seat of government, that any city getting it would have to put up $50,000 and two acres of land for the new state buildings. It does not seem at all unethical, yet there was much talk about this "bribe" at the time, even by Sangamon County residents. As late as 1881, Dr. Alexander Shields of Sangamon County wrote, "They finally accomplished the end by Springfield giving a bribe, in the name of a bonus, of fifty thousand dollars, to the State."[56] Undoubtedly adding to the talk over the $50,000 was the fact that Springfield pledged the money, but then, because of the economic chaos of the times, was not able to pay the money on time. It looked like a promise made but not kept.

Mrs. Browning wrote a letter in which she refers to "the bargain" on the seat of government, perhaps referring to the $50,000 Springfield was to raise or to the improved conditions promised by Springfield, for she comments with irony, "Your feet have been taken out of the mire clay of Vandalia and placed on the beautiful mossaick [*sic*] pavements of Springfield."[57]

A more significant kind of trade or bribery took place in which there was no immediate exchange of money. Land speculators and

---

[56] *History of Sangamon County, Illinois,* written by various citizens (Chicago, Interstate Publishing Co., 1881), 202–203.

[57] Mrs. Orville H. Browning to four legislators, December 20, 1839. Letter at Chicago Historical Society Library.

people interested in the money to be acquired from engineer's fees and attorney's fees were pushing hard for the legislation, as did some contractors. It would have passed without this, but these people who expected tremendous income from the project were most enthusiastic and added to the public clamor for the bill. People who owned land saw this as a means of raising the price of their property. A typical reaction was that of a Macon County farmer who wrote to his brother in Ohio, "The Railroad will come in sight of my place I expect from Springfield to Danville which will make my property valuable. Land is raising verry [*sic*] fast in this state."[58]

There is some truth to the charge made three years later by Senator Sidney H. Little of the western part of the state in a lengthy speech on the subject that internal improvements was caused by "a mania for speculation."[59]

The *Peoria Register and North Western Gazatteer* ran a remarkable series of articles from August through December, 1838, going into depth on the weaknesses of the Internal Improvements Act and why it passed. This series of articles laid the chief blame for passage on those who were out after some personal profit. But it is equally interesting to note that in this long series, and with many letters from readers on the subject, no hint anywhere was made that there might be a tie-up of internal improvements with the moving of the seat of government. If there had been any truth to such a charge, it is difficult to imagine such a penetrating series of articles missing it completely.

The correspondence between John A. McClernand, one of the chief backers of internal improvements, and Henry Eddy gives no hint of any deal on the seat of government. McClernand believed popular opinion strongly behind the measure, for he commented on some members who opposed it, "Their days I think are no^d."[60] Nor does correspondence of others in this period indicate any deal.

The *Vandalia Free Press* was one of the few newspapers that

---

58 Isaac Williams, April 23, 1836, IHL.
59 *SgJ*, January 21, 1840.
60 McClernand to Eddy, February 19, 1837, IHL.

was opposed to internal improvements and after passage of the act published a lengthy speech by Browning attacking it. This journal made no mention of the moving of the capital other than a small one-paragraph item, on page 3, telling of the vote for Springfield and noting, "The removal is to take place after 1840, provided some subsequent Legislature does not interfere."[61] There was no hint at any trade of the seat of government for internal improvements.

John Henry, representative from Morgan County (Jacksonville), in 1839 introduced the measure to repeal the Internal Improvements Act, but in his "Memoirs" gives no hint that a trade for the seat of government was responsible for the passage of the bill.[62]

In later years, Stephen A. Douglas was in a position to gain politically by charging internal improvements to Lincoln in a deal for Springfield. Instead Douglas wrote, "The people were for the system—almost en masse. So strong was the current of popular feeling in its favor that it was hazardous for any politician to oppose it. Under these circumstances it was easy to obtain instructions in favor of a measure so universally popular, and accordingly the friends of the bill got up instructions, I did not feel myself at liberty to disobey. I accordingly voted for the bill under these instructions. That vote was the vote of my constituents and not my own."[63]

Even when the Lincoln-Douglas debates would have given Douglas an ideal opportunity to make charges against Lincoln of trading for Springfield and causing the tremendous debt which the state had because of internal improvements, Douglas made no such charge.

Hardin—in one speech made in 1839—talked of "acts of bargain and sale which . . . may have been made out of doors."[64] What he was referring to is not clear from the speech. The day after the Internal Improvements Act passed with all its additions, Hardin

[61] March 4, 1837.
[62] "The Memoirs of John Henry," *ISHSJ*, April, 1925.
[63] "Autobiography of Stephen A. Douglas," *ISHSJ*, October 1912, 341.
[64] *Vandalia Free Press*, February 21, 1839.

wrote to his wife from Vandalia, "A man has no business here unless he will debase himself to bargain and trade for his rights or his desires."[65] Here again there is no reference to what he was talking about, but from what others have written, it may have been the fight for position and the money that went with it. From all other evidence, this last conclusion seems the proper one.

Hardin, of course, opposed the internal improvements plan, but his position was attacked by many back home. A letter Hardin received in Vandalia from a Jacksonville friend illustrates the feeling on the proposal: "A petition a few weeks ago was put in circulation for signers requesting our members to vote for the [Internal Improvements] Bill. It was presented to me for my signature, I refused, and have offended some of my friends; After the mail arrived last night, I stepped into an office. A Gentleman was reading a letter he had just recd from one of our members. *He stopped*, on my entering the room and said you are against Internal Improvements, and quit reading."[66]

Jacksonville was as excited about internal improvements as the rest of the state.

Did opponents of Springfield charge a trade in behalf of internal improvements?

Obviously many were unhappy with the selection of Springfield. The *State Register* of Vandalia within a few months started making charges, most of them wild and reckless. However, they centered chiefly on the financial pledges of Springfield. Significantly, there is no charge of a vote trade in behalf of internal improvements—and this was an era in American journalism when even a rumor of that kind would have been published without any compunction. The few editorials in the state critical of internal improvements made no mention of any leader or any trade.

The *State Register* of Vandalia, in the weeks following the close of the legislative session, paid but little attention to the matter of moving the seat of government. To it, internal improvements was the big issue. It was not until a month later that the *State Register*

---

65 February 26, 1837, Chicago Historical Society Library.
66 Melendy to Hardin, January 29, 1837, Chicago Historical Society Library.

referred to Springfield as a city of "arrogance and aristocracy" and as the "Whig metropolis of Democratic Illinois."[67]

The *Alton Telegraph* did not seem to mind the Springfield selection, even though Alton itself once headed a public vote on the measure. Here, too, the big thing was internal improvements.

A year afterwards, the *Sangamo Journal* commented, "Every effort that ingenuity could devise . . . was made by the friends of Vandalia to defeat its passage. The editor of the *Register* and kindred spirits made the most baseless charges against Springfield," including calling Springfield "the hotbed of federalism. . . . All charges against the moral and political honesty of the Long Nine . . . were unavailing."[68] Again, no suggestion of a trade of the capital for internal improvements.

A meeting held in Vandalia in July, 1838, "of all those who feel interested in the pending seat of government question," was a last desperate effort to halt the moving of the capital from Vandalia.[69] After that meeting, several issues of the *Register* (then published in Vandalia) covered the capital issue in detail. Every possible charge was aired; references suggested the Long Nine to be "firm and united" and as having "swapped off and exchanged"; but they are quite incidental and the charges general.[70] A lengthy appeal on the capital issue appeared in the *Register*, signed by prominent Vandalia citizens, including William L. D. Ewing. The charges were not specific. Vaguely, the statement accused the Long Nine of "every art, device and argument."[71] The State Bank's activities were mentioned and corruption was strongly hinted at as the cause for the move to Springfield, although the *Register* conceded that some of those who voted for Springfield "may have been honorable." It made no specific tie-in of the Long Nine with internal improvements. In none of these issues of the *Register* is Lincoln even mentioned.

If there had been hints of a tie-in of the Long Nine or Lincoln with the trade suggested in later years, the newspapers would not

[67] *ISR*, March 25, 1837.
[68] *SgJ*, February 24, 1838.
[69] *ISR*, July 6, 1838.
[70] *Ibid.*, August 10, 1838.
[71] *Ibid.*

have hesitated to print it. Extreme and baseless charges were printed readily. For example, the editor of Vandalia's *State Register*, a few weeks after the passage of the Internal Improvements Act and the moving of the seat of government measure, referred to the local opposition editor, Lincoln's friend of the *Free Press*, as a "hypocrite" and a man of "singularly contemptible character." He was described as "not a member of any religious society . . . [he] left the Church rather than settle an honest debt. . . . [He was] a wretch, whom no charity can soften, no religion reclaim, no miracle convert . . . cold as the snows of Russia and putrid as the dead." The *State Register* editor also noted an item in the opposition paper about a dog losing its tail. The *Register* editor commented in print to his fellow journalist, "Don't fret about that, neighbor, you carried so close between your legs before you lost it, that it will never be missed."[72] All of this in one issue! Editors of that stripe would not have hesitated publishing the least rumor about Lincoln and his colleagues in the Long Nine.

The only tie-in of the Long Nine with internal improvements ever suggested by the newspapers was the one already mentioned in this chapter, a small one by the *Vandalia Free Press* in 1839. By then, the internal improvements issue had started to lose its popularity, and Lincoln was leading the fight to keep the capital in Springfield, something not designed to endear him to the Vandalia newspapers. In that one edition, the *Free Press* said that Lincoln "admitted" that internal improvements were traded for Springfield.[73] No other edition of that newspaper mentions it, and no other newspaper picked it up. A Vandalia legislator may have suggested it. In any event, Lincoln authorities believe the report at best contains exaggeration.[74] It does not sound like a Lincoln statement.

The *Sparta Democrat* in 1840 often denounced the folly of in-

---

[72] *Ibid.*, March 25, 1837.

[73] "Mr. Lincoln admitted that Sangamon county had received great and important benefits, at the last session of the Legislature, in return for giving support, thro' her delegation to the system of Internal Improvements; and that though not legally bound, she is morally bound, to adhere to that system, through all time to come!" *Vandalia Free Press*, February 21, 1839.

[74] *CW*, I, 144, footnote.

ternal improvements. Rabidly Democratic, it preferred Vandalia to Springfield, yet never suggested that Springfield by unfair barter became the seat of government. There was no such intimation even when one of the legislators discussed the "mad and visionary specu-- lations of 1836 and 1837."[75] In an 1841 issue, internal improvements were said to have been "established by logrolling legislation," but did not accuse Springfield, a natural foe.[76]

In Morgan County, one of the candidates for re-election to the House contended in the Jacksonville *Gazette and News* that the legislature chose Springfield because of "bargain and sale."[77] Here again there is, significantly, no amplification of the charge. It apparently was little more than an attempt to show Jacksonville constituents why Springfield became the capital rather than Jacksonville, in the hope that a vague, general charge would satisfy them. Or he may have been referring to the $50,000 Springfield had agreed to put up. The *Sangamo Journal* immediately refuted the charge, stating that "no sensible man would believe it," and showing that the same legislator had previously been talking much differently. It had a letter to prove that the legislator, R. S. Walker (whom they called "a dunce"), changed his tune when dealing with Jacksonville constituents.[78] Walker did not reply.

Stephen A. Douglas, also of Jacksonville, in a letter to the *Illinois Patriot* of Jacksonville, had to defend himself for failing to bring the capital to Jacksonville. Douglas replied that the newspaper's assertion that he had helped Springfield was not true, and then he credited the Sangamon delegation with working extremely hard for Springfield. They had used "every exertion and . . . every necessary sacrifice."[79] But in Douglas's reply there is no mention of any trading engaged in by the pro-Springfield group, and Douglas was not a man to deal in vague language.

In a handbill distributed in Vandalia, the champion of Vandalia, William L. D. Ewing, appealed to voters to support his candidacy to the legislature. He pointed out "the foul corruption by which

[75] *Sparta Democrat*, November 6, 1840. Letter by Richard G. Murphy.
[76] *Ibid.*, November 26, 1841.
[77] Quoted in the *SgJ*, May 20, 1837.
[78] *Ibid.*, May 20 and 27, 1837.
[79] Quoted in the *SgJ*, April 22, 1837.

the seat of government, contrary to justice and the constitution, was removed to Springfield." This may have gone over well in Vandalia, but there was nothing unconstitutional about the move. It was not contrary to justice, and there was no "foul corruption" involved. Again, Ewing made all three charges without stating specifics. There is no hint of a trade with internal improvements, and there is nothing of substance in the handbill to indicate that Ewing's charge is anything more than campaign oratory.[80]

When Lincoln spoke in Vandalia in 1856, published reports of questions from the audience gave no hint of any adverse public reaction to the moving of the capital. If Lincoln had made the "massive trade" and was so clearly responsible, as some biographies declare, it seems probable that opponents among the newspapers or in the audience would have mentioned it.

In 1840 in the State Senate there was extensive debate about the issues of the seat of government and internal improvements but no suggestion of any connection between the two. Vandalia and Alton both had legislators there who could have made such charges.

Another minor piece of evidence is the fact that logrolling would be common knowledge among politicians and could hardly fail becoming a major election issue. But it did not. As to the special elections in 1838—immediately after the vote for Springfield—the Galena newspaper commented, "The only political question which has been raised in any of these elections, that has come to our knowledge, is the one whether our present Bank and Banking system shall be sustained or destroyed."[81]

Was Lincoln the hero of Springfield?

One of Lincoln's abler biographers, Senator Beveridge, writes substantially what many have written: "Lincoln was the hero of the hour. . . . [Springfield's] victory gave 'new life and energy to our citizens' proudly declared the *Sangamo Journal*. All knew that they owed their good fortune to the representative from New Salem more than to anybody else. . . . Seldom has a young man gone to any town to make his way, with so many friends awaiting

[80] *Ibid.*, July 14, 1838.
[81] *North West Gazette and Galena Advertiser*, July 15, 1837.

him, as Lincoln found when on an April day in 1837 he rode into Springfield."[82]

It must be pointed out, however, that no newspaper of that day gave Lincoln such credit. Lincoln received credit along with other members of the Long Nine, but was not singled out. If anything, the newspapers regarded Senator Browning of Quincy—sponsor of the Senate bill to vote on moving the capital—responsible. The official records—the *House Journal* and the *Senate Journal*—do not warrant giving Lincoln a position of lonely eminence in this matter either, although he was one of the leaders. The original motion in the House, on January 2, 1837, to have a committee report to the House on the matter of capital relocation was made by Gideon Minor of Edgar County. When the seven committee members were named, Springfield's interests were not represented by Lincoln but by his colleague Dan Stone. The selection of the other members of the committee indicates that the men regarded as the leaders for each community were named—Cloud of Jacksonville and Dement of Vandalia, for example.

Moreover, the Hardin letters, the David Davis letters, and other papers written by men on the scene in Vandalia do not assign to Lincoln any such role or prominence as do more recently written works. Hardin referred to Vandalia as a "den of legislative trading," but in his letters he does not implicate Lincoln.[83]

If Lincoln was "the hero of the hour," as Beveridge states, it seems strange that he would write, two months after the passage of the bill and less than a month after moving to Springfield, that "living in Springfield is rather a dull business after all, at least it is so to me. I am quite as lonesome here as [I] ever was anywhere in my life. I have been spoken to by but one woman since I've been here, and should not have been by her if she could have avoided it."[84] Does this sound like the "hero of the hour"? Where is the host of friends awaiting his entrance into town?

The choice of Springfield was celebrated in Springfield in late July and in Athens in early August. At Springfield the toast to

---

[82] Beveridge, *Abraham Lincoln*, I, 206–207.

[83] Letter of Hardin to his wife, December 14, 1835, Chicago Historical Society Library.

Browning was, "When the column and the dome of the capital shall be reared aloft, as we gaze upon its beauty and its grandeur, Sangamon in her gladness will remember him as introducing into the Senate, the bill locating the seat of government. That pillar, that dome, shall be his monument." Browning, in response, praised the Sangamon delegation for their work, but did not single out Lincoln. There were a number of planned toasts to various individuals and causes, and then there were "volunteers." Third among the volunteer toasts, Lincoln saluted "all our friends. They are too numerous to be now named individually, while there is no one of them who is not too dear to be forgotten or neglected." Lincoln received no particular recognition during the affair, less attention in fact, than that given to two other legislators. Stephen T. Logan made the most sensible of the toasts: "The system of Internal Improvements adopted by the late Legislature—the best mode of rearing it to perfection would be a liberal pruning of its superflous branches." Lincoln's friend David Prickett made the most unusual toast: "The State Capitol—may it be built of rum."[85]

At the Athens affair Lincoln was toasted twice like the other legislators that evening. "He has fulfilled the expectations of his friends and disappointed the hopes of his enemies," and "one of nature's nobility," was said in praise of him. But the newspaper account shows nothing of his having been singled out for honors or feted as "the hero of the hour."[86]

No doubt a colleague of Lincoln in that session was right when he wrote in later years, "My readers will perhaps be astonished when I say to them that at that time Mr. Lincoln did not give promise of being the first man in Illinois, as he afterwards became."[87]

Lincoln did exert greater leadership in the special session held in July, 1837. Here he stopped the bill which would have repealed the Springfield move. But the election returns in Springfield—particularly those in 1840, when he ran last among the elected representatives from Sangamon County—prove that Lincoln received little

[84] *CW*, I, 78.

[85] *SgJ*, July 29, 1837.

[86] *Ibid*., August 12, 1837.

[87] Linder, *Reminiscences*, 58.

credit from the public for bringing the state's headquarters to Springfield. Whatever gratitude there may have been disappeared, for Sangamon County gave Douglas a majority over Lincoln when the two were running for United States Senator in 1858, and Sangamon County gave Douglas a majority over Lincoln when the two were running for President in 1860.

Is the case against logrolling airtight?

No, although the evidence that no trade took place is overwhelming. What makes it impossible to state with complete certainty is that on many amendments and bills there was no record roll call. There was a roll call and record vote on controversial measures, and non-controversial bills, of course, require no trading. But since the record is incomplete, it cannot be established beyond doubt that Sangamon's seven in the House did not trade on internal improvements. Besides, there are always actions taken and arrangements made which a simple study of the record does not reveal. However, any such massive trading as previously was said to have occurred is completely out of the question. This would have shown on the record.

The case against the usual accounts of trading comes near being airtight. The weight of evidence is heavily on the negative side. There likely was some trading by various local and personal interests, but nothing in the record indicates that Springfield's legislators were a prominent part of that. If there had been a brazen swap of Springfield for internal improvements, it would certainly have been mentioned in the mass of correspondence and pertinent source material available; but it is neither mentioned nor even hinted at.

Every session of the legislature has some trading, but there is no evidence that Lincoln supported any measure with which he was in basic disagreement in order to secure votes for Springfield. Lincoln knew of the process of logrolling. But his service in the session which acted on the seat of government and internal improvements was not that of the crafty leader constantly making deals to achieve his objective. Nevertheless, this image of him probably will live on: Lincoln the logroller, the head of a united Long Nine, who voted as a unit; Lincoln the sly politician who worked devious deals on internal improvements to secure the capital for Springfield.

Like the story of George Washington's cherry tree and the legend of Ann Rutledge, it makes fascinating reading. But that kind of reading is fiction, not history.

5

Lincoln's First Encounter with Douglas

Twenty-two years ago Judge Douglas and I first became acquainted. We were both young; he a trifle younger than I. Even then, we were both ambitious; I perhaps, quite as much so as he. With me, the race of ambition has been a failure—a flat failure; with him it has been one of splendid success.—ABRAHAM LINCOLN, 1856[1]

THE PATHS OF Abraham Lincoln and Stephen A. Douglas crossed frequently. One was to become a much-loved President; the other a famous and powerful United States Senator and candidate for President—better known to most Americans than many of our Presidents.

They opposed each other for President of the United States in 1860.

They opposed each other in their famous debates of 1858. The debates, historian Paul Angle notes, gave Lincoln "the nationwide reputation without which he could not have been nominated for the presidency two years later. But for the debates, it is conceivable that in the next two or three years American history might have run a far different course."[2]

Lincoln and Douglas met each other twenty-four years before those debates took place. Twenty-two years before the famous debates and race for United States Senator, Lincoln and Douglas

[1] *CW*, II, 382–83.

[2] Paul Angle, *Created Equal* (Chicago, University of Chicago Press, 1958), 5.

were prominent members of the Illinois House of Representatives. An observer at that early meeting hardly would have guessed the important role these two Illinois legislators would play in developing and directing the nation.

Born in Vermont, Douglas grew up on a farm there. In addition to country schooling, he had a year of academy training and a short course in law. Then he went west, arriving in Jacksonville, Illinois, with $1.25 and a few books. He sold the books, went to nearby Winchester, and taught school for one quarter. When at the end of the quarter he had a little more money, he returned to Jacksonville, determined to practice law.

"I applied to the Hon. Samuel D. Lockwood, one of the justices of the Supreme Court," writes Douglas, "and after a short examination, obtained a license, and immediately opened an office, being then less than 21 years of age."[3]

Of twelve lawyers in Jacksonville, Douglas was the only Democrat. His reputation, law practice, and political influence grew rapidly. Captain John Wyatt, a Morgan County (Jacksonville) political leader, saw in Douglas an opportunity to take the office of state's attorney away from his political rival John J. Hardin. Hardin was well known, tall and handsome. Douglas was five feet, four inches tall, and weighed ninety pounds. Short legs and a large head gave him a dwarfed appearance. Wyatt thought it would be great sport to defeat Hardin "with little Douglas."

On a horse lent him by Wyatt, Douglas took off for Vandalia. There he drafted a bill which made the state's attorney an appointee of the legislature rather than the anti-Jackson governor, a friend of Hardin. The legislature was controlled by adherents of President Andrew Jackson. Douglas's bill was introduced by Wyatt, adopted, vetoed, and then passed over the veto. Lincoln voted against the measure and voted for Hardin, but twenty-one-year-old Douglas won.

Lincoln and Douglas met during this 1834–35 session, but did not become well acquainted. An observer who saw both described Douglas as "a very short man, almost a dwarf. But he had more

[3] *Autobiography of Stephen A. Douglas*, ed. by Frank E. Stevens (Springfield, Illinois State Journal Co., 1913), reprinted from the *ISHSJ*, October, 1912.

presence than had Lincoln in his six feet four. . . . His whole bearing showed the custom of command."[4] A strong-looking jaw and
bushy dark-brown hair, together with his uncommonly large deep-
blue eyes and his massive eyebrows, made Douglas appear all the
more impressive. "Here indeed was a lion, by the very looks of
him master of himself and of others," remarked the wife of a
political rival.[5]

The famous session of 1836–37 brought Lincoln and Douglas
face to face regularly. Only twenty-three when he took his seat in
the House of Representatives, Douglas was four years younger
than Lincoln. Douglas "looked like a boy with his smooth face
and diminutive proportions," reminisced a colleague, "but when
he spoke in the House of Representatives, as he often did in 1836
and '37, he spoke like a man, and loomed up into the proportions
of an intellectual giant, and it was at that session he got the name
of the 'Little Giant.' "[6] Ten years later, at thirty-three, he became
a United States Senator.

There were numerous contrasts between the two.

Lincoln was tall, unusually tall; Douglas was short, unusually
short.

Lincoln was the son of an unlettered farmer and cabinetmaker;
Douglas the son of a doctor.

Lincoln was born in a southern state; Douglas in Vermont.

Lincoln had little formal education; by comparison, Douglas
was well educated.

Lincoln had a high-pitched, penetrating and not too pleasant
voice; Douglas had a resonant, bass voice, so that he was called a
"lion-voiced orator."[7]

Lincoln spoke slowly and deliberately; Douglas was fiery.

Lincoln generally did not go out of his way to take in social life,

[4] E. S. Nadel, "Impressions of Lincoln," *Scribner's*, March, 1906.

[5] Beveridge, *Abraham Lincoln*, IV, 174. Quoting Mrs. Roger A. Pryor, wife of
Congressman Pryor of Virginia, from her book, *Reminiscences of Peace and War*.

[6] Linder, *Reminiscences*, 78.

[7] Wilson, *Lincoln Among His Friends*, 68. Quoting from Thomas Hall Shastid's
article in *The Nation*, February 20, 1929.

he was somewhat of a "loner;" Douglas thoroughly enjoyed parties and social life.

Lincoln did not drink; Douglas indulged freely, sometimes too freely.

Lincoln felt awkward around women, and at least once was a frustrated suitor; Douglas was the center of attraction for women. One young lady wrote in 1839, "I almost forgot to grieve over the loss of the 'Little Judge' or to sigh that I could not have captivated him, ere he was courted by the beauties of the Washington belles."[8] She wanted to go to "the capital to see the Judge"—a wish she apparently shared with many of her sex.

Lincoln was somewhat melancholy by nature, Douglas jovial and bouncy. Lincoln seemed sad in victory, in defeat even more depressed. After the 1858 defeat, a visitor noticed him "steeped in gloom," and Lincoln commented that he expected "everyone to desert me now, but Billy Herndon."[9] In 1854 the Douglas Democrats took a stunning defeat. The next evening Douglas "with that curious mingling of courage and optimism which distinguished him . . . actually sounded a note of triumph."[10] When Douglas was twenty-two and running for his first elective office, he wrote with the confidence typical of him, "I ent[er]tain no doubt of my success in the election. I find no difficulty in adopting the Western mode of Electioneering by addressing the people from the stump."[11]

Lincoln was a storyteller; Douglas did not have that ability.

Lincoln was not the dynamic type of personality that makes a strong first impression; Douglas struck people as "the most daring and forthright personal political force that had held the American stage since Andrew Jackson stepped off."[12]

Lincoln was awkward and unimpressive in appearance; Douglas of majestic mien and bearing. Even one of Lincoln's closest

[8] Matilda Edwards to John Hardin, April 9, 1839, Chicago Historical Society Library.

[9] William H. Herndon, *The Hidden Lincoln*, ed. by Emanuel Hertz (New York, Viking Press, 1938), 10. Lincoln's remark is quoted by Henry C. Whitney in a letter to Herndon.

[10] Beveridge, *Abraham Lincoln*, III, 273.

[11] *Letters of Stephen A. Douglas*, April 8, 1836, 36. Written to his brother-in-law, Julius Granger.

[12] Sandburg, *The Prairie Years*, II, 7.

friends admitted that he was "not so ready or ingenious as Douglas."[13]

Lincoln "mingled with the common workers with the familiarity of a comrade," while Douglas "moved among his worshippers of the rank and file with the haughtiness of a conqueror."[14]

There was a saying that "with a good case Lincoln is the best lawyer in the state, but in a bad case Douglas is the best lawyer the state ever produced."[15]

Lincoln "shrank from any controversy with friends;"[16] Douglas reveled in it.

Lincoln achieved notice gradually; Douglas almost at once became "by far the most conspicuous member of his party."[17]

Lincoln was moral and deeply concerned with human need; Douglas had a more flexible moral code and was not, like Lincoln, preoccupied with human welfare. Their respective attitudes toward slavery illustrate this difference.[18] Lincoln felt a strong sympathy for the slave, while Douglas "cared little, relatively, for the fate of the Negro and audaciously declared his indifference."[19]

In response to a question about Douglas's truthfulness, Lincoln replied, "Well, Judge Douglas don't tell as many lies as some men I have known. But I think he *keers* as little for the truth *for the truth's sake* as any man I ever saw."[20]

[13] Recollections of John Allen, RTL, not dated, but written prior to the 1860 election.

[14] *Congressional Record*, February 22, 1929. Extension of remarks by Henry T. Rainey in the House of Representatives.

[15] Sandburg, *The Prairie Years*, II, 12.

[16] Rufus Rockwell Wilson, *Intimate Memories of Lincoln* (Elmira, N. Y., Primavera Press, 1945), 24, quoting Joshua Speed.

[17] Carl Schurz, *The Writings of Abraham Lincoln* (New York, Collier & Son, 1905), 27.

[18] Many writers feel that Douglas's lack of moral direction was his real weakness. Horace White wrote, "The one thing lacking . . . was a moral substratum. . . . He had no conception of morals in politics, and this defect was his undoing as a statesman." (Wilson, *Lincoln Among His Friends*, 173. Quoting the *New York Evening Post*, February 12, 1909.)

[19] Albert Watkins, "Douglas, Lincoln and the Nebraska Bill," *American Historical Magazine*, May–July, 1908.

[20] Wolcott Hamlin, Amherst, Mass., May 17, 1887, recalling a visit by Lincoln to Exeter, N. H., in the winter of 1859–60, in the Nicolay and Hay Collection, IHL.

Lincoln's wife was ambitious for him, but she was at least somewhat of a political liability. Many of Lincoln's closest friends thought her strange. Douglas married twice; his first wife died six years after their marriage. Both of his wives were political assets. Reporters covering the Lincoln-Douglas debates of 1858 noted that Mrs. Douglas was "very helpful to Judge Douglas in the campaign. . . . Republicans considered her a dangerous element."[21] His second wife, a strikingly beautiful woman, was the great-niece of Dolly Madison, one of the nation's most colorful First Ladies.

Standing out among the things Lincoln and Douglas had in common was a shared desire to save the Union. When the nation faced its greatest crisis, Douglas ignored the differences he and Lincoln had and boldly espoused the cause of the Union.

How do their records in the Illinois House of Representatives compare?

An observer at the session of 1836–37 endeavoring to pick a likely winner for a race for the highest office in the land would have picked Douglas.

Although only a first-termer, Douglas was already known to the membership because of his previous activities in Vandalia. He served as chairman of the Committee on Petitions, the busiest and most important standing committee. He had membership on the relatively unimportant Penitentiary Committee. Lincoln was a leading member, though not chairman, of the important Finance Committee and was also on the Penitentiary Committee.

Douglas's prominent committee assignment cannot be explained by party affiliation or the vote for House speaker. The speaker appointed the standing committees, but Douglas had with Lincoln voted for the same candidate for speaker—a losing candidate. Yet, with four others who had voted against the speaker, Douglas was made a chairman, but Lincoln was not. The vote for the wrong man as speaker did not by itself disqualify anyone from a chairmanship.

---

[21] Beveridge, *Abraham Lincoln*, IV, 282. A report by Horace White; other reporters had similar accounts.

Douglas played a more prominent role than did Lincoln throughout the session. He was more active in debate and in specially assigned committee work. Douglas was named to eighteen special committees; Lincoln to eight. Douglas served as chairman of seven special committees; Lincoln on three.

No recorded vote was taken, except on something controversial. On issues on which their votes were recorded, the two voted differently 119 times and alike 75 times. Lincoln failed to vote on issues sixteen times; Douglas, ten times. Twice they are both recorded as not voting on the same issues. There is no particular pattern to Lincoln's absences from voting in this session or any session, but Douglas tended to be absent on the first roll call at the beginning of the day or after lunch, perhaps because of committee work, but more likely because of not being too punctual. In voting on issues, the record of sixteen absences for Lincoln and ten for Douglas was well below the average of 32.18 absences for House members during that session.

In voting to fill vacancies, Lincoln and Douglas followed the general trend in American politics—to divide more on men than on issues. They voted twenty-four times for different men, and twelve times for the same men.[22]

What were some of the issues on which the two differed?

Most significantly, they clashed on a proslavery resolution calling the right to own slaves a "sacred" right of slave-holding states and supporting the institution of slavery in the District of Columbia. The resolution carried 77–6. Lincoln was one of the six voting against it; Douglas voted for it. But both voted against an amendment declaring the abolition of slavery in the District of Columbia "unconstitutional." Douglas took the position that abolition of slavery there would be "unwise."

Douglas generally took a stronger position in support of education. On a motion to lay the main school bill "on the table until July 4th"—which meant killing it—Lincoln voted for killing it,

---

[22] Not figured in these calculations were the four votes for the seat of government since this did not fall completely in the issue category and was not voting for an individual. Douglas voted for Jacksonville on all four ballots and Lincoln for Springfield on all four ballots.

and Douglas supported the bill. Douglas favored using the entire school fund for schools immediately; Lincoln favored using only the interest. Douglas, a former school teacher, was secretary to a state-wide educational convention at Vandalia when the session opened; Lincoln was one of the delegates.

Lincoln favored having the legislature retain the power to grant divorce; Douglas felt that only the courts should handle this. Douglas introduced a resolution that called for an end to the legislature granting divorces. The resolution received consideration twice, and Lincoln opposed it both times. Only once after that was a divorce ever granted by the legislature.

On national issues, Lincoln and Douglas were almost always in opposition. Douglas upheld the Jackson administration; Lincoln opposed it. Regarding the state attitude toward banks, they were again generally in disagreement. Douglas wanted the banks investigated; Lincoln did not. A bank bill sought to limit banks to 10 per cent interest on their loans. Lincoln was for it; Douglas against it. Both favored the establishment of branch banks so that more communities could have banking facilities.

Both supported the Internal Improvements Act, introduced by Douglas. But when it came to voting for amendments expanding the act, Douglas was the more conservative. The record of neither man in this field is good, but Lincoln's all-out support makes his worse. (Ironically, an 1860 Lincoln campaign biography asserts just the opposite and makes Douglas appear more all-out in support of this ridiculous program.) Both Lincoln and Douglas voted to override the veto of the Internal Improvements Act. Both men voted against having a state-wide referendum on the Internal Improvements Act before it could become effective.

Major issues were not the only ones on which they disagreed. Douglas wanted to reduce the bounty for a wolf scalp to fifty cents; Lincoln favored one dollar. Both opposed an amendment calling for the payment of "the sum of 50 cents for every hawk scalp, and the sum of ten cents for each crow, opposum, raccoon, and wild cat."[23] Both finally voted against the whole measure.

Douglas did not want a vote on relocating the seat of govern-

[23] *HJ*, 1836–37, p. 324.

ment. His Jacksonville colleagues were divided on this matter. Lincoln, who felt that Springfield might get the capital, advocated a vote on relocation.

Douglas supported the move for a convention to draw up a new state constitution; Lincoln voted against it. It is possible that Lincoln wanted to forestall bringing up the slavery issue at this time.

On some measures their background was inadequate. How could they vote intelligently on the proposal to "locate a state road from Mr. Anderson's bridge, in Madison County, to B. Johnson's in Bond County"? Yet Lincoln voted yes; Douglas, no.

Lincoln supported an increase in pay for the circuit judges; Douglas opposed the increase.

The two disagreed on many more minor things. As in any modern state legislature, the majority of things which came before the assembly of 1836–37 were matters of little importance, concerned with specific local problems.

Both voted to repeal the "Little Bull" Bill, which had become very unpopular and which Lincoln had opposed from the beginning. Douglas did not serve in the legislature at the time it was originally presented and passed. Douglas and Lincoln supported a bill to permit popular election of the clerks of the courts and county treasurers. In later years, Douglas thought that the clerks of the courts should be appointed by the judges.

In matters of court procedure and matters concerned with justices of the peace, Douglas and Lincoln tended to vote the same.

About noon on February 6, Douglas moved to adjourn until two o'clock. Lincoln is recorded as voting against the motion, and so is Douglas! Why the motion became a matter of controversy, and why Douglas voted against his own motion, is a mystery the official records do nothing to clarify.

Both men opposed a clause restricting those eligible to appointment as canal commissioners. A proposal was made that no member of the legislature could be appointed to the office "nor to any office or appointment under and from the Board of Canal Commissioners,"[24] and that no former commissioner could be eligible. Lincoln and Douglas cast negative votes, and in this instance history would judge both men wrong. Possibly some of the abuse and improvident

24 *Ibid.*, 614–15.

spending would have been avoided had the proposed amendment passed. One of the men named canal commissioner was their colleague John A. McClernand.

During the early part of the session, Douglas moved to amend a resolution by adding, "and also to enquire into the expediency of adding another member to the Supreme Court."[25] It is likely that the exceedingly ambitious Douglas had himself in mind when he made the motion. The House may have recognized this, for his motion was defeated.

In the only recorded direct clash between the two on the floor of the House, Lincoln came off the winner. This fight revolved about the proposal to divide Sangamon County. Douglas moved to present the petitions of the Sangamon County residents to the Committee on Petitions of which he was chairman. Lincoln wanted the matter referred to a select committee of five. Lincoln and some of his Sangamon colleagues were aware that their political futures might be hanging in the balance because this bill had aroused public opinion in Sangamon County. The Douglas motion failed and the Lincoln proposal carried. Lincoln served as chairman of the committee—and one of his committee members was Douglas.

Douglas, the more prominent member of the legislature, also was more widely known at this time throughout the state. Even the *Sangamo Journal*, with views sympathetic to Lincoln, mentioned Douglas of neighboring Morgan County much more than it did Lincoln of Sangamon County. One Whig newspaper said that Douglas is "but a shadow—no one knows him—no one cares about him."[26] But newspaper accounts of that day show this particular judgment to be wishful thinking.

Political leader John Wentworth wrote about a year after Lincoln's death, "I came to Illinois 25th Oct 1836. He [Lincoln] & Douglas were both in the Legislature. . . . During that session Douglas made himself known all over the State and got himself made a Land Officer. . . . Lincoln at that time was scarcely known though having the same chance as Douglas."[27]

25 *Ibid.*, 68.

26 *North West Gazette and Galena Advertiser*, January 13, 1838.

27 John Wentworth to Herndon, February 4, 1866, Herndon-Weik Collection, Library of Congress.

A Douglas biographer comments about their session together, "The reputation of Lincoln, for anything he accomplished at that session, did not get beyond the confines of his judicial circuit. On the contrary the reputation of Douglas reached the four corners of the state."[28] There is much evidence to support this.

In political matters Lincoln and Douglas were opponents from the start. A few months after serving together in the legislature, Lincoln wrote to a colleague, "We have adopted it as part of our policy here, to never speak of Douglas at all. Isn't that the best mode of treating so small a matter?"[29]

When the regular session of 1836–37 ended, Douglas resigned to accept the federal appointment as Register of the Land Office in Springfield. So at the special session, called during the summer of 1837, Douglas did not serve, but was there lobbying and getting better acquainted with men of influence around the state. One generally reliable source says that Douglas went to the special session "and urged that work on Internal Improvements be suspended until a more favorable season; but even his support of the Whig Governor's request was unavailing."[30] From 1837 to 1841, Lincoln's last years of service in the Illinois House of Representatives, Douglas did not serve but was frequently around lobbying and consulting with political leaders.

In 1839, when writing to Stuart in Washington about the Stuart-Douglas congressional fight which Stuart barely won, Lincoln said:

> Douglas has not been here since you left. A report is in circulation here now, that he has abandoned the idea of going to Washington; though the report does not come in a verry authentic form. . . . Though, by the way, speaking of authenticity, you know that if we had heard Douglas say that he had abandoned the contest, it would not be very authentic.[31]

In the 1840–41 session, a proposal was made to increase the membership of the Illinois Supreme Court, in effect making it a

[28] Frank E. Stevens, "Life of Douglas," *ISHSJ*, October 1923, 306–307.
[29] *CW*, I, 107.
[30] Beveridge, *Abraham Lincoln*, I, 237. Beveridge apparently relied somewhat upon Douglas's biographer, Stevens, for this information.
[31] *CW*, I, 154.

Democratic court instead of a Whig court. The son of one member recalls Douglas being "particularly active and efficient as a lobbyist in passing the revolutionary measure for reforming the courts."[32] Another House member in that session recalls Douglas's activities as "decisive for the court measure."[33] The result: a state Supreme Court seat for Douglas at the age of twenty-seven.

In 1840, when Lincoln was a presidential elector for Harrison, Lincoln ran two hundred votes behind the other Whigs in the Mormon center of Nauvoo. The *Chicago American* had a report from Warsaw about it: "There is something connected with the vote at Nauvoo precinct, which needs explanation. Two hundred Mormon voters were induced to erase the name of A. Lincoln, from the Whig electoral ticket, and substitute the name of James R. Ralston, in his stead. Rumor says that the Hon. Richard M. Young, of the U. S. Senate, and the 'little giant,' Stephen A. Douglas, who wants to go to Congress, were present at this election, and of course their names are freely used in connection with this little petty trick."[34]

The climax of the Lincoln-Douglas relationship came during the race for United States senator in 1858. Lincoln lost this race, but became a national figure. But Douglas had been nimble enough politically so that some of the leading Republicans, including Horace Greeley of the *New York Tribune*, suggested that Illinois Republicans should take Douglas as candidate because of his changed attitude. The suggestion was rejected, and one Republican leader commented, "A penitent prostitute may be received into the church, but she should not lead the choir."[35]

During the course of the 1858 compaign there were occasional references to their mutual experiences in the state legislature. Douglas apparently had not been too impressed with Lincoln's service in the state legislature after 1836 because in the first debate he recalled that they "both retired" from the legislature that year—five years before Lincoln's legislative service ended.[36] Refer-

---

[32] Snyder, *Selected Writings*, 365.

[33] Letter from A. Cavarly, Ottawa, Ill., to Lincoln, September 10, 1858, RTL.

[34] November 16, 1840.

[35] Willard King, *Lincoln's Manager, David Davis* (Cambridge, Mass., Harvard University Press, 1960), 117.

[36] *CW*, III, 6.

ences frequently were made to legislative colleagues during the 1858 race.

A final touch of irony in the 1858 race for United States senator was that Douglas carried Lincoln's home county of Sangamon (not normally Democratic), and Lincoln carried Douglas's home county of Cook.

In 1860, Sangamon County again broke its usual custom of going against Democrats when in the presidential race Sangamonites gave Douglas 1,035 votes and Lincoln 962.

When Douglas lost the 1860 race to Lincoln, he did it graciously. A national magazine quoted Douglas as saying with pleasure, "We Springfield people will take the capital next year. Lincoln in the White House, Baker, M'Dougal and I in the Senate—we will make Washington jolly in spite of politics."[37]

When the Civil War was suddenly thrust upon the country, Douglas ignored the advice of many of his friends and close associates and stood firmly with Lincoln and the Union. It is only speculation, but it is possible that the bonds of mutual respect which were first established in Vandalia may have played a part in the Douglas decision.

At the Lincoln inauguration in 1861, it was Douglas who stepped forward to hold Lincoln's hat. The day after news arrived in Washington that Fort Sumter had been fired on, Douglas called on Lincoln and the two had an animated discussion of how to proceed with the war. The man who brought them together that day later recalled: "I venture to say that no two men in the United States parted that night with a more cordial feeling of united, friendly and patriotic purpose than Mr. Lincoln and Mr. Douglas."[38]

More important than his immediate visit with Lincoln was Douglas's trip to Illinois where pro-Southern feeling still existed, particularly within Douglas's party. The famous reporter and editor Horace White recalled: "I heard him [Douglas] deliver the

[37] "Colonel Baker," *Harper's New Monthly Magazine*, December, 1861. No author indicated.

[38] Quoting George Ashmun of Mass., *The Lincoln Reader*, ed. by Paul Angle (New Brunswick, N. J., Rutgers University Press, 1947), 357.

speech in Springfield April 25, 1861, which saved Illinois from the fate which befell Kentucky and Missouri, that of secession sympathies and guerilla warfare. That speech was beyond comparison the greatest that I ever listened to from anybody. I cannot believe that Demosthenes, or Mirabeau, or Patrick Henry, or any orator the world ever saw, could have surpassed that speech in its effect upon the men who heard it. It did more, far more, than consolidate the State of Illinois for the Union. It consolidated the Democratic party of the North as supporters of Lincoln in that great struggle that ensued."[39]

Douglas died a few months after the start of the Civil War, but Lincoln showed through many acts after Douglas's death a warm feeling for the memory of his longtime friend and foe. In June of 1861, Lincoln wrote to the Secretary of War, "Because of his relationship to the late Senator Douglas, I wish James Madison Cutts, Jr., to be a captain in some part of this new corps."[40] Cutts was a brother-in-law of Douglas. In November of the same year Lincoln acted to safeguard the property of the Douglas heirs in the South.[41]

Two years later, when the brother-in-law of Douglas, whom Lincoln had befriended, was charged with striking a senior officer and being a "peeping tom," Lincoln remitted the sentence given Cutts because of his "previous good character . . . and gallant conduct in battle." Lincoln then wrote this piece of advice to Cutts:

Although what I am now to say is to be, in form, a reprimand, it is not intended to add a pang to what you have already suffered upon the subject to which it relates. You have too much of life yet before you, and have shown too much of promise as an officer, for your future to be lightly surrendered. You were convicted of two offenses. One of them, not of great enormity, and yet greatly to be avoided, I feel sure you are in no danger of repeating. The other you are not so well assured against. The advice of a father to his son "Beware of entrance to a quarrel, but being in, bear it that the opposed may beware of thee," is good, and yet not the best. Quarrel

[39] Wilson, *Lincoln Among His Friends*, 173, quoting from the *New York Evening Post*.
[40] *CW*, IV, 409.
[41] *Ibid.*, V, 32.

not at all. No man resolved to make the most of himself, can spare time for personal contention. Still less can he afford to take all the consequences, including, the vitiating of his temper, and the loss of self-control. Yield larger things to which you can show no more than equal right; and yield lesser ones, though clearly your own. Better give your path to a dog, than be bitten by him in contesting for the right. Even killing the dog would not cure the bite.[42]

Lincoln added the hope that "the unpleasant events . . . will not have been profitless to you."

If the hard and plain-spoken Little Giant had lived to read that note, he would have been touched by what had been written and done by the man with whom he grew up in politics.

[42] *Ibid.*, VI, 538–39.

6

Lincoln and the Slavery Issue

[In the family Bible] not only were the blank leaves where usually are bound between the testaments written to the full but others had been inserted, for the purpose of recording not only the issue of some couple of white peoples but also the offspring of some of their negroes. One page was filled with "Sarah's Children," and another with "Anna's Children," together with their respective ages and a catalogue of prices. One Boy, for example, eleven years of age was valued $200, and others in proportion. This part of the Book was evidently most worn for it probably was a ready reconer by which to compute their wealth. The sum total of their negroes would show how rich they were.—Notes from a diary of a visitor to Carlinville, Illinois, in 1835.[1]

ILLINOIS was not as "free" a state as many imagine during the period when Lincoln served in the legislature, 1834–42, nor Lincoln as neutral on the slavery issue as his Kentucky background might suggest.

When Ninian Edwards was territorial governor of Illinois, slavery was illegal, but Edwards ran this advertisement:

Notice: I have for sale twenty-two slaves, among them are several of both sexes between the years of ten and seventeen; if not shortly sold, I shall wish to hire them in Missouri territory. I have

[1] Alexander Blakie Diary, entry of May 5, 1835, IHL.

also for sale a full blooded horse, a very large English bull and several young ones.[2]

The will of the first governor of Illinois also tells something of the atmosphere of the "free" state:

> I give to my loving wife, Achsah Bond, all of my personal property ... my negro Frank Thomas. ... I give to my daughter Julia Rachel five hundred dollars and my negro girl Eliza. And to my daughter Achsah Mary five hundred dollars and my negro girl Harriet and to my wife Achsah I give all the rest of my negroes to be disposed of as she thinks best having entire confidence that she will make proper use of it.[3]

Illinois became a state in 1818. Slavery "remained the main topic of discussion at the constitutional convention."[4] The constitution of 1818 technically prohibited slavery, but this was with the understanding that it had to be done to get Illinois admitted as a state. The constitution, however, permitted a Negro to sell himself under a system of "indenture," which for all practical effects retained a modified system of slavery. The 1818 constitutional convention went as far as it could to retain slavery and still permit Illinois to be admitted as a state.

Prior to 1818 and for approximately twenty years after statehood, most of those coming into Illinois came from the South. They brought Southern attitudes with them.

Technically, Illinois was a free state, but there were enough loopholes in the law so that slavery could be retained on a limited scale. As one writer says: "Slavery was winked at."[5]

French settlers who had slaves were allowed to keep them. Free Negroes were permitted to sell their labor for a period of about twenty years (and frequently more), marking an "X" on an agree-

[2] Ethan A. Snively, "Slavery in Illinois," photostat at IHL, 55.

[3] "Will of Shadrach Bond, First Governor of Illinois, Under Statehood. Found in the County Clerk's Office of Randolph County," *ISHSJ*, April, 1927.

[4] John Barnhart, "The Southern Influence in Early Illinois," *ISHSJ*, September, 1939.

[5] Eudora Hamsey Richardson, "The Virginian Who Made Illinois a Free State," *ISHSJ*, Spring, 1952.

ment which few ever had the ability to read. It was a sort of legalized slavery, except for the fact that the children born to such a slave would be free.

A typical arrangement like this, entered on the county's records, would call for a man leasing a Negro to provide "good and sufficient meat, drink, lodging and apparel, together with all other needful conveniences fit for such a servant"; the Negro—in this case a woman—pledged herself "faithfully to serve, obey, not to absent herself from her work and not to embezzle or waste or lend her master's property."[6] That this procedure virtually amounted to slavery can be seen from the case of "Linda, last out of Missouri Territory," who bound herself to William Wilson for a period of ninety-nine years.[7] She was approximately nineteen years old when the legal document was signed and recorded. She would have to be 118 years old before she could be free again.

One case discovered by the able southern Illinois historian, John Allen, shows a free Negro woman buying her own son and holding him technically in slavery for four months before filing a document for his freedom.[8]

Anti-Negro sentiment was strong.

In 1837 a mob killed the Abolitionist newspaper editor, Elijah P. Lovejoy in Alton for his antislavery views. A few weeks before Lovejoy was killed, when a minister announced he was going to speak against slavery at the First Presbyterian Church in Springfield, a "crowd collected and swore that it would mob him."[9] Courageous action by Lincoln's colleague Edward D. Baker saved him.

A paragraph from a history of Saline County is an example of prevalent attitudes:

> There were a number of Negroes in Gallatin County. They were
> slaves or indentured servants who had been freed or had bought

[6] Gallatin County Records, quoted by John W. Allen in *Legends & Lore of Southern Illinois* (Carbondale, Southern Illinois University Press, 1963), 256.

[7] *Ibid.*, 256.

[8] *Ibid.*, 257.

[9] Paul Angle, *"Here I Have Lived": A History of Lincoln's Springfield* (Abraham Lincoln Association, Springfield, 1935), 79.

their freedom. Most of them were peaceful, law-abiding people; but their presence caused friction. Every crime committed was attributed to them. In 1840 a band of men calling themselves Regulators ranged over the whole of what is now Massac, Hardin, Saline and Gallatin counties attempting to force all of these Negroes out of the state. They kidnapped the children of these free Negroes and sold them into slavery. When Benjamin Hardin was murdered, the Negroes were accused. It was subsequently believed that a Negro might have done it, but at a white man's request. Harmless colored people were whipped and terrified in an unpardonable way.[10]

As late as 1853—twelve years after Lincoln left the Illinois House of Representatives—a law was passed in Illinois that a free Negro entering the state could be sold into slavery. The measure was sponsored by John A. Logan, future Civil War general and son of John Logan, Lincoln's House colleague. Ten years after that, in 1863, when Lincoln as President issued his Emancipation Proclamation, the Illinois General Assembly by resolution condemned that action.

In 1862, by a majority of 107,650 votes, the people of Illinois voted not to admit additional Negroes into the state. By a majority of 176,271, they voted not to allow Negroes to vote or hold office. That same year in Hancock County a Negro "was arrested for being in the state ten days and intending to remain permanently. He was found guilty and fined. Interested citizens appealed his case to the State Supreme Court, which in 1864 upheld the verdict of the lower court."[11]

Slavery was an old institution in Illinois. The first slaves were known to have worked in Illinois under the French in the 1720's. By the time of the Revolution, there were about one thousand slaves in the state. The area which later became Illinois was considered slave territory both when held by France and when held by Great Britain.

The Ordinance of 1787 outlawed slavery. But since the terri-

[10] The staff of the Mitchell-Carnegie Library in Harrisburg, Ill., "A History of Saline County," *ISHSJ*, April, 1934.

[11] John W. Allen, "Slavery and Negro Servitude in Pope County, Illinois," *ISHSJ*, December, 1949.

torial governors were worried about slaveowners' leaving, they assured them that this law meant only that new slaves could not be brought into the state.

Slavery increased in Illinois despite the laws. The 1820 census showed more than six times as many slaves in Illinois as were shown by the 1810 census. The 1820 census showed more than twice as many slaves in Illinois as free Negroes.

Lincoln's Sangamon County differed from the state picture somewhat, having only a small number of Negroes and most of these free. In 1835 there were seventy-six free Negroes and twenty who were either slaves or "indented or registered servants."[12]

The Illinois constitution of 1818 was more proslavery than were the constitutions of the states of Ohio and Indiana. The constitution was similar to that of Tennessee. The president of the constitutional convention, Jesse B. Thomas, was a slaveowner. There were enough slaveowners among the delegation that "slaves held by the members of the convention were more numerous than the delegates themselves."[13]

Almost immediately after statehood was granted, Illinois enacted "Black Laws." One historian describes these laws:

They provided that no negro or mulatto should settle in the State until he had first produced a certificate of freedom under seal of a court of record. . . . The overseers of the poor were empowered to expel such negroes or mulattos whenever they desired. Any person bringing slaves into the State with a view of emancipating them was required to execute a bond in the sum of one thousand dollars as a guaranty . . . and if he neglected to execute the bond, he was liable to a fine of two hundred dollars. . . . To harbor any slave or servant, or to hinder the owner in retaking any slave was made a felony punishable by a fine two-fold the value of the slave and a whipping not to exceed thirty stripes. . . . A slave found ten miles from home was subject to arrest and to be punished by thirty-five stripes. . . . In all cases where free persons were punished by a fine, slaves were to be punished by whipping at the rate of twenty stripes for each eight dollars of fine.[14]

12 *SgJ*, December 12, 1835.
13 Barnhart, "The Southern Influence in Early Illinois," *ISHSJ*.

The first legislature of Illinois declared as law that persons who "should permit slaves or servants to assemble for dancing or revelling, by night or day, were to be fined twenty dollars. It was made the duty of all sheriffs, coroners, judges, and justices of the peace, on view of such assemblage, to commit the slaves to jail, and to order each one of them to be whipped, not exceeding thirty-nine stripes, on the bare back, to be inflicted on the next day, unless the same should be Sunday, and then on the next day after."[15]

Most of Lincoln's legislative colleagues were men of Southern background. All but one of the first judges in the state were from the South. At least three of the first governors were themselves slaveowners. Several United States senators and congressmen from Illinois were slaveholders.

To whatever extent there was antislavery sentiment, it also came largely from Southerners. New Englanders and others who moved to Illinois tended to follow the two Southern camps until the heavier numbers started moving in from New England. When Lincoln served in the legislature, the population was mostly Southern in origin. This was true of New Salem (founded by two Southerners) and of Springfield. Except for Jacksonville, it was also true of surrounding areas. Records show that in neighboring Macon County "as late as 1840 at least three-fourths of the population" was Southern in background.[16] The Illinois population was so Southern that many believed the state "was on its way to becoming a transplanted Southern commonwealth, with all the institutions, including slavery, of its sister states south of Mason and Dixon's line."[17]

The laws, as a result, were to a large extent influenced by Southern laws and attitudes. There were even laws "for the inspection of hemp and tobacco, when there was neither hemp nor tobacco raised."[18]

---

[14] Snively, "Slavery in Illinois," 56.

[15] Ford, *History of Illinois*, 32–33.

[16] Aretas A. Dayton, "The Raising of Union Forces in Illinois During the Civil War," *ISHSJ*, December, 1941.

[17] Ray A. Billington, "The Frontier in Illinois History," *ISHSJ*, Spring, 1950.

[18] Ford, *History of Illinois*, 33–34.

There were a few pockets of strong antislavery sentiment. In 1836, for example, there were "antislavery prayer meetings" held in Galesburg.[19] About this same time others were speaking out in Alton, Jacksonville, and Quincy. But these were voices of the future, not of the 1830's.

Thomas Ford, who became governor immediately after Lincoln retired from the legislature, stated in his memoirs that it would have been "dangerous" for a politician to be sympathetic to the Negro cause.[20] Illinois was a state of strong prejudice against Negroes in 1834–42, Lincoln's years in the Illinois legislature.

Contrary to what many biographers have indicated, Lincoln did not suddenly become opposed to slavery after a trip to New Orleans. The authority for that statement did not make the trip to New Orleans and what we know about Lincoln's background shows the account to be incorrect.

Lincoln's family tended to be antislavery. Trips to New Orleans, talks with New Salem's Dr. John Allen, and other factors undoubtedly helped to mold and reinforce his opinions, but the basic direction was cast before he ever reached New Salem.

Lincoln historians are indebted to Dr. Louis A. Warren for his detailed study of the antislavery background of Lincoln's family. Warren's studies show that Lincoln's mother grew to womanhood in a home where there were slaves. Lincoln's father, Thomas Lincoln, was born in Virginia and grew up in Jefferson County, Kentucky, where slavery caused debate. During Thomas Lincoln's childhood, he heard about the severe punishment inflicted on a Negro slave who stole some cloth, thread, and ribbon. He was ordered to be "taken back to the jail of said county and from thence to the place of execution, and then be hung by the neck until he be dead, dead, dead."[21]

Warren gives additional important information about the Lincoln family background on slavery:

[19] Herman R. Meulder, "Galesburg: Hot-Bed of Abolitionism," *ISHSJ*, September, 1942.

[20] Ford, *History of Illinois*, 34.

[21] Louis A. Warren, *Slavery Atmosphere of Lincoln's Youth* (Fort Wayne, Lincolniana Publishers, 1933, pamphlet), Jefferson County (Kentucky) Court Order Book No. 2, p. 32, quoted.

Thomas Lincoln's brother, Mordecai, acquired a slave in 1803, about the time Thomas left Washington County [Kentucky]. . . . It is likely that Thomas Lincoln got his first close contact with the slavery system as it existed in the more southern states (when he visited his Uncle Isaac). . . . When Isaac's widow died in 1834, forty-three slaves were listed in the inventory of her estate. Another Thomas Lincoln, for whom the president's father was named, was also a slave holder, having as many as six black men in his possession at one time. There is no dependable evidence that the father of Thomas Lincoln was an owner of slaves, and the inventory of his estate does not list any.[22]

Despite this type of proslavery background in both of Abraham Lincoln's parents, Mr. and Mrs. Thomas Lincoln soon were part of the Kentucky population that opposed slavery. Their attitude may have partly been due to their living on the old Cumberland Road going from Louisville to Nashville. Here the parents—and young Abe—saw human beings herded and treated like animals. In 1811, when the future President was only two years old, the tax list for Hardin County showed "1,007 slaves listed for taxation. The white male population above sixteen years of age, this same year was 1,627."[23] Lincoln and his parents saw slavery firsthand.

When the Baptist churches of Hardin County, Kentucky, were split on the slavery question, Abraham Lincoln's parents affiliated with the antislavery church. About six months before the birth of Abraham, Lincoln's parents moved into the community where he was to be born; they moved in the fall of 1808. Warren relates:

A few months before, the minister of the South Fork Baptist Church, not far from their cabin home, had become greatly disturbed over the slavery question. Finally the minister, William Whitman, declared himself an "amansapater" as an entry in the church record for Dec. 19, 1807 reveals. When Abraham Lincoln was born the church was closed because of the controversy over human bondage, and fifteen members had gone out of the church "on account of slavery" to organize the Little Mount Anti-Slavery Baptist Church. It was this organization with which the parents of Abraham Lincoln became affiliated.[24]

22 *Ibid.*   23 *Ibid.*
24 Louis A. Warren, "Lincoln's Baptist Background," *Lincoln Lore*, March 28, 1949.

In 1860, Lincoln wrote that his family moved from Kentucky to Indiana "partly on account of slavery."[25]

When the Lincoln family moved to Indiana, they again were in contact with antislavery Baptist preachers and laymen. The minister at the Pigeon Creek Baptist Church, which the Lincolns attended, was noted for his foot-washing and for his antislavery sermons.

Lincoln's father supported Clay, and Clay favored gradual emancipation in the original Kentucky constitution and was the father of the Missouri Compromise, which eventually would have meant the end of slavery.

All of this had some effect on young Abraham Lincoln. Many years later he wrote, "I am naturally anti-slavery. If slavery is not wrong, nothing is wrong. I can not remember when I did not so think and feel."[26] In 1852, one week after Clay's death, Lincoln delivered a eulogy to the man his father had supported and Lincoln supported, and he noted of Clay, "He ever was, on principle and in feeling, opposed to slavery."[27]

This attitude was Lincoln's also. And this viewpoint soon caused Lincoln to face a dilemma. His viewpoint was in conflict with the opinion of the public and of his fellow legislators—some of whom were slaveowners.

Slavery in the official *House Journal* during Lincoln's service was first referred to when a state representative from Montgomery County, Christian B. Blockberger, introduced a resolution calling for an amendment to the state constitution prohibiting slavery within the state. This was in Lincoln's first term in office. Unfortunately, there was no roll call on the issue. If two legislators had asked for a roll call, there would have been one. Getting someone to join in a request for a roll call was a routine matter, and Lincoln could have forced a roll call had he wanted one. It can be assumed that the resolution was defeated overwhelmingly, since no one asked for a roll call.

The second session of his first term a more significant action took place. On a resolution regarding voting procedures, an amendment was introduced with the following language:

25 *CW*, IV, 61. 26 *Ibid.*, VII, 281. 27 *Ibid.*, II, 130.

Resolved, that the price of the public lands ought to be reduced.

Resolved, that all white male citizens of the age of 21 years and upward, are entitled to the privilege of voting whether they hold real estate or not.

Resolved, that the elective franchise should be kept pure from contamination by the admission of colored votes.

Resolved, that we approve of the granting of re-emption rights to settlers on the public lands.[28]

The amendment carried 35–16, and Lincoln voted for it. It is probable that Lincoln favored the portions dealing with land problems more than he opposed—if he did—the portions dealing with the rights of the Negro. In view of his criticism of President Van Buren in the 1840 campaign for Van Buren's permitting the Negro to vote in New York, it seems fair to conclude that this resolution contained Lincoln's sentiments at this early stage in his political development. At this point in his life he opposed slavery but favored restrictions on Negroes.

When Lincoln announced his candidacy for state representative for his second term, he stated in the second paragraph of that announcement that he favored "admitting all whites to the right of suffrage."[29] Here he added that he favored giving women the right to vote. Possibly Lincoln took this stand against Negroes voting because one of his legislative colleagues, William Carpenter, was receiving public criticism for suggesting that free Negroes should be permitted to vote.

Lincoln was not alone in taking this stand against Negro voting. In the same issue in which Lincoln's announcement of candidacy appeared, the *Sangamo Journal* carried letters from John Dawson, R. L. Wilson, and Andrew McCormick. Dawson said, "I believe in the great principle of civil liberty, that all white men, rich or poor, have an equal right to elect or be elected to office." Wilson said that he believed that "all white male inhabitants" should be able to vote. McCormick was even more clear: "Some of the supporters of Van Buren have declared themselves in favor of extending the right of suffrage to free blacks. I am opposed to this doctrine."[30]

28 *HJ*, 1835–36, p. 236.   29 *SgJ*, June 18, 1836.   30 *Ibid*.

Both the votes in the legislatures and the pre-election stands of his colleagues indicate that in this matter Lincoln was following almost unanimous public opinion, and at this point he probably shared that opinion.

As the antislavery forces around the nation started to pick up strength, so did the proslavery forces. The issue was coming more and more to the front of the national political stage. The same year that Lincoln announced for re-election to the Illinois legislature, the Mississippi legislature passed a resolution calling on free states to prevent citizens "under suitable and sufficient penalties, from writing, speaking, printing or publishing sentiments and opinions . . . calculated in temper and spirit . . . to endanger our right of property or domestic repose."[31] The same year Connecticut, through its legislature, passed a resolution that slavery was "secured by the Constitution of the United States" and that no state "has any right to interfere." The same year, only weeks before Lincoln's announcement of candidacy, the New York legislature passed a similar resolution.

Lincoln also saw advertisements like the following, which appeared in a Vandalia newspaper he ordinarily read:

$100 Reward. Ranaway from the subscriber, in Washington County, Mo., on the night of the 3d of October, a negro man named
BILL
about five feet, eight or nine inches high, of a black complexion, bowlegged, a small scar near one of his ears, beard light, and down cast when spoken to. Bill is about twenty-nine years old, and had on when he left home a brown cassinet coat, dark pantaloons and vest and took with him a shot gun, and butcher knife. I will give one hundred Dollars to any person that will apprehend said negro and deliver him to me at my residence, near Potosi, or secure him in some jail in this State, so that I may get him again.

JACOB BOAS[32]

About a month after Lincoln started his second term in the House there was a debate on a controversial resolution about

[31] Adopted February 27, 1836. From notes of Sen. Albert Beveridge, Library of Congress. The references which follow in the same paragraph from Connecticut and New York are also from Sen. Beveridge's notes.

[32] *Vandalia Register*, March 6, 1837.

slavery, but neither official nor unofficial accounts record either Lincoln or his new colleague, Stephen A. Douglas, taking part in the debate. When the resolution was referred to a committee of five, neither served on the committee, although both were recognized as leaders and could have been named had they requested it.

A week later the committee reported and proposed an amendment to the resolution. What the committee amendment was is not known for sure. From the context of motions, it appears probable that the committee added something about Congress not taking away the right of slavery from the District of Columbia.

Suddenly the future Lincoln is seen momentarily. He moved to insert after the word "Congress" the words, "unless the people of the said District petition for the same."[33] At twenty-seven, Lincoln proposed an amendment aimed at clearing a path for making the District of Columbia free territory. His motion failed without a roll call, probably overwhelmingly; if there had been support for his position, a roll call would have been requested.

Another amendment was attempted to call Congressional action on slavery "unconstitutional" instead of "unwise." Lincoln voted with the overwhelming majority to reject the motion. Illinois was not willing to follow the most extreme of the proslavery forces.

The resolution that finally was adopted condemned Abolitionists, was sympathetic to the moves for colonization of free Negroes in Africa, and ended with these resolutions:

> *Resolved* by the General Assembly of the State of Illinois, That we highly disapprove of the formation of abolition societies, and of the doctrines promulgated by them. ·
>
> *Resolved*, That the right of property in slaves is sacred to the slave-holding States by the Federal Constitution, and that they cannot be deprived of that right without their consent.
>
> *Resolved*, That the General Government cannot abolish slavery in the District of Columbia, against the consent of the citizens of said District without a manifest breach of good faith.
>
> *Resolved*, That the Governor be requested to transmit to the States of Virginia, Mississippi, Alabama, New York and Connecticut, a copy of the foregoing resolutions.[34]

[33] *HJ*, 1836–37, p. 309.   [34] *Ibid.*, 241–44.

The House adopted the resolution 77–6, and among the six voting against it were Abraham Lincoln and Dan Stone. It was unanimously approved by the Senate. Six weeks later, on March 3, 1837, Lincoln and Stone used the right given to them in the constitution and entered the following protest on the record:

> Resolutions upon the subject of domestic slavery having passed both branches of the General Assembly at its present session, the undersigned hereby protest against the passage of the same.
>
> They believe that the institution of slavery is founded on both injustice and bad policy; but that the promulgation of abolition doctrines tends rather to increase than to abate its evils.
>
> They believe that the Congress of the United States has the power, under the constitution, to abolish slavery in the District of Columbia; but that power ought not to be exercised unless at the request of the people of said district.
>
> The difference between these opinions and those contained in the said resolutions, is their reasons for entering this protest.
>
> DAN STONE
A. LINCOLN
Representatives from the county of Sangamon[35]

What motivated Lincoln and Stone to file the protest is not clear. It probably was a desire to go on record firmly against slavery. It may have been a desire to make clear to their constituents that in voting against the earlier resolution they were not aligning themselves with the Abolitionists—whom neither favored at this time; siding openly with the Abolitionists would have been political suicide, and future opponents might interpret their earlier votes on the resolution that way.

It is significant that Lincoln and Stone waited until the measure to bring the seat of government to Springfield had passed. The controversial views expressed in their protest might have caused a storm in the legislature and sent the seat of government to some other city.

During Lincoln's 1860 campaign for the presidency, he referred to this protest in an autobiography, saying that the statement

[35] *Ibid.*, 817–18.

"briefly defined his position on the slavery question; and so far as it goes, it was then the same that it is now."[36]

During the 1836–37 session, the committee assigned to work on a proposal for a constitutional convention recommended favorable action and listed as the first reason for having a new constitution "to prevent domestic slavery" within the state.[37] Lincoln voted against a new state constitution, perhaps out of fear that a new constitution might bring more slavery. During his final term in the House, he supported proposals for a new state constitution.

During each session the slavery matter often came up incidentally. School funds, for example, were specified in the law to be distributed on the basis of the white population rather than the total population. This never became a matter of debate. On these matters Lincoln voted on the basis of the central issue rather than the racially restrictive clause. Even if his opinion was contrary to the racial clause, it would not have been possible to eliminate it. Whether he was being practical, or whether the common use of such language had his agreement, the student of the record can only guess.

One exception to this appears in his third term. He was in all likelihood present for roll calls and simply refrained from voting on the phrase that limited school funds to white children.

Negroes were not excluded when a bill was under consideration to require all white male citizens to do one day of roadwork; a motion was adopted to eliminate the word "white" from that bill.[38] Legislators were reluctant to give Negroes the opportunities of citizenship, but had no hesitation in giving them the obligations.

In Lincoln's third term, Illinois received a letter from the governor of Georgia complaining about the antislavery activity in the northern states. What caused his immediate anger was the refusal of the governor of Maine to give up two men who had "kidnapped" a slave in Georgia, brought him North and given him freedom. What the Illinois response to this should be became a matter of controversy.

The Judiciary Committee was assigned the task of replying to the Georgia chief executive. The result was a soft agreement with

[36] *CW*, IV, 65. [37] *HJ*, 1836–37, p. 684. [38] *Ibid.*, 1837, 128.

the Georgia governor. It said that the governor of Maine did the wrong thing. It agreed that the Abolitionists were doing their own cause damage, but, significantly, it did not treat the Abolitionists like thieves and murderers. They were "misguided" people whose aim was to "better the condition of a portion of the human family."[39]

When the resolution first came up, Lincoln took the floor and said that he "inclined to vote in favor" of the portion which criticized the governor of Maine; the second part of the resolution stated that free states should not "interfere with property of slaveholding states," and on that Lincoln said he wanted more time to consider the matter.[40] He moved to postpone the entire resolution "indefinitely," a motion which virtually would have killed it. His motion was defeated without a roll call.

When the matter finally came up for full House consideration after an adjournment motion temporarily postponed it, Calhoun brought in a resolution much stronger than the original. It stated that slavery should not be abolished in the District of Columbia; it favored admission of slave states into the Union; and it called moves to give Negroes equal rights in Illinois "unconstitutional."[41] Calhoun's amendment was killed 44 36, Lincoln being among those who voted to kill it.

In the 1838–39 session, Lincoln supported a measure which called for revenue on the assets of Illinois citizens, and among the items to be taxed were "slaves and servants of color." This can even be construed as an antislavery move, since it placed a tax on them, but the listing of items to be taxed in the law does not indicate a humanitarian cause. Items to be taxed were:

> Stock in incorporated companies, money actually loaned, retail stores, wholesale stores, carts, wagons, carriages, watches, clocks, slaves and servants of color, cattle, horses and mares, mules, jinnies, asses, stud horses, acres of land, town lots.[42]

In one of the last days of a session in Lincoln's third term, Edwards introduced a resolution calling the abolition of slavery in

[39] *Ibid.*, 1838–39, 170.
[40] *Vandalia Free Press*, January 10, 1839.
[41] *HJ*, 1838–39, p. 323.
[42] *LIll*, 1838–39, p. 5.

the District of Columbia "inexpedient, unwise, and unconstitutional."[43] Lincoln's friend Dubois moved to strike the word "unconstitutional," which was agreed to, and then the resolution was passed without controversy and without a roll call.

During the 1840 campaign, Lincoln went through the state working for the Whigs and William Henry Harrison and against Van Buren. Lincoln was aware that Van Buren came from New York, where Negroes had the right to vote, and this Lincoln used in speeches against Van Buren. There is no reason to believe that at this point he believed in Negroes voting. Lincoln also must share the responsibility for the constant use of "the Negro issue" against Van Buren in the campaign newspaper of 1840 which Lincoln and several other Whigs edited—the *Old Soldier*. The issue of July 28, 1840, for example, devoted most of the front page to attacking Van Buren in intemperate ways for the New Yorker's support of Negro rights. One of the things which appeared to shock them most was that Van Buren "is in favor of allowing FREE NEGROES and SLAVES to swear in Courts against WHITE MEN!"

When Lincoln spoke at Tremont during this 1840 campaign, the newspaper reported that Lincoln "reviewed the political course of Mr. Van Buren, and especially his votes in the New York Convention in allowing Free Negroes the right of suffrage."[44]

During Lincoln's final session a bill passed, introduced by Lyman Trumbull of Belleville—eventually one of the nation's leaders in the United States Senate—which made it easier for a Negro to establish his status as a free citizen. Surprisingly, no roll call was needed on this measure, and it slipped through easily; many of the members did not understand its significance. Helping to get the measure through was the final sentence that "nothing herein contained shall be construed to bar the lawful claim of any person or persons to any such negro or mulatto."[45]

Two years after Lincoln retired from the legislature, he frequently went over to the same halls to listen to debates. He heard a new member talk on the floor against slavery. When the remarks

43 *HJ*, 1838–39, p. 485.
44 *SgJ*, May 15, 1840.
45 *LIll*, 1840–41, p. 190.

were finished, Lincoln shook his hand warmly and was "emphatic in his commendation."[46]

The significance of Lincoln's votes on slavery can be summed up in the word "growth." He came from a family which was opposed to slavery, but did not get excited about the issue. Lincoln tended to accept that family attitude; he was not a crusader on the issue. But gradually, session by session, he became a little more concerned and a little more courageous.

[46] Moses Coit Tyler, "One of Mr. Lincoln's Old Friends," *ISHSJ*, January, 1936.

7

Two Mobs and Two Deaths
Shake Lincoln and the Nation

A community deeply involved in the commission of evil loves neither disturbance, repentence, nor rebuke. Their language is: Let us alone. And any exhibition of the truth, however well meant, which reaches the conscience will cause bitterness and reaction. —Rev. Edward Beecher, 1837.[1]

During Lincoln's legislative years, national attention focused on angry mobs which caused the deaths of two men.

Mob action in St. Louis made Lincoln speak up. He denounced it. When a newspaper editor was killed by a mob in Alton—on Illinois soil—eighteen months later, Lincoln spoke on the issue of mob rule in a general way, but made no specific mention of the incident. Why?

An examination of the fascinating but gruesome details of these incidents may provide an answer, at the same time giving further insight into Lincoln's legislative service.

Frank (or Francis) McIntosh, a young, free Negro, worked on the steamboat *Flora*, which had docked in St. Louis. When the boat had discharged its cargo, McIntosh left the boat to call on a young Negro girl he had met.

What happened next is not clear; accounts differ. What is certain is that McIntosh knew that he was in the slave state of

---

[1] Edward Beecher, *Riots at Alton* (Alton, George Holton, 1838), 13.

138

Missouri, where free Negroes occasionally were seized and sent back to slavery.

McIntosh hardly had stepped on land when he was arrested. McIntosh resisted arrest and in the ensuing fight pulled out a knife and killed one officer and wounded another. He then tried to escape but was quickly caught and placed in jail.

Even before he reached jail, a mob of several thousand persons formed, and law enforcement officers quickly gave up their attempt to save McIntosh. McIntosh was tied to a tree and burned to death.

Elijah P. Lovejoy, the second area victim of mob violence, was born in Maine. His New England background and Princeton theological training seemed to make him a natural Abolitionist and militant foe of slavery. But at first he opposed the Abolitionists as fanatics. He began his newspaper work with the *St. Louis Times*, first as a reporter and eventually as the publisher. His opposition to slavery gradually increased. Lovejoy's editorials were hard-hitting and plain. All attempts to silence him on the slavery issue failed.

When mob action took the form of physical violence, he was equally courageous. But the destruction of his printing equipment finally resulted in his moving across the river to Alton, where his newspaper became the *Alton Observer*.

Even before Lovejoy started operating in Alton, his first printing press was destroyed. Before long, three more were destroyed. He was finally killed by a mob and became the first martyr to freedom of the press in the United States.

Reaction to this tragedy was immediate—except in the state of Illinois. Even many Southern newspapers condemned the mob action. Two Northern newspapers said that the murder brought forth from every part of the land "a burst of indignation which has not had its parallel in this country since the battle of Lexington in 1775."[2] Everywhere editorials were being written, sermons delivered, and mass meetings called. The death of Lovejoy had rallied the antislavery forces as nothing before it had ever done.

[2] *Boston Recorder* and *Philadelphia Observer*, quoted in several Alton area newspapers, but no dates given.

What was Lincoln's reaction? It was the reaction of the Springfield newspapers and all Illinois newspapers, except the *Peoria Register* and the *Galena Advertiser*—silence. Governor Duncan, seemingly ever ready to champion an unpopular cause, stated simply, "The outrage at Alton must be disapproved and regretted by all good citizens."[3] All other Whig and Democratic leaders in the state maintained silence.

The first and only public notice Lincoln took of either the Lovejoy or the McIntosh murders was in a speech before the Young Men's Lyceum of Springfield on January 27, 1838, almost three months after Lovejoy's slaying. It is a speech denouncing mob violence in general terms, pointing out examples in New England, Louisiana, Mississippi, and St. Louis. But there is no mention of Alton or of Lovejoy, except for one small phrase.

Lincoln went into detail on the McIntosh murder, pointing out its tragedy and the danger of mob action on our constitutional processes, but the nearest he came to mentioning Lovejoy is in one sentence in a lengthy speech: "Whenever the vicious portion of population shall be permitted to gather in bands of hundreds and thousands, and burn churches, shoot editors, and hang and burn obnoxious persons at pleasure, and with impunity; depend on it, this government cannot last."[4]

Lincoln's whole address was caused by the public agitation which followed the Lovejoy incident. Obviously, in the minds of any Illinois audience, the Lovejoy murder was uppermost during Lincoln's talk, one of his finer speeches. Perhaps nothing Lincoln said during his legislative years indicated his potential as much as this talk, with the exception of the protest he and Dan Stone filed on the slavery question. Listen to the young legislator, not yet turned twenty-nine:

> There is, even now, something of ill-omen amongst us. I mean the increasing disregard for law which pervades the country; the growing disposition to substitute the wild and furious passions, in

[3] Elizabeth Duncan Putnam, "The Life and Services of Joseph Duncan," *Illinois State Historical Society Transactions*, 1919.

[4] *CW*, I, 111.

lieu of the sober judgment of Courts; and the worse than savage mobs, for the executive ministers of justice. This disposition is awfully fearful in any community; and that it now exists in ours, though grating to our feelings to admit, it would be a violation of truth, and an insult to our intelligence, to deny. . . .

But you are, perhaps, ready to ask, "What has this to do with the perpetuation of our political institutions?" I answer, it has much to do with it. . . . The innocent, those who have ever set their faces against violation of law in every shape, alike with the guilty, fall victims to the ravages of mob law; and thus it goes on, step by step, till all the walls erected for the defence of the persons and property of individuals, are trodden down, and disregarded. . . .

I know the American People are *much* attached to their Government. . . . Yet, notwithstanding all this, if the laws be continually despised and disregarded, if their right to be secure in their persons and property, are held by no better tenure than the caprice of a mob, the alienation of their affections from the Government is the natural consequence. . . .

The question recurs "how shall we fortify against it?" The answer is simple. Let every American, every lover of liberty, every well wisher to his posterity, swear by the blood of the Revolution, never to violate in the least particular, the laws of the country; and never to tolerate their violation by others. . . . Let every man remember that to violate the law, is to trample on the blood of his father, and to tear the charter of his own, and his children's liberty. Let reverence for the laws, be breathed by every American mother, to the lisping babe, that prattles on her lap. . . . In short, let it become the political religion of the nation; and let the old and the young, the rich and the poor, the grave and the gay, of all sexes and tongues, and colors and conditions, sacrifice unceasingly upon its altars.[5]

It is not as simple and direct as Lincoln would later become, and considering the terrible tragedy that had occurred on Illinois soil, it is somewhat surprising that Lincoln did not talk more plainly.

[5] *Ibid.*, I, 109–12.

Why did Lincoln not speak out more forthrightly? Answers to that question must be speculative, but these seem reasonable possibilities:

1. Lincoln's thinking was still maturing on the whole question of slavery, and Lincoln did not detail his ideas before he had come to some solid conclusions. Particularly he did not want to associate himself with what he regarded as extremists, the Abolitionists. One study comments on Lincoln's silence, "The answer must be that, while he detested mob violence and considered Lovejoy murdered, he did not approve of Lovejoy's methods nor of the Abolitionist cause.... It is probable that Lincoln thought of Lovejoy as he afterwards thought of John Brown, a sincere but misguided fanatic."[6]

2. In the protest he had signed with Dan Stone in the House a few months earlier, Lincoln had already taken an unpopular stand against slavery. By opposing mob violence and mentioning the McIntosh case, he stood on the side of law and order without being charged with being an Abolitionist, which he was not. Too forthright a statement might offend public opinion.

3. Lovejoy's extreme religious views, with his attacks on various denominations, were not in keeping with Lincoln's convictions. It is possible—although not probable—that Lincoln feared that defending Lovejoy and denouncing mob violence would associate him in the public mind with Lovejoy's religious views. Lincoln was sensitive to public feelings in this area, so this is possible; it is not likely, however, since he could have stated clearly that he did not necessarily endorse the religious views of Lovejoy, but was defending his right to freedom of speech.

4. But while conceding the preceding points, it does not appear too difficult to speak out against mob action in the Lovejoy case and still not be associated with the Abolitionists, with Lovejoy's religious views, or arouse much public opposition. A fourth possibility strongly suggests itself. Lincoln was not without political ambition and did not want to alienate some of Lovejoy's influential opponents who were Lincoln's friends and potential supporters of his political aspirations. He felt so strongly on the subject that he

[6] Ernest C. Marriner, "The Springfield Lawyer and the Alton Martyr," *Colby Mercury*, Colby College, Waterville, Me., February 12, 1941.

had to speak out, but wanted to do this without stepping on powerful toes. He simply temporized for political reasons.[7]

Who were these political leaders, and what was their role?

One of these was Usher F. Linder, attorney general of Illinois, who actively fought Lovejoy. He thought it his duty, after Lovejoy's death, to prosecute those who helped Lovejoy defend his press and to defend those who were the mob leaders! Although Lincoln did not vote for Linder for attorney general, the two had served together in the Illinois House of Representatives, and there was a cordial relationship between them. Linder, in age and size similar to Lincoln, was an influential member of the House and used his influence to get himself elected attorney general. He appeared to have a bright future in Illinois politics.

A second Lincoln friend and colleague involved in the Lovejoy affair was the Rev. John Hogan of Alton. Five years older than Lincoln and Linder, "Honest John" Hogan, a former Methodist circuit rider, had become a respected Alton businessman. In the legislature he had frequently used his booming, loud voice to aid his friend Lincoln. He had not voted for Linder for attorney general, but this did not prevent a friendly relationship between Linder and himself. Hogan's city of Alton had been considered for the state capital, but when it became clear that Alton could not make it, Hogan voted on the fourth ballot for Lincoln's town of Springfield.

The third Lincoln friend involved was State Senator Cyrus Edwards, uncle of Lincoln's Springfield colleague in the House, Ninian W. Edwards. Cyrus Edwards was the youngest brother of former Governor Ninian Edwards who had been a slaveholder. Cyrus Edwards became the Whig candidate for governor in 1838. A hero of the Black Hawk War, Cyrus Edwards had a large personal following throughout the state. Edwards was "a man of commanding presence, six feet, four inches tall, always elegantly dressed."[8] The Whigs had high hopes that Edwards would soon be

[7] The editors of the *Collected Works* add a fifth possibility that strikes this author as unlikely. They suggest that Lincoln was attempting by a subtle approach to be more effective. It seems more likely that Lincoln wanted to be effective, but without mentioning the Lovejoy incident specifically.

[8] Edwards described by his granddaughter, Alice Edwards Quigley, *Allentown* (Pa.) *Morning Call*, February 9, 1936.

governor. There were many ways a governor could help a young legislator like Lincoln.

By avoiding direct comment on the Lovejoy murder because of his three friends, Lincoln gained but little.

Linder co-operated with Lincoln in some legal work, but probably would have done so regardless of what Lincoln had said. Even though in later years Linder spoke kindly of Lincoln, in 1858 he supported Douglas and in 1860 again actively worked against Lincoln. The cordial feeling between Lincoln and Hogan continued, although Hogan left his Whig moorings and became an active Democrat and worked against Lincoln.

If Lincoln wanted to seek the favors of a potential governor in Cyrus Edwards—and the favors a governor could dispense were many—it did Lincoln no good, for Edwards was defeated by 926 votes. Edwards thought he pleased the public by his Lovejoy stand, and perhaps he did, but at least one Whig organ thought differently.

The Lovejoy Slaying

A mob attacking the warehouse of Godfrey Gilman & Company, Alton, Illinois, on the night of November 7, 1837, at the time Lovejoy was murdered and his press destroyed.

From *The Martyrdom of Lovejoy*, by "An Eye-Witness" (Chicago, 1881)

The *Hennepin Journal* commented, "Had it not been for the Abolitionists, we should, also, at the last August election have elected a Whig Governor—These gentry could not be brought to vote for Edwards because they thought he had been a participator in the tragical occurrences in the city of Alton. . . . Although we believed Mr. Edwards guiltless, the great body of the Abolitionists in this State did not, and their Whig principles were sacrificed upon the altar of their fanaticism. This we know to be a fact, in our own neighborhood, at least."[9]

When Lincoln was in Congress, he unsuccessfully tried to get a Land Office job for Edwards. By 1858, Edwards was a prominent Douglas supporter in the Lincoln battle with the Little Giant.

Lovejoy failed in his immediate objective, but in his tragic failure he shocked the nation and achieved eventual success. One of the reasons for his success was his influence on men who were to influence the Great Emancipator, Abraham Lincoln.

The silence of Lincoln on the Lovejoy incident is not Lincoln's most shining hour. But he was learning that improperly directed public opinion could be dangerously wrong, literally dead wrong.

[9] December 22, 1838.

8

A Third Term and Leadership

This has been a stormy session and a very unpleasant one.
—JOHN J. HARDIN, February 21, 1839.[1]

THE FEBRUARY, 1838, announcement that Lincoln was seeking his third term in the House of Representatives did not slow down his law practice. The firm of Stuart and Lincoln was kept busy—busier than most Springfield law firms—and Lincoln did most of the paper work for them. Lincoln also took care of the maintenance chores. On the various pages of the fee book can be found, "Lincoln paid for stove pipe. Lincoln paid for wood. Lincoln paid for wood-saw. . . . Lincoln paid for candles."[2] When fees were split, at least occasionally the large share went to the senior partner, John Stuart. One entry, for example, reads, "$5.00. Paid Stuart $3.00. Paid Lincoln $2.00."

Lincoln did not, as some biographies hint, secure powerful clients who might benefit from his House leadership.

On March 22, Lincoln was one of 101 citizens of Springfield who signed a bank note for $16,666.67 at 6 per cent—one-third of the $50,000 Springfield had pledged as its share for being made the state capital.[3]

Lincoln and Stuart were both more interested in politics than in law, and in April, the race for Congress between Stuart and Doug-

---

[1] Letter from Hardin to his wife, Chicago Historical Society Library.

[2] Stuart-Lincoln Fee Book, owned by Mrs. Edna Orendorff Macpherson, Springfield, Ill.

[3] CW, I, 116.

las began in earnest. In May, Stuart was ill, so Lincoln substituted for him and debated with Douglas, not a new task for Lincoln.

Lincoln also took an interest in the gubernatorial race. Cyrus Edwards, the Whig candidate who had been involved in the Lovejoy incident, was opposed by Thomas Carlin for the Democrats. The electorate turned Edwards down—30,648 to 29,722.[4] Issues in the governor's race centered mainly on the national picture, with Carlin a "Democrat of the straightest sect."[5]

For a while Lincoln campaigned mostly by conversation or correspondence rather than speeches. He tried to prod his correspondents to action. "If we relax an iota, we shall be beaten," he wrote.[6]

Four meetings were held in Sangamon County, with all legislative candidates present and speaking. The first was held on Sugar Creek, five miles from Springfield. Other meetings were held at places with equally rural-sounding names—William Colburn's mill on Lick Creek, Water's Camp Ground on Spring Creek.[7] What Lincoln said at these meetings is not known.

When the *Sangamo Journal* endorsed seven House candidates, it listed Lincoln's name fourth, possibly because it felt he would win anyway and additional support should be given the other candidates.[8]

Division of Sangamon County was the major concern in the legislative race. All agreed that the county should be divided; the question was how. People in the outlying areas of Sangamon County were unhappy with their legislators because the county had not been divided already. Some favored dividing the county into four equal portions, but Springfield residents particularly disliked this suggestion because it would put their city in one corner of the new county. A candidate's position on revision and the vigor with which he supported it, determined where his strength at the polls lay.

On August 6, the election was held. Lincoln headed the field of seventeen candidates in the race for the Illinois House, and Stuart

---

[4] Pease, *Story of Illinois*, 264.

[5] George W. Smith, *A Student's History of Illinois* (Carbondale, Ill., Smith, 1907), 334.

[6] *CW*, I, 120.   [7] *SgJ*, June 23, 1838.   [8] April 28, 1838.

beat Douglas for Congress by only thirty-six votes. Wild charges and countercharges followed the congressional vote count.

With the exception of Robert L. Wilson of Athens, all of the Long Nine were returned to office. Wilson was defeated by John Calhoun, the only Democratic winner. Lincoln, the top vote-getter, was not far ahead of the others. Both the winners and leading losers ran close. Lincoln received 1,803 votes; Ninian W. Edwards came in second with 1,779, only twenty-four less than Lincoln.

Those within the Whig Party in Sangamon County who resented the leadership of Lincoln and his friends—whom they called "the junto"—ran as Anti-Junto Whigs, but ran far behind the other Whigs and Democrats.

The increased Democratic strength could be traced largely to the division of the county question. In New Salem, where Lincoln usually ran strong, he received only thirty-one votes, while the other Whigs trailed him—and the Democrats received 95 to 107 votes, more than three times the vote of Lincoln.

It was much the same story in Petersburg, where many of the New Salem residents and friends of Lincoln had moved and he could be expected to run well. But Lincoln received fifty-five votes, about one-fourth the Democratic vote.

In his own Springfield precinct Lincoln voted for Whigs at the legislative and state level, except that he voted for Thomas Vance, a Democrat, instead of himself. In 1838 it was still the custom for a candidate not to vote for himself. In earlier elections he had voted for Calhoun, but not this time. In the State Senate race between his friends "Whiggish" Archer G. Herndon, one of the Long Nine, and Democrat Bowling Green, who had helped him in his start at New Salem, Lincoln voted for Herndon.

There is at least a strong possibility that Lincoln himself, in an editorial which appeared immediately after the election in the *Sangamo Journal*, explained his vote:

> We believe the interest of our country required that Herndon should be elected; and, therefore, we are gratified with his election. On the other hand, to see our old friend, Bowling Green, beaten, and to have been under the necessity of aiding in defeating him,

we confess is, and has been extremely painful to us. Under other circumstances, we would have been glad to do battle for him; but as it was, he threw himself in the ranks of our enemies, and therefore we could do no less than we did.[9]

Herndon won in a close race, 1,476–1,429.

The clerk of the election wrote "Hon. Lincoln" when Lincoln came to vote, but he recorded the first and last names of the other legislators.[10]

A month before he started for Vandalia and the meeting of the legislature, Lincoln was one of eight speakers at a big barbecue at Porter's Grove celebrating Stuart's victory over Douglas. More than two thousand were in attendance, and one newspaper took note of Lincoln's remarks and described his speech as "pithy in its own peculiar style."[11]

On November 30, Lincoln again made the trip to Vandalia and another legislative session, the last in Vandalia, to the capitol which the *Peoria Register* said "looks more like a Pennsylvania barn than anything else."[12] An Eastern visitor reported that he was "somewhat disappointed" with Vandalia: "It is passing strange that a town like Vandalia, with all the natural and artificial advantages it possesses; located nearly twenty years ago, by state authority, expressly as the seat of government, situated upon the banks of a fine stream . . . in the heart of a healthy and fertile region, should have increased and flourished no more than seems to have been the case."[13]

Members of the House delegation from Sangamon County, besides Lincoln, were John Dawson, William F. Elkin, John Calhoun, Edward D. Baker, Ninian W. Edwards, and Andrew McCormick —all men Lincoln had known and worked with.

Lincoln's leadership was well established by this time, and he became the Whig candidate for speaker of the House. His chief

[9] July 14, 1838.

[10] Precinct voting is on file with the Illinois Archives.

[11] *Alton Telegraph*, October 17, 1838.

[12] *Peoria Register and Northwestern Gazetteer*, December 29, 1838.

[13] Edmund Flagg, *The Far West: or, A Tour Beyond the Mountains* (New York, Harper & Brothers, 1838), quoted in *ISHSJ*, September, 1948.

opponent, William L. D. Ewing, had had some fiery moments of debate on the House floor with Lincoln. Short, auburn-haired, and muscular, Ewing—a former governor, United States senator, and brigadier general—had campaigned on the platform that he would "be a thorn in the sides of the Long Nine."[14] He became that for at least one of the Nine on the opening day.

There were eighty-five possible votes for speaker, the winning candidate needing a majority of forty-three. The Whigs controlled the Senate. It is difficult to determine what the lineup in the House was, with newspaper accounts varying. Apparently it was almost a tossup between the two, with fourteen independents (in greater or lesser degree) holding the balance of power. One historian gives the Whigs a 46–40 majority, with five independents.[15] None gives the Democrats (administration men) a majority, although the Democrats secured the speakership. Three candidates ran for the House as Conservatives, all three winning, but Lincoln did not get a single vote from them.

For the first time in Lincoln's legislative service, the number of men who had already served in the legislature outnumbered the newcomers. Some of these House veterans felt that a man who had served in high positions merited the top House post more than a man like Lincoln, who had served in the House only two terms.

Three ballots were taken in the morning, Ewing leading Lincoln 41–38 on the first ballot, six other votes scattered. Three Whigs were absent. Lincoln voted for Henry Webb of Alexander County, who called himself a Conservative. On the second ballot the votes were unchanged.

On the third ballot Ewing received forty-one votes; Lincoln slipped to thirty-four. Then the House adjourned until two o'clock in the afternoon. During the lunch hour two votes were switched to Ewing, and he received the bare majority he needed to win, forty-three, while Lincoln received thirty-eight.

The Jacksonville *Illinoian* credited Ewing's victory to pressure from a congressman and "a certain *judicial* officer of the state" and to the fact that two Whigs supported Ewing because of "local

14 *SgJ*, July 14, 1838.
15 Snyder, *Selected Writings*, 267.

influence."[16] The two who supported Ewing because of "local influence" were from counties next to Ewing's.

The next day a committee was appointed to draw up the rules for the House; Lincoln was named one of the seven members.

Retiring Governor Joseph Duncan gave his farewell message to the legislature. It was an "I told you so" speech. He stated: "Experience has now sufficiently shown that all my objections to [Internal Improvements] must in time be fully realized. . . . How to correct this mistake, and get rid of the evils with which we are threatened by this improvident act . . . should occupy your serious and patriotic deliberations. That there should have been many mistakes committed and much waste of public money . . . was to have been expected. But I confess they have occurred to an extent never anticipated by myself—and whether by mistake or design, it is very manifest that large sums have been squandered."

Governor Duncan called patronage "a thing which belongs only to ambitious tyrants, to reward the servility of their dependents; a word and principle which should be scowled by every freeman in our country."

He finally assured his listeners that "the violence with which I have been assailed by my political opponents, during the whole time I have been in office, has caused no rankling in my bosom."[17]

On December 6, the Rules Committee to which Lincoln belonged brought in recommendations for House Rules, including a rule that "every member who shall be in the House when a question is put, shall vote on one side or the other, unless the House, for special reasons, shall excuse him."[18] The legislators were having difficulty with some members who preferred to avoid voting on the more controversial measures, a problem not foreign to legislative bodies of today.

The next day Governor Thomas Carlin took his oath of office. Not highly educated, he had served as sheriff of Greene County and for two terms in the State Senate. An all-out Democrat, his views on national issues, such as the United States Bank, reflected this background. A muscular man of medium height, he was not brilliant "but well stocked with strong, practical sense and determina-

16 *Illinoian*, December 15, 1838.   17 *HJ*, 1838–39, pp. 10–17.   18 *Ibid.*, 23.

tion."[19] Even a political opponent described him as "courageous as a lion."[20]

Carlin was something of a political accident. The Democrats were forced to switch at the end of the campaign from James W. Stephenson, their nominee for governor, caught embezzling funds from the federal treasury. After Stephenson had been nominated, one of the Democratic leaders of Vandalia wrote to a friend, "For my own part I am much, very much, pleased with the result. Stephenson is of that breed of men—rare bands on earth—in the defense of whom a man feels the consciousness of occupying high and elevated ground. In giving your unbought testimony to the character of such a man, you don't apprehend that hereafter your words will be repeated to you in irony."[21]

Within six months Stephenson was caught. This forced the Democrats to switch to Carlin, who had a reputation of being honest. He was, however, accurately described by one of the Democratic state senators as "a most unexceptionable man."[22] Governor Duncan was known as a man who wrote his own speeches, while Carlin depended "upon the services of a 'penny-a-liner.' "[23] In his message to the legislature, Carlin said that "in the principles and policy of this plan [Internal Improvements], I entirely concur."[24] However, he would have recommended its adoption "on a less extensive scale." His speech was much more optimistic, but less realistic than that of Governor Duncan. Carlin received some assistance in writing the speech, and when some of his friends, who hoped he would be as courageous as Governor Duncan on internal improvements, heard the speech, their reaction was one of "astonishment and disgust."[25] However, the large majority of Illinois citizens welcomed his falsely reassuring words.

[19] Snyder, *Selected Writings*, 270.

[20] Joseph Gillespie, *Recollections of Early Illinois and Her Noted Men* (Chicago, Fergus Printing, 1880), 23.

[21] Dr. I. G. Armstrong, Vandalia, to Major Daniel F. Hitt, Ottawa, December 14, 1837, IHL.

[22] A. W. Snyder, probably written to G. P. Koerner, May 7, 1838, IHL.

[23] *Quincy Whig*, December 15, 1838.

[24] *HJ*, 1838–39, pp. 26–30.

[25] Snyder, *Selected Writings*, 271.

On Saturday, the first legislative week closed with the appointment of committees, Lincoln being named to the powerful Finance Committee and to the Committee on Counties. The latter was important because of the Sangamon County division question.

That day the legislators also heard a report blaming the escape of four convicts from the state penitentiary on the warden, a man Lincoln had opposed for the position two years earlier. The inspectors reported that the prison physician is "allowed 50 cents for bleeding and 50 cents for extracting teeth. . . . Twenty-four [prisoners] attribute their present misfortune to the use of intoxicating liquor."[26]

During the first week, Lincoln came out in favor of a resolution by his fellow Whig Hardin asking for more information on the internal improvements operation. In supporting Hardin's resolution Lincoln told the House, "If there is extravagance or wrong, make it known, and correct it—now is the best time to do this; there is no imputation cast on the Commissioners, they are not perfect."[27] Lincoln by this time had some misgivings about the whole thing. He is quoted in a newspaper story as saying that the legislature had "gone too far to recede, even if we were disposed to do so."[28]

Internal improvements continued to dominate the Illinois picture. A resolution passed which called for "a prudent and economical prosecution of the public works."[29] For a state with a multimillion dollar program on its hands, this was a modest enough statement of policy even though too late. By the time this session of the legislature met, opposition to internal improvements had grown. The *Peoria Register* commented:

> Were all the roads projected by our last legislature now completed, and locomotives and cars placed upon them ready for business; where, let me ask, would be found the passengers and tonnage necessary to raise a revenue to keep these roads in repair? . . . Let us take a glance at our central railroad, upon which the sum of

26 *HJ*, 1838, pp. 33–38.
27 *Illinoian*, December 15, 1838.
28 *SgJ*, December 15, 1838.
29 *HJ*, 1838–39, p. 94.

three millions five hundred thousand dollars is authorized to be expended, which sum will probably pay about one half the cost of the whole road. . . . Galena is the only town on the whole route which is anything more than a mere name. It is situated near the Mississippi on a navigable branch, containing about twelve hundred inhabitants, and has a constant intercourse with Saint Louis and other markets on the Mississippi.[30]

However, the Board of Public Works reported confidently to the legislature that if internal improvements is "persevered in, [it] will enable the State to carry out the system to its full completion without imposing burdens on the people."[31]

The report of the auditors showed a balance on hand at the end of the fiscal year of $92.16 for the state of Illinois! A further illustration—even aside from the internal improvements extravaganza—that the Illinois financial picture was not what it should have been was the fact that the auditor's report showed an estimated total state income for the year of $67,000 and an estimated expenditure of $80,000.[32]

With a balance of $92.16 in the state treasury, one newspaper made a study of the internal improvements debt and came to the figure of $15,146,444. With forty thousand taxpayers in the state, the paper pointed out, this "makes the indebtedness amount to $378.66 per man!"[33] This made the per taxpayer debt more than four times the total balance in the state treasury.

Despite the looming financial crisis, the legislature itself was not so "prudent and economical" as they had urged others to be regarding internal improvements. Not only was the internal improvements program not curtailed, projects were added—usually with Lincoln's agreement.

Among items agreed to by the legislators were extension of Indiana's railroads into Illinois, the improvement for navigation purposes of the Embarrass River, the improvement of the Big Muddy River, construction of a railroad from Rushville to Erie,

[30] *Peoria Register and Northwestern Gazetter*, August 25, 1838.
[31] "Report on the Board of Commissioners of Public Works," December 28, 1838.
[32] *HJ*, 1838–39, pp. 75–76.
[33] *Illinoian*, February 16, 1839.

the improvement of the Spoon River, as well as several other projects totaling almost $1,000,000—if done at the prices the legislature guessed, and their cost estimates were almost always low. In addition, $4,000,000 was appropriated for the Illinois and Michigan Canal.

To compound their folly, the legislators refused to grant the right to a private railroad firm to construct track in the state. To Lincoln's credit in this instance, he joined the minority who favored giving the private corporation permission to build.

Lincoln consistently supported bigger and more internal improvements. In some instances no vote is recorded, but there is no evidence to suppose that Lincoln changed his course on these. In two instances the recorded vote showed Lincoln absent. Otherwise, the unbelievably reckless course followed by the legislature had Lincoln's approval and encouragement. For a Washington County representative, Lincoln drafted the legislation calling for a survey for two additional small railroad lines. This legislation became law.

When Lincoln made a report for the Committee on Finance regarding "Public Lands in Illinois," one of his first statements was, "We are now so far advanced in a general system of Internal Improvements that, if we would, we cannot retreat from it without disgrace and great loss."[34]

One saving action—if it can be termed that—on Lincoln's part was a resolution urging the federal government to sell federally owned land to the state at twenty-five cents an acre, the state hoping to resell it at a profit. Lincoln placed the total cost of such a purchase at $5,000,000.[35]

Lincoln thought the investment a good one because "Illinois surpasses every other spot of equal extent upon the face of the globe." To those who thought the federal government would not be interested in selling the land at that price, Lincoln's response was that $5,000,000 represented one-third of the cost of the Louisiana Purchase, and compared with that, the federal government would do well by getting $5,000,000.

The federal government paid no attention to the request. If it

[34] *Illinois Reports*, 1838–39, n.p.
[35] *HJ*, 1838–39, p. 224.

had agreed, it is not clear how the state of Illinois with all its financial problems could have raised an additional $5,000,000.

This resolution is one of the few examples of Lincoln's showing original thinking and leadership in the sense of introducing legislation of more than local interest. His role was not particularly creative in this or in any other session. For the most part his leadership was provided in reaction to legislation introduced by others, by amendment to these proposals, and in the ability to get along with his colleagues and to sense what they would support and would not support.

To raise some state revenue for meeting the mushrooming costs of the government, a property tax of twenty cents per $100 worth of taxable property was suggested by a committee. The House rejected this in favor of a fifteen-cent figure. Lincoln supported the higher figure, which the House and Senate finally adopted. It brought in only a small per cent of the money Illinois needed. The auditor's report showed that taxable lands in Cook County (Chicago) were worth $2,500 and in Sangamon County $335,097.[36] The same report noted that so far in the biennium, $423.84 had been spent for running the attorney general's office and $389.50 for killing wolves.

Illinois banking problems and the national issue of whether there should be a United States Bank dominated much of this session. A move to have the state collect its revenue in gold or silver exclusively was defeated, Lincoln voting to defeat it. In the banking field, his actions were largely influenced by his desire to help the State Bank at Springfield.

The minority report of the Finance Committee favored money in specie because "the dangers from fire and robbery are less, as the precious metals, though melted, would still retain their intrinsic value; and the difficulties of carrying off and concealing gold and silver are much greater than purloining and secreting paper money."[37] Lincoln did not share this thinking.

A resolution of the Senate, expressing displeasure that some federally collected Illinois money was in the Bank in Missouri in St. Louis, received a great deal of amendment and discussion. Lin-

[36] "Report of the State Auditor," *Illinois Reports*, 1838–39.
[37] *HJ*, 1838–39, p. 107.

coln agreed with the Senate resolution but then had the resolution and amendments tabled "until July 4th"—long after the legislature adjourned. It is not clear why he did this; perhaps because of the adoption of one of the amendments which he opposed or because the resolution took up too much time. With a Democratic legislator he debated whether the federal government had shown "partiality" in this matter.

During a series of amendments and debates on the question of a national bank, one legislator introduced an amendment which said "that it is inexpedient to consume the time of the Legislature and waste the money of the people in acting on resolutions which merely involve national politics."[38] The amendment carried in the House, with Lincoln against it. The Senate defeated it.

The endless debate on the national banking policies was almost meaningless. It convinced nobody, changed no votes in Washington, and probably had little, if any, effect on public opinion.

Lincoln voted against a proposal to prohibit the use of paper money in Illinois "of less denomination than five dollars," a resolution which carried 63–20.[39] He was the only Sangamon member to vote against it.

With the majority, Lincoln killed a move to appoint a legislative committee to examine the state banks. His chief interest—protecting the Springfield bank.

Some legislators were taking an interest in banking legislation because they saw it as the way to solve their financial problems. One who tried to get on the board of directors of the bank at Shawneetown was "so deeply in debt that he can see no prospects, or if he can see any, his friends can see none of his getting out soon, if ever. He owes I understand between 16 or 1700S to the Br[anch] of [the] State Bank at Alton about or full as much more to eastern merchants all now due or soon to be due. I have no doubt he owes much besides. If he is made a director he will possess the means ... of transferring his debts from the State B[ank] to the Illinois B[ank at Shawneetown]."[40]

---

38 *Ibid.*, 260.

39 *Ibid.*, 254.

40 David J. Baker, speaking of John Hogan, in a letter to Henry Eddy, September 25, 1837, IHL.

While internal improvements and banking matters dominated the legislative session, there were a host of other concerns Lincoln and his colleagues had. One member introduced a resolution that "we deprecate the practice of the General Assembly of electing members of their own body to fill state offices, as corrupting in its tendencies."[41] It was adopted by the narrow margin of 44–42, Lincoln supporting it. Calhoun tried in vain to table the resolution. One courageous legislator wanted to add "or their relatives or connexions" to the resolution. He lost 66–18, but Lincoln was one of the eighteen to support him.

The next day a motion by a Bond County legislator to reconsider this resolution got Lincoln into a conflict with some of his colleagues. The original motion was to refer the resolution to the Judiciary Committee. Lincodn moved that instead it be sent to the Internal Improvements Committee. The men on the latter committee took this as a personal attack. The *Alton Telegraph* stated, "Mr. Lincoln replied, he did not move the reference with any such design as had been attributed to him. He had always been the friend of both the gentlemen; and at the last extra session he had voted against such a proposition because his friend from Wabash was personally interested then in the decision, being at that time in the employ of the state. . . . But he was glad he had made it [the motion]: the hydra was exposed; and all the talk about settling this matter at another tribunal, he had no objection to, if the gentlemen insisted on it. He was always ready, and never shrunk from responsibility."[42] The motion to reconsider failed.

Later in the session there was an exchange over legislators accepting federal positions, contrary to the state constitution. The move was aimed at Adams County Democrat William G. Flood who had been named to the Quincy Land Office. Lincoln entered into the discussion, trying to maintain the principle and to avoid a personal attack on the man.

An unsigned letter from Vandalia to the editor of the *Sangamo Journal*—perhaps written by Lincoln—declared that after the appropriation bill for the new state capitol in Springfield passed the Senate, for some reason Sangamon's Democratic member, John

[41] *HJ*, 1838–39, pp. 120–21.   [42] December 29, 1838.

Calhoun, got hold of it and took it to Springfield, delaying passage for about ten days. The letter concluded: "I suppose the workmen employed on the state house at Springfield, who are thus kept out of the reward of their labor for ten days longer, will feel themselves particularly indebted to Mr. Calhoun."[43]

A motion to have a detailed explanation of "the contracts for the construction of the State House at Springfield" was immediately seized by Lincoln.[44] This happened so quickly as to justify the suspicion that it was prearranged. Lincoln moved to refer the matter to a Committee of the Whole House and this was approved. Chairing the Committee of the Whole was Representative Richard G. Murphy of Perry County, a Springfield supporter.

At no time during the session was there any serious effort to halt the move to Springfield. Usually such efforts were designed to satisfy some local constituents. Representative William J. Hankins, the author of the motion cited above, was one of the two representatives from the Vandalia area, where strong sentiment opposed the Springfield move.

A motion to have another state-wide election was defeated 62–26. During the debate, Lincoln and the speaker of the House, William L. D. Ewing of Vandalia, exchanged words in debate. A month later Lincoln wrote to his law partner, "Ewing won't do anything. He is not worth a damn."[45] This was unusually strong Lincoln language and revealed some bitterness toward the man who defeated him for speaker—as well as a protest against some of the irresponsible statements Ewing had made since the 1836–37 session. The one-sided vote on the measure indicates that Ewing merely went through the motions for local consumption. All similar motions to halt the moving of the capital to Springfield were defeated by wide margins. Ewing even appointed a majority of pro-Springfield men to the Finance Committee, a move which legislators and newspapers considered a clear indication that the capital issue had been decided.

Lincoln handled the House side of things for the $128,300 appropriation to complete work for the new capitol. The State House Commissioners, who were in charge of erecting the new capitol in

43 January 5, 1839.   44 *HJ*, 1838–39, p. 127.   45 *CW*, I, 143.

Springfield, reported that the costs would include: 28,182 feet of cut stone, 303,000 bricks, 9,519 pounds of nails, 12 large and 16 small stoves.[46]

An act to incorporate the town of Danville passed 47–33, Lincoln voting for it.

Lincoln handled a Senate bill which authorized General Assembly committees to swear witnesses. The measure passed without difficulty.

In this session Lincoln again showed no leadership in the field of education. A bill to make the office of school commissioner in each county an elective one passed the House 54–17, with Lincoln's one of the seventeen votes against it. Supporters of the measure felt it would give increased emphasis to education, and legislators like Ninian W. Edwards (later the first state superintendent of public instruction) and others who had been showing more interest in the cause of education than Lincoln had, lined up against the future President.[47] Perhaps one reason for Lincoln's action was the report of the auditor which showed seventy-eight schools in Sangamon County. But others had far less. Cook County, for example, had only six schools.[48] An act to incorporate the Springfield High School Association was handled not by Lincoln but by two of the other Sangamon County representatives.

As in other sessions, when it came to the cause of educating the handicapped, Lincoln voted "on the side of the angels." A bill to establish "the Illinois Asylum for the education of the deaf and dumb" was supported by Lincoln, both at the amendment stage and in final passage.[49]

When it came to the matter of distribution of funds entrusted to the state for the cause of education, Lincoln was cautious, but again not a leader. Of the many amendments introduced on this subject, not one was introduced by Lincoln. When it came to final passage, Lincoln voted against the bill.[50] In view of the state's

[46] "Report of State House Commissioners," December 8, 1838.

[47] *HJ*, 1838–39, p. 235.

[48] "Report of Auditor Showing the Condition of Schools for the Year 1837," *Illinois Reports*, 1838–39.

[49] *HJ*, 1838–39, pp. 327, 391.

[50] *Ibid.*, 396.

financial situation, Lincoln's caution on distributing any funds that the state had to its credit is understandable despite the pressing need for education. During the final full day of the session, Representative Robert Smith of Alton introduced an amendment which called for the state to pay to the schools interest on the school funds it held, since it obviously would not distribute them. A move to kill the amendment carried 38–27, Lincoln helping to kill the measure.

Once during debate someone suggested that the number "nine" was favored by old women. Lincoln replied that he had been one of the nine from Sangamon County at a previous session and added, "If any woman, old or young, ever thought there was any peculiar charm in this distinguished specimen of number 9, I have, as yet, been so unfortunate as not to have discovered it."[51] The young bachelor's comments were greeted by a roar of laughter.

Several times during the session resolutions were introduced to hear special speakers, such as an evening lecturer from McKendree College, a former officer of Napoleon's army, or a temperance lecturer. Lincoln never presented one of these resolutions. He did, however, make the motion "that the use of the hall of the House of Representatives be tendered to the ladies and gentlemen resident at and visiting the town of Vandalia" for the evening of George Washington's birthday "for the purpose of any public amusement they may choose to indulge in."[52]

There was a lighter side to Vandalia activities, everything from hard drinking parties to the more educational. During the session there were at least three lectures on phrenology given in the evening.[53]

One legislator's wife, who had been at a previous session but did not accompany her husband this time, wrote, "I miss the intellectual feasts I enjoyed at Vandalia."[54] The frontier town of Vandalia and its legislators were polished enough for one traveling reporter to note that the legislature "as a body will lose nothing in

[51] *SgJ*, January 15, 1839.
[52] *HJ*, 1838–39, p. 476.
[53] *Peoria Register and Northwestern Gazetteer*, January 26, 1839.
[54] Letter from Sarah Hardin to John Hardin, February 19, 1839, Chicago Historical Society Library.

personal appearance" in comparison with other states he had visited.[55]

Jesse W. Fell, a friend of Lincoln, noted in his *Bloomington Observer*: "Our Legislature is composed of a very respectable and talented body of men; and it gladdens the heart of the patriot to behold that talent nobly exerting itself."[56]

Newton Walker, a House member from Fulton County, later recalled: "I used to play the fiddle a great deal. . . . He [Lincoln] used to come over to where I was boarding and ask me to play; and I would take the fiddle with me when I went over to visit him, and when he grew weary of telling stories he would ask me to give him a tune, which I never refused to do."[57]

Lincoln's work in this session ranged over a wider scope of activities than in earlier sessions, partly because he was now one of the leaders of the House, and partly because the state was growing and the legislature had more to consider. This also necessitated a speed-up in the legislative process. A Lincoln suggestion to hasten the procedure on amendments was adopted.

One of his legislative pets from his first days in the House appeared again in this session. This time Lincoln called for an act "repealing all laws in relation to a state road leading from William Crow's in Morgan County to Musick's bridge in Sangamon County."[58] In earlier sessions he had favored anything leading to Musick's bridge. Why he had the change of heart is not known.

The division of Sangamon County Lincoln handled cautiously. He exerted more leadership on this matter than appears in the record. Since this was an explosive matter among his constituents, he did not want to project himself publicly into the matter more than necessary. When petitions for divisions of Sangamon County were presented, they went to the Committee on Counties. Lincoln then brought the measure to the House as a committee recommendation rather than his own personal bill. He suggested that it

[55] *SgJ*, December 15, 1838.

[56] December 22, 1838.

[57] Ida Tarbell, *Life of Lincoln* (2 vols., New York, Lincoln Memorial Association, 1900), I, 146.

[58] *HJ*, 1838–39, p. 197.

be referred to a special committee. He was named as a member of the committee but not the chairman. Lincoln drafted the entire bill.

When it came to final passage in the House, Calhoun handled the measure. The first name of a commissioner of Fulton County had been omitted, and Lincoln made the motion to insert his first name, "Newton."[59] At another point Lincoln disagreed with a colleague on an expense figure to be inserted; Lincoln won out in the House, but the Senate eliminated the figure entirely.

The issue of the division of Sangamon County involved Lincoln in an unpleasant exchange of letters with a close friend and benefactor, William Butler. Lincoln was getting his meals in Springfield at the Butler residence. Butler was clerk of the Sangamon County Circuit Court. He had once signed a note at the bank so Lincoln could get some money. Butler was a man of mercurial temperament, and when he thought Lincoln had done him an injustice in drawing the county lines, he sent some torrid letters to Lincoln and to Edward Baker. He felt he had been "badly treated."[60] He hinted corruption was the cause.

Baker replied, "If you believe the charges you make to be true, I say most flatly you are a fool. . . . This is a short letter, but it is longer than one having so little truth, or reason or justice as yours, deserves as an answer."[61] Baker dictated that letter and signed it but Lincoln penned it. In Lincoln's letter, the future President made a very Lincolnesque reply: "You were in an ill-humor when you wrote that letter, and, no doubt, intended that I should be thrown in one also; which, however, I respectfully decline being done. All you have said . . . I know you would not say seriously in your moments of reflection; and therefore I do not think it worth while to attempt seriously to prove the contrary to you. I only say now, that I am willing to pledge myself in black and white to cut my own throat from ear to ear, if, when I meet you, you shall seriously say, that you believe me capable of betraying my friends for any price. . . . Your friend in spite of your ill-humor. Lincoln."[62]

59 *Ibid.*, 234.
60 *CW*, I, footnote on 142.
61 *Ibid.*, 138.
62 *Ibid.*, 139.

Butler soon got over his "ill humor" and offered to send Lincoln a horse to bring him back to Springfield after the session. Lincoln declined the offer.

Lincoln knew the county division matter was a "hot potato" not only with his friend Butler. In other cases he found himself between "one party of the new-county men against another."[63] Lincoln felt relieved when the whole matter was out of the way. The newly created counties were named: Menard, in which New Salem is located; Logan, which now bears the name of Lincoln for its county seat; and Dane, which later had its name changed to Christian. After the Senate passed this county division bill, Lincoln entered debate on Senate amendments. By an amendment he placed on the measure, the boundaries were changed. After accepting the Senate amendments with the one change introduced by himself, Lincoln later that same afternoon changed his mind. "On motion of Mr. Lincoln, the vote taken on concurring in the amendments of the Senate . . . was reconsidered."[64] The Senate later agreed to some of Lincoln's amendments. The final result was largely a Lincoln-constructed bill. It passed without a roll call in either house, a compromise in boundaries reasonably satisfactory to most of the county's residents. It gave Sangamon County the large population.

In this session there were the usual bills to incorporate businesses, some of which became matters of controversy. Lincoln, for example, supported the move to incorporate the Alton Marine and Fire Insurance Company, a motion which carried 42–38.

The Senate adopted a resolution which, if actually carried out, would have had far-reaching effects on the life of Lincoln. The resolution would amend the federal Constitution to limit the President of the United States to serving only four years in any eight-year period. The House passed the resolution 65–8; Lincoln did not vote on it.[65]

A bill to establish a $1,000 fine for anyone betting on an election passed, Lincoln voting for it.[66] Prior to getting the bill to passage stage, an amendment was offered prohibiting federal and state

---

[63] *Ibid.*, 141.
[65] *Ibid.*, 284.

[64] *HJ*, 1838–39, p. 347.
[66] *Ibid.*, 319.

employees from political participation. This amendment was defeated 63–20, with Lincoln among the sixty-three who voted to kill it.[67]

The legislature passed the bill to incorporate McKendree College at Lebanon. There was no controversy for this already well-known institution in the state.

Lincoln acted prominently in moves to restrict certain abuses by limiting the jurisdiction of justices of the peace and the mileage allowances for constables. The bill to accomplish this was written by him but introduced by James T. Cunningham of Coles County.[68] Cunningham either was given the measure by Lincoln to introduce or had heard of Lincoln's views in this field and came to him to draft it.

Lincoln reported favorably for the Committee on Finance on a bill limiting to 6 per cent the interest which the state must pay on its obligations. This was in line with Lincoln's policy of restricting interest rates. When Lincoln presented this measure, one of his Sangamon County colleagues who had been a member of the Long Nine the previous session, William F. Elkin, moved to strike a section of the bill—probably at Lincoln's suggestion—and there was no protest. When another member wanted to add an amendment permitting no maximum interest on money used by the state for the erection of the new capitol, that motion was tabled.

Hardin "made a long and a very able report on the subject of intemperance, presenting its evils in a very strong light."[69] The anti-liquor *Illinois Temperance Herald* published at Alton reported: "Petitions to have the license laws repealed, are pouring in upon our legislators. There are at this early day, memorials to which are appended the names of some 500 or 600 petitioners in the hands of the members."[70]

Petitions signed by 631 Sangamon County citizens were presented by Lincoln to the House and referred to the Judiciary Committee—petitions calling for "the repeal of all laws authorizing the

[67] *Ibid.*, 318–19, 283.
[68] *CW*, I, 124.
[69] *Northwestern Gazette and Galena Advertiser*, February 14, 1839.
[70] February, 1839.

retailing of intoxicating liquors."[71] Presenting petitions to the House was a courtesy generally extended, whether one agreed with the particular petitions or not. There may have been some significance, however, in the fact that the petitions were given to Lincoln. While he was never militant on the subject, it was generally known among his constituents that he did not drink. During the campaign which preceded this legislative session, Lincoln and the lone member of the Long Nine who was defeated in 1838, Robert Wilson, together canvassed the northern part of Sangamon County. Wilson recalled that Lincoln "being personally acquainted with everyone, we called at nearly every house. At that time it was the universal custom to keep some whiskey in the House, for private use, and to treat friends. The subject was always mentioned as a matter of etiquette, but with the remark to Mr. Lincoln, 'You never drink, but maybe your friend would like to take a little.' "[72]

The other side of the picture is that in this session Lincoln opposed a measure supported by anti-liquor forces which authorized counties to collect a license tax of $25 to $500 from tavern operators. The measure also authorized justices of the peace to issue the licenses. In line with his general disapproval of giving much authority to justices of the peace, Lincoln supported an unsuccessful amendment which would have taken that power from them.

Without controversy a bill was passed authorizing a lottery to raise funds "for the purpose of draining the ponds of the American bottom" in the vicinity of what is now East St. Louis, an area which to this day has a severe drainage problem.[73]

Lincoln supported a bill to "more effectually apprehend horse thieves," but the measure lost 51–28.[74]

Another measure written into law premitted carpenters and contractors to take a lien against property when a debt is not paid. Lincoln voted in favor of it.

The day before his thirtieth birthday, Lincoln reported an unusual bill to the House for the Committee on Counties—a measure still part of the laws of Illinois. It states that if a sheriff does not perform his duties, the coroner can assume them.

[71] *HJ*, 1838–39, p. 319.
[73] *HJ*, 1838–39, p. 359.

[72] Wilson, *Intimate Memories*, 31–32.
[74] *Ibid.*, 372.

On the day of his birthday, Lincoln came to the afternoon session late, missing some debate and the first roll call.

Lincoln voted for an amendment to reduce the pay of jurors from seventy-five cents a day to fifty cents a day.

Much of this session, as of other sessions, was taken up with matters that in no sense had state-wide importance. An example is the "act for relief of John Winstanley and Hugh Duffy," which passed 46–36, with Lincoln's vote for it.[75] Another measure that passed and not surprisingly evoked little controversy was an act "to permit William Jackson to insert a middle letter in his name."[76] This resident of McHenry County wanted to sign his name William M. Jackson—and it took an act of the legislature to get the "M" there!

A bill was introduced authorizing "any religious society in this State to purchase, or receive by a donation, and hold any real estate, not exceeding forty acres, for the purpose of camp-meeting ground."[77] This became controversial, but Lincoln supported the measure, which passed.

Not surprisingly, when a proposal was made to pay the presiding officers of each house seven dollars a day instead of six, it was defeated by a voice vote; but when a roll call was demanded, it carried. Legislators hesitate going on record against their legislative leaders. Lincoln voted favorably. At the same time, Lincoln appears to have favored a move to lower the pay of sitting legislators. On that he and his friends were decisively outvoted!

Lincoln handled a Senate bill setting up a calendar for the courts; the measure passed.

On the matter of the many positions which the legislature had to fill, vacancies continued to be filled on other than strictly party lines, although partisanship had become more common. In many instances Lincoln voted for a Democrat, but usually he had a Whig choice.

With few exceptions, there was nothing unusual about Lincoln's voting for officeholders. For president of the Board of Canal Commissioners, Lincoln was one of ten who voted for Cyrus Walker, the lawyer who had just been associated with him in a murder

---

[75] *Ibid.*, 409.   [76] *LIll*, 409.   [77] *Ibid.*, 267.

trial. In the case of acting commissioner of the Board of Canal Commissioners, Lincoln did not vote for either of his friends and colleagues Hardin or Baker, but for Jacob Frey, a Democrat, who had been one of Lincoln's commanding officers in the Black Hawk War. For state's attorney in the Eighth Judicial District, Lincoln voted for David Davis, the losing candidate. Davis wrote to a friend after watching a session at Vandalia, "Legislation in our Western States is generally based upon barter, trade, and intrigue."[78]

On seventeen occasions in this session, Lincoln voted for the losing candidates for an office, and in eleven cases for winners. He missed no roll calls on filling offices.

In procedural matters Lincoln was much more in evidence. This—his third term in office—was to be the high point of his four-term legislative career in terms of influence on his fellow legislators.

This session was the first in which he missed roll calls on bills and procedural matters almost as much as his colleagues. The average House member missed twenty-four roll calls, and Lincoln missed twenty-three. This was not due to a lack of diligence. He involved himself in more than his share of committee work, and this frequently took place when some unexciting legislation was being debated on the floor. This meant missing roll calls occasionally. It is also possible that he left Vandalia during the Christmas holidays to be in Springfield since his name is absent from the record for several days.

No greater indication of Lincoln's increased effectiveness can be given than that during the course of the session he was named to fourteen committees. In addition to being an influential member of the Finance Committee and the Committee on Counties, midway in the session he served on the Committee on Elections, a standing committee, and had enough influence with that committee that on one occasion he made the report for it. Once he served as the chairman of the "Committee of Whole," meaning that he presided over the entire House when a matter came up for consideration. In four instances during this term, Lincoln also presided as the chairman of special committees.

[78] Davis to William P. Walker, January 26, 1839, quoted in King, *Lincoln's Manager*, 35.

On March 2, 1839, the Saturday he left Vandalia for Springfield, Lincoln was handed a letter questioning his support of the new tax measure adopted in this session. Lincoln answered by letter:

> The passage of a Revenue law at this session is *right* within itself; and I never despair of sustaining myself before the people upon any measure that will stand a full investigation. I presume I hardly need enter into an argument to prove to you, that our old revenue system, raising, as it did, all the state revenue from nonresident lands, and those lands rapidly decreasing, by passing into the hands of resident owners, whiles [*sic*] the wants of the Treasury were increasing with the increase of population, could not longer continue to answer the purpose of its creation. That proposition is little less than self-evident. The only question is as to sustaining the change before the people. I believe it can be sustained, because it does not increase the tax upon the "many poor" but upon the "wealthy few" by taxing the land that is worth $50 or $100 per acre, in proportion to its value, instead of, as heretofore, no more than that which was worth $5 per acre. This valuable land, as is well known, belongs, not to the poor, but to the wealthy citizen.
>
> On the other hand, the wealthy can not *justly* complain, because the change is equitable within itself, and also a *sine qua non* to a compliance with the Constitution. If, however, the wealthy should, regardless of the justness of the complaint, complain of the change, it is still to be remembered, that they are not sufficiently numerous to carry the elections.
>
> Verry Respectfully,
> A. LINCOLN[79]

For his services in this session Lincoln received four dollars a day, and four dollars for each twenty miles of travel. House members were paid for all days they were in session, as well as thirteen Sundays and Christmas day when they were not in session. In the middle of December, Lincoln received $100. When the session ended he got a check for $302, also picking up checks for Ninian W. Edwards and Archer G. Herndon, who had left before the checks were ready.[80]

[79] *CW*, I, 147.   [80] Pratt, *Personal Finances*, 23, 144.

The final voting took place on Saturday, March 2, 1839. Monday, March 4, the last session convened, but Lincoln was not there. That day, already back in Springfield, he handled four cases in the Sangamon County Circuit Court.

From now on Springfield would be the meeting place for the legislature.

9

Slowly Facing the Illinois Crisis

Mr. Lincoln . . . has, however, a sort of assumed clownishness in his manner which does not become him, and which does not truly belong to him. It is assumed—assumed for effect. Mr. L. sometimes makes his language correspond with this clownish manner, and he can thus frequently raise a loud laugh from his Whig hearers; but this entire game of buffoonery convinces the mind of no man, and is utterly lost on the majority of his audience.

We seriously advise Mr. Lincoln to correct this clownish fault, before it grows upon him.—*Illinois State Register*, November 23, 1839.

WHEN LINCOLN RETURNED to Springfield, his primary emphasis between the end of the regular session and the special session called by the Governor in December was his law practice. Lincoln found himself much busier than most of his fellow attorneys in the new Illinois capital.

About a month before a special session of the legislature opened, Lincoln's partner Stuart left for Washington to take his seat in Congress. This increased Lincoln's legal load, and he noted in the law firm's fee book: "Commencement of Lincoln's Administration, November 2, 1839."[1]

During these months between sessions, Lincoln and Douglas opposed each other in a case of slander. Lincoln successfully defended his client. Only one case Lincoln and Douglas handled dur-

[1] Stuart-Lincoln Fee Book, owned by Mrs. Edna Orendorff Macpherson, Springfield, Ill.

ing these months was of some political significance. It involved Secretary of State A. P. Field, a colorful, heavy-drinking Whig leader. Field, "six feet three inches tall, perfectly formed, had an erect soldierly bearing, and the polished manners of a born courtier. His otherwise handsome features were marred by a nodular potato-like nose."[2] Field was considered arrogant by many Whigs and Democrats; the *Illinois State Register* called him "King Alexander I."[3] The Democrats were particularly eager to get rid of Field because they regarded him as the most effective speaker in the state.

When Carlin came in as governor, he appointed one of Lincoln's former House colleagues, Democrat John A. McClernand, as secretary of state, but Field refused to yield the post. McClernand filed suit in Fayette County Court, demanding that Field yield the office to him. The court ruled in McClernand's favor, and Field appealed to the Illinois Supreme Court, where the Whigs had a majority. Just to play it safe, Field moved his files as well as the state seal to the new state capital, Springfield, where he would be out of reach of the Fayette County Court with its Democratic leanings. Douglas, representing McClernand, sued in behalf of the state to get these documents and the state seal from Field. This case was tried in the circuit court. Lincoln appeared in behalf of Field, before Judge Samuel H. Treat, a Democratic judge but Lincoln's friend, and successfully got Field recognized as secretary of state, until the Supreme Court ruled, which it did that same day, in favor of the Whig. Field's friends were jubilant over "a signal triumph over the panderers and parasites of power."[4] Ironically, the next year Field resigned, and Governor Carlin appointed Douglas secretary of state.

Judge Treat, before whom Lincoln appeared in this case, in June had resigned from the Board of Trustees of the town of Springfield, and Lincoln was appointed in his place. In the same meeting Lincoln's House colleague, E. D. Baker, resigned as attorney for the town board. Lincoln probably did not seek the position on

---

2 Snyder, *Selected Writings*, 431.

3 November 16, 1839.

4 Virgil A. Bogue in a letter to Field, August 10, 1839, Chicago Historical Society Library.

the town board but felt reluctant to decline it when asked. At the first meeting he served on a committee of two to see whether the trustees could "cause the drain now passing through the block south of the public square, to be so divided, that it may not longer run beneath certain houses."[5] At another meeting he served on a committee to "investigate names on petitions for and against liquor licenses."[6] He helped decide how wide Fourth Street should be; he was one of nineteen assistant marshals for the Fourth of July parade.

Lincoln served only a short period on the Board of Trustees with little opportunity to show much leadership, although at one point he did serve as temporary chairman.

The big political headache was internal improvements. It was obvious that action was needed to save the solvency of the state. In addition to the adverse national economic situation that was hurting internal improvements projects, the plans in Illinois were riddled with corruption. The state could not meet its operating expenses, let alone the multimillion dollar debt with which it was saddled.

A lot of money went into unbelievable schemes and found its way into the pockets of unconscionable rascals in public office or in charge of operations. The minutes of the Board of Public Works contain a letter from Orin Hamlin, one of the contractors for building railroads, who received a "large amount of money over and above the sum due him." He sent this story to Illinois from Kentucky, notifying Illinois officials that he was fleeing the country:

> I started on a boat up the river (forever to my shame be it spoken) and on my way there I got engaged in playing Poker for the first and last time in my life for money. I got a hand I supposed to be the best in the pack, and I commenced betting, and my opponent backed me up, until he had got up to eight thousand dollars, and then called me, and to my astonishment and ruin, he held the best hand, whereas mine was second best.[7]

[5] Minutes of the Corporation Proceedings of Springfield, published in *SgJ*, June 28, 1839.
[6] Miers, *Lincoln Day by Day*, I, 123.   [7] *SgJ*, September 6, 1839.

The state indebtedness on internal improvements soon exceeded $15,000,000.[8] To even the most casual political observer, it was evident that drastic action was necessary.

Some newspapers, including the *Sangamo Journal*, urged Governor Carlin to call a special session of the legislature to face up to the problems. This newspaper, with which Lincoln worked so closely, called not for repeal, but for "action" to save the state's finances. The *Sangamo Journal*'s editorial stand is significant because seldom is its opinion different from Lincoln's. It certainly reflected a change in public attitude, even in the Springfield area which benefited—if it can be called that—from the only completed stretch of railroad in the entire internal improvements' scheme.

The Northern Cross Railroad ran from Meredosia to Jacksonville to Springfield, a total distance of fifty-six miles. Jacksonville residents were in a storm because the railroad skirted their town instead of through it. The citizens won out—to their ultimate regret. The trustees passed a resolution "that no railroad could be built in Jacksonville unless it ran through the public square and along State Street."[9]

The total cost of the railroad from Meredosia to Springfield, only part of a track planned to run across the state, was over $800,000. That averaged about $14,500 per mile, well above a Midwest railroad construction cost of between $7,000 to $12,000 per mile. In the fall of 1839 the track opened between Meredosia and Jacksonville. Two years later the line was completed to Springfield.

There were some difficulties, however.

Between Jacksonville and Springfield—thirty-six miles apart—there were three stops for water. If the train developed a need for water other than at those three points, passengers had to get out and carry water from the nearest source. Male passengers often had to help fuel the train. The light track, which competent engineers even at that time knew would not work, developed "snake

[8] Message of Governor Ford, *HJ*, 1842–43, 38–51. Others placed it in excess of $15 million already at this time.

[9] H. J. Stratton, "The Northern Cross Railroad," *Proceedings of Trustees of Town of Jacksonville, Ill.*, May 15, 1838, quoted in *ISHSJ*, July, 1935.

heads." The ends would turn up, and conductors moving at a slow pace would stop the train to fix a rail occasionally. If they did not catch it, the train might miss the track, and a rail come shooting up through the floor. Occasionally farmers found the rails useful and simply took some. Sometimes engine trouble meant that the big iron engine had to be pulled by horses. Senator Orville H. Browning noted in floor debate in the special session of 1839–40 that the Governor's message was a day late "because snow enough had fallen upon the railroad to powder a gentleman's wig; and the locomotive could not run."[10] Mechanical difficulties finally forced a maximum speed of six miles an hour—slower than the "outdated stage coaches." This was finally lowered to five miles an hour between Springfield and Jacksonville and three miles an hour the rest of the trip.

Not surprisingly, all of this meant that revenue was exceeded by expenses. "The road now finished does not furnish enough money to buy oil to grease the wheels," a state senator reported.[11] In 1847 the state was forced to sell the railroad for $21,000, about one dollar for every forty originally invested. This was the lone "successful" railroad of the Gargantuan internal improvements scheme!

Everything had not collapsed completely in 1839, but generally the popularity of internal improvements had waned considerably. The state was full of digging and equipment—and no results.

Governor Carlin and the Board of Commissioners of Public Works were exchanging letters, each trying to place the blame on the other. Carlin at no time displayed either much strength or much wisdom on this whole issue. When the board voted to curtail all but essential activities, the Governor wrote to them, "I only regret that the Board had not arrived at this determination at an earlier period." He mentioned nothing about his own lack of leadership, but stated that their move to slow construction postponed the necessity for calling the legislature in session immediately. Their action "will afford me more time to ascertain public sentiment. . . .

[10] *SgJ*, January 17, 1840.
[11] Sen. Sidney H. Little of Hancock County. Statement referred to by Sen. Byrd Monroe of Coles County, *ISR*, February 1, 1840.

I am persuaded the same members would generally adhere to their former course, unless they were imperatively instructed to the contrary by their constituents."[12]

A House vacancy in Lincoln's district was caused by the resignation of Calhoun, and the change in public temperament can be seen in the statements of the candidates. John Bennett of Petersburg, remembered for always wearing a skullcap, said, "I was then as I am now, opposed to the whole system."[13] Whether he opposed it previously is not known, but there were many who now claimed they had taken that position. Another candidate who later withdrew tried to please everyone. He favored "practical common sense" on internal improvements; he said he could "see errors and excellencies on both sides."[14] The man who won, Democrat T. J. Nance, is not known to have taken a public position on the matter.

The Whig *Sangamo Journal* in issue after issue now quoted from statements made by the Democratic *Illinois State Register* after the initial passage of the Internal Improvements Act. The *Register* at that time tried to claim credit for the Democrats for its passage, and the *Sangamo Journal* was willing now to give the "credit."

However, even as late as November 1, 1839, the *Sangamo Journal* had a letter from "Citizen" which praised the legislators for approving internal improvements. Under "this highly judicious and benevolent system . . . the sower and the reaper have rejoiced together. All have profited by it; and if it continues, all will more or less continue to profit." The money that was brought into the state will do everyone some good, "like the rain from Heaven."

When the state Whig convention met in Springfield early in October, Whig delegates passed resolutions supporting Henry Clay and William Henry Harrison as possible Whig candidates for President. They passed resolutions on other subjects but were silent on internal improvements. On the second day of the Whig convention, Lincoln was named one of the Whig presidential electors, but, surprisingly, he did not serve on a committee to prepare "an address to the citizens of this State" for the Whigs, the kind of

[12] Minutes of the Board of Commissioners of Public Works, published in *SgJ*, September 6, 1839.

[13] *SgJ*, November 15, 1839.   [14] *Ibid.*

task he usually enjoyed doing and did well.[15] During this whole convention, there is no indication that Lincoln or any of the other Whigs wanted to provide leadership on the vital problem of internal improvements.

A Democratic convention held for Sangamon and Kane counties in April at least had the courage to pass a resolution calling for the repeal of the Internal Improvements Act.[16] The state Democratic convention avoided the issue.

By December of 1839, even the Whigs had to take some note of the internal improvements problem, and at a state-wide meeting in Springfield the group adopted a resolution presented by Lincoln's House colleague for Jacksonville, John J. Hardin, which stated: "We are opposed to the creation of so large a debt, as it is now discovered, would be entailed. . . . We believe that the system needs classification, curtailment, or suspension."[17] That was vague enough to please everyone! At this meeting Lincoln was named to a committee of ten to "prepare an address to the people of the State" for the Whigs.

Newspapers in the state were divided on the internal improvements issue. The *Vandalia Register*, for example, said it was "decidedly in favor of the Internal Improvements System" and the *Illinois Republican* called in capital letters for the "DESTRUCTION OF THE SYSTEM."[18] The *Chicago Democrat* called the plans "insane projects."[19]

Lincoln and his colleagues from Sangamon County called a public meeting to explain the new revenue law enacted at the previous session. Both Lincoln's Whig colleagues and Democrat John Calhoun signed the call for the meeting. During the meeting Calhoun came out against the internal improvements system. The Whig *Sangamo Journal* lost no time in pointing out that Democrat Calhoun was the secretary of the original state internal improvements convention. "It now appears that he was opposed to the system— at the time he recommended its adoption," commented the paper.[20]

The *Sangamo Journal*, like everyone else, found some cause for

15 *Ibid.*, October 11, 1839.
17 *Ibid.*, December 20, 1839.
19 Quoted *Ibid.*, July 19, 1839.

16 *Ibid.*, April 26, 1839.
18 Both quoted *Ibid.*, April 26, 1839.
20 *Ibid.*, May 3, 1839.

the internal improvements fiasco, other than its own advocacy of it. At one point the newspaper traced all troubles to "the destruction of the United States Bank," putting the blame for the Illinois folly on Andrew Jackson.[21]

The *Mt. Carmel Register* reported a duel between two men over differences on internal improvements: "Three shots were exchanged with pistols, but without taking effect. One of the parties then went to his house . . . loaded his rifle, and returned to the battle field, where his antagonist was waiting, and took deliberate aim at him; the ball passed through ,his hat and grazed his head. The parties no doubt concluded that they were both miserable shots, and separated."[22]

On October 14 of that year (1839), Governor Carlin announced a special session of the legislature for December 9, with no indication in the call for the session as to the purpose, though everyone understood that it was to deal with internal improvements. It would also be the first legislative session to be held in rapidly growing Springfield.

Springfield became the focus of attention of newspapers in the state and from neighboring states. While there was much that was attractive about the town, there was also much that was unattractive. The *Marietta* (Ohio) *Intelligencer* reported that "one of the most beautiful places in the West is Springfield, the capital of Illinois."[23] The *Sangamo Journal* reprinted the story, and then the next issue candidly admitted that the Ohio reporter must have had his "glorification spectacles" on when he passed through Springfield.[24]

A more accurate picture of Springfield said that "its houses were mostly frame and poorly constructed. . . . Its streets and most of its sidewalks were unpaved, and in the spring and fall its normal condition was that of unfathomable mud. Indeed, for many years, it was far from being an inviting city."[25]

[21] *Ibid.*, December 20, 1839.
[22] Quoted *Ibid.*, July 12, 1839.
[23] Quoted *Ibid.*, October 25, 1839.
[24] *Ibid.*, November 1, 1839.
[25] John Moses, *Illinois, Historical and Statistical* (2 vols., Chicago, Fergus, 1887), I, 431–32.

The *Chicago American* editor visited Springfield in 1839 and found work on the new capitol the center of interest. "Thirty or forty men are engaged on the building. . . . It is going up on the public square, which embraces an area of two or three acres. Its length is to be 123 feet. The first story is 16 feet high. The second, 22. The basement 8½. . . . The State of Illinois deserves a good capitol, and she is likely to soon have one, in this beautiful and magnificent structure."[26]

In local elections Lincoln voted for Whigs; sometimes his men were losers, sometimes winners. The *Illinois State Register* accused Lincoln (whom they called the longest of the Long Nine) and his Whig "junto" of trying to dictate politics in the area. They asked, "Would Mr. Lincoln be likely to urge a candidate upon the people, unless he were well assured that he would, if elected, go the whole hog with the Springfield Junto members?"[27] When Lincoln responded, calling them liars, the *Register* was filled with righteous indignation, censuring Lincoln for what he said: "Such was the language of the man selected by the Whig Party to be an elector of the high office of President of the United States."[28] Little did they dream that he would one day become not an elector but the holder of that high office! The *Register* supported the winning T. J. Nance for the House vacancy, but had a good word for Samuel Wyckoff, a Whig fighting Lincoln and his friends: "Although he is a Whig, we believe him to be an honest one. Although opposed to us, he is even more hostile to the junto, and is determined in the future not to submit to their dictation."[29] Wyckoff withdrew his candidacy a few days after he announced for office.

In this election the Whigs had once again turned down Lincoln's old friend from New Salem, Justice of the Peace Bowling Green, as a candidate for state representative. Four friends from the New Salem area wrote to Lincoln and explained that Douglas was pushing for Green's candidacy. They also thought Green would be a loser. "To start a man who we believe must be defeated and one

26 Quoted in *SgJ*, August 16, 1839.
27 *ISR*, November 16, 1839.
28 *Ibid.*, November 23, 1839.
29 *Ibid.*, November 16, 1839.

too selected by our enemies is a matter we will be slow to do," they wrote.[30]

Green was not selected—and the Whigs lost anyway.

About three weeks before the special session began, a series of political debates was held in Springfield, Lincoln being one of the speakers for the Whigs and Douglas one of the Democratic debaters. Not surprisingly, the Democratic *Illinois State Register* was not impressed by Lincoln's performance:

> Lincoln [in replying to Douglas] misrepresented Douglas, as was apparent to every man present. . . . [Douglas] literally swamped his adversaries. . . . [He] delivered one of the most powerful arguments against an United States Bank that we ever listened to. It sunk deep into the hearts of his hearers. . . . A settled gloom covered the countenances of the Whigs. They saw how utterly hopeless must be the attempt to answer him. Mr. Lincoln, was, however, again put forward; but he commenced with embarrassment and continued without making the slightest impression. . . . He could only meet the arguments of Mr. Douglas by relating stale anecdotes and old stories, and left the stump literally whipped off of it, even in the estimation of his own friends.[31]

The editorial concluded that Lincoln is "smart enough," but the cause he represents is "rotten to the core." A week later the same newspaper noted that Baker did better than Lincoln or any of the other Whigs.

As of July 4, 1839, the official state capital was Springfield, so the December special session met there. The new capitol not being completed, the House, Senate and Supreme Court met in churches in the city, the House meeting in the Second Presbyterian Church. The newly built church was "the largest church edifice in the whole central and northern part of the State. It was built of brick, had a square belfry and a gallery around three sides of the interior, but had not yet been occupied for church purposes."[32]

[30] Letter from D. H. Rutledge and three others to Lincoln, October 23, 1839, Chicago Historical Society Library.

[31] November 23, 1839.

[32] Bateman, *Historical Encyclopedia*, 651.

A Jacksonville newspaper noted with pleasure that the Springfield citizens "have done themselves credit by their exertions to make the Legislature comfortable."[33] The *Quincy Whig* was less impressed: "The public houses here [Springfield] are but shabby affairs, the only particular in which they have the least appearance of corresponding with the good hotels of our country, is in their bills."[34]

An advertisement in one of the local newspapers informed the General Assembly that "members of the legislature . . . can have their horses kept on moderate terms in good stables and fed on the best" at C. M. Polk's.[35]

Lincoln took part in the social life in Springfield, and a week after the special session began he and Stephen A. Douglas were two of the sixteen who signed their names as hosts to the "Cotillion Party," which was scheduled "at the American House on tomorrow evening at 7 o'clock P.M."[36]

The *Alton Gazette* had little regard for the legislators and suggested adjournment "immediately after it assembles."[37]

On the first day, Lincoln got into debate on who would be seated from Pike County.[38] That day the Governor, who had called the session, was not in Springfield, and the *Sangamo Journal* said that the "members appear anxious to learn why they were called here."[39]

On the second day of session there was still no word from the Governor, but Lincoln's friend Archibald Williams of Adams County introduced a resolution calling on the federal government to turn over "proceeds of the sales of the public lands" to the states. The resolution, which was turned over to the Finance Committee on which Lincoln served, had the same general idea Lincoln had been advocating.

The Governor was on his way to Springfield, but one newspaper noted: "It is said that the good citizens of Meredosia read Gov.

---

33 *Illinoian*, December 21, 1839.
34 January 18, 1840.
35 *SgJ*, December 20, 1839.
36 Facsimile in Tarbell, *Life of Lincoln*, I, 171.
37 Quoted in *SgJ*, December 10, 1839.
38 *SgJ*, December 10, 1839.
39 *Ibid.*

Carlin a moral lesson for traveling on the Sabbath, whilst on his way to the seat of Government."[40]

The next day Governor Carlin delivered his message and called the internal improvements situation "truly alarming. The public credit has been . . . extended to exhaustion."[41] He said that the amount the state was then paying interest on was $10,630,000 and the estimated debt on completion of the authorized projects would be almost $22,000,000. Newspapers reported the debt at that time as at least $11,107,919.74.[42] The Jacksonville *Illinoian* placed it in excess of $15,000,000. Carlin's suggestion: "I would most earnestly recommend the concentration of all future labor and expenditures upon the most useful and promising [rail]road and to the improvement of such of the larger class of rivers as may be susceptible of steamboat navigation, and to suspend operations and expenditures upon all others." He also recommended "an investigation of the accounts and proceedings of the Board of Public Works, and the conduct of all officers and agents connected with the System."[43] It was the first governor's message during Lincoln's legislative service which did not mention national politics.

The *Missouri Republican* of St. Louis said the Governor's message "subjected him to the sneers of some and pity of others."[44] The newspaper also spoke of his "ignorance." The *Chicago American* commented toward the end of the session on the Governor's performance, "All agree in believing him honest, but few think him capable."[45]

A resolution introduced by Wyatt B. Stapp of the northern part of the state denounced internal improvements. "Instead of railroads to every corner of the State, we have nothing but deep cuts and high embankments, in many instances stopping up entirely the public highways leading from one neighborhood to another, and the prospect of increased taxation. . . . *Resolved*, that the committee . . . report a bill to this House, repealing the law establish-

---

[40] *Illinoian*, December 14, 1839.
[41] *HJ*, 1839–40, p. 14.
[42] *SgJ*, December 20, 1839.
[43] *HJ*, 1839–40, pp. 16–18.
[44] December 25, 1839.
[45] January 23, 1840.

ing and maintaining a general system of Internal Improvements."[46]
It was moved to lay the resolution on the table, and that was done,
43–40, Lincoln being one of the forty-three who helped defeat the
resolution. The next day a resolution was introduced calling for
"construction of not more than one [rail]road." It lost 44–42,
Lincoln voting to kill it.

Two weeks later, on December 28, John Henry of Jacksonville
suggested that the House take off three days to see the railroad in
operation from Meredosia to Jacksonville, the only operational
portion of the internal improvements system. However, the days he
suggested taking off ("to see whether the said Railroad answers
the expectation of the Legislature") were December 30, and January 1 and 2.[47] He may have wanted an excuse to get off for the
New Year's holidays. His motion was defeated 44–34; Lincoln
voted against it.

The same day the Finance Committee, on which Lincoln served,
was asked to check into the possibility of creating a sinking fund to
apply to the payment of the interest on the bonds and the retirement of them.

During committee hearings on internal improvements, Hardin
told the House that he thought it was "unnecessary to abuse the
Internal Improvement system. It was like abusing a horse after he
was dead and commenced stinking."[40] Many years later another
legislator recalled that Hardin predicted the fate for internal improvements "with an accuracy that looks to me almost like
prophecy."[49]

Probably the most sensible vote Lincoln cast on internal improvements during this session came on a motion which would have
set up "joint stock companies," the state becoming a stockholder
"to the extent of its expenditures on all the roads," the remainder
of the needed capital coming from private investment; these corporations then would run the railroads.[50] Whether any would have
successfully operated the railroads is doubtful, but it was worth

[46] *HJ*, 1839–40, p. 29.
[47] *Ibid.*, 98.
[48] *SgJ*, January 3, 1840.
[49] Linder, *Reminiscences*, 61.
[50] *HJ*, 1839–40, p. 128.

a try. The motion, however, lost 49–28, Lincoln one of the twenty-eight voting for it.

Lincoln's vote for joint government–private business operation for internal improvements was viewed by the *Illinois State Register* as action that "has blown his pledges to the winds, and has left the system to shift for itself. What an example of good faith! Do Mr. Lincoln and his colleagues stand in no dread of the consequences of this act of political perfidy?"[51] The *Sangamo Journal* replied, with undoubted accuracy, that Lincoln did not try to destroy the system but to rescue it.[52] Lincoln still favored the idea but recognized in a limited way that the state was in financial trouble, and thought that "at least some portion of our Internal Improvements should be carried on."[53]

A resolution "to suspend all action and operation in the construction of railroads" passed.[54] Lincoln and Edward M. Daley of Greene County demanded a roll call vote on the resolution. It passed 41–37; Daley and Lincoln voted against it. An amendment permitting only three river projects to be completed lost 40–37, Lincoln again voting against it. A motion to "require all work upon the rivers to be suspended" carried 46–37, Lincoln voting in the negative.

Two weeks later three votes were taken on internal improvements questions, with Lincoln absent because of committee work. The next day he was again absent part of the day, possibly for the same reason, and missed five more roll calls on internal improvements questions.

This absenteeism caused an embarrassing moment for Lincoln. A Vermilion County legislator asked for a "call of the House," meaning that absent members should be brought in by the sergeant at arms. He said he did it because of Lincoln's absence. The *Illinois State Register* continues:

> Mr. Lincoln entering during the proceedings under the call, said that he had been absent attending to his duties on the Bank Investi-

51 January 8, 1840.
52 January 10, 1840.
53 February 7, 1840.
54 *HJ*, 1839–40, p. 129.

gation committee; that while the committee was progressing with
the business, a call of the Senate had been ordered, and the Senate
members of the committee leaving, they had not had a quorum left,
and he had voluntarily come down to the House. Since he had entered he had been gibed by different members as absenting himself
with a view to avoid voting; he therefore asked liberty to record his
vote on the various propositions that had been before the House,
declaring he was not afraid of voting on any question relating to
Internal Improvements.[55]

There seems no reason to doubt his statement. He firmly stood
on the side of internal improvements. At one point in debate he
indicated that he would compromise for completion of only the
central railroad—down the middle of the state and through
Springfield—"if those gentlemen will agree upon that road."[56]
That proposal lost.

Two weeks before the legislature adjourned, there was in one
day nine recorded votes on internal improvements, and Lincoln's
vote with one exception was on the side of continued internal improvements. The one exception was on an amendment by Edward
D. Baker, which proposed letting the Governor select one railroad
or turnpike to complete. Baker lost by a lopsided vote of 61–27.
By placing the responsibility squarely on the Governor, the Whigs
hoped to avoid the politically dangerous issue and Democratic
Governor Carlin would be forced to make the people along one line
happy and all the others unhappy.

Lincoln supported a measure to "further the prosecution of the
Illinois and Michigan Canal."[57] It lost 50–35. Two days later the
House reconsidered that vote, and on the motion of Lincoln, a
select committee of five considered it, Lincoln serving as chairman.
Interest in the canal bill increased, and when the issue was de-
bated, the galleries were crowded.

Once when the bill to further work on the Illinois and Michigan
Canal was stymied, Lincoln's motion revived it, and he again
served as chairman of the committee to look over the legislation.

[55] January 22, 1840.
[56] *Ibid.*
[57] *HJ*, 1839–40, p. 201.

In House debate Lincoln said that stopping canal construction would be like stopping "a skiff in the middle of the river—if it was not going up it would go down."[58]

Lincoln supported a move to examine thoroughly "the accounts, books, papers and everything else" of the officials connected with internal improvements.[59] But when the committee to make that examination reported, stating that bonds were illegally sold and that "any such sale or negotiations will be and is void," Lincoln opposed the committee.[60]

In one of the rare sensible moves Lincoln made on the whole question of internal improvements, he placed an amendment on the Illinois and Michigan Canal bill which said that "no more than $500,000 of said certificates shall be at any time outstanding."[61] The House agreed to this. The next day he successfully opposed an amendment on this bill, and again his was a reasonable motion; he moved to table a proposed amendment adding another river project to the canal bill.

But sensible Lincoln actions on internal improvements were few. Some of his votes are difficult to understand. For example, a resolution disapproving payments of interest by the state, until the state received the money, carried overwhelmingly, 76–8, but Lincoln was one of the eight against it.

There were a number of other Lincoln votes on internal improvements and related legislation. Viewed from the perspective of the present, Lincoln was almost always wrong. In all discussion on this issue, he rarely entered into debate.

The legislature did its best to deal with the difficult financial crisis the state faced by passing a bill "to provide for the settlement of debts and liabilities incurred on account of Internal Improvements in the State of Illinois" and by placing an amendment on the appropriations bill prohibiting any further contracts for "any rail road, turnpike road, or river in this State."[62] Complete repeal was the effect of this legislative action, although a separate measure

[58] *SgJ*, January 28, 1840.
[59] *HJ*, 1839–40, pp. 218–19.
[60] *Ibid.*, 271–75.
[61] *Ibid.*, 236.
[62] *LIll*, 1839–40, pp. 85, 93.

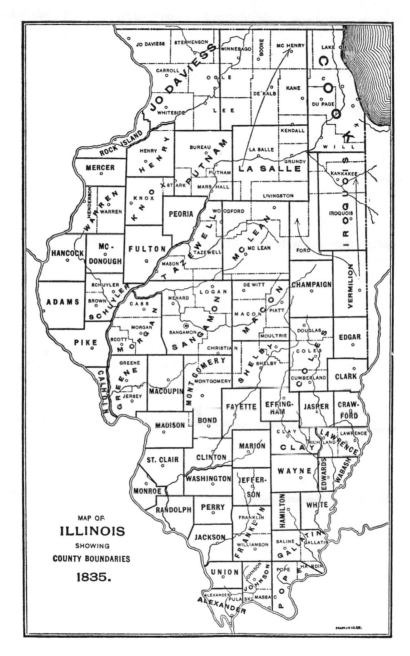

Courtesy Illinois Secretary of State

187

to repeal the Internal Improvements Act did not become law, even though passed by both houses. An amendment made in the Senate was lost in carrying the bill to the House, so that the Senate and the House did not pass the repeal measure in exactly the same language and the Internal Improvements Act was not officially repealed. Officials caught the error before the session adjourned, but the two houses could not agree on the form of repeal, and there were some who opposed repeal entirely. The *Lacon Herald* reported: "After it was discovered the bill was lost [because of the technical error] the House passed another bill to repeal the system. It was sent to the Senate and there indefinitely postponed. Several of the old friends of the system, who had voted for repeal, voting against it when the House bill was before them."[63] For all practical purposes, however, internal improvements had been buried.

Not until seventeen years after Lincoln's death did the state finally free itself from this tremendous load.

Other issues during this special session were small in comparison. Banking ranked next in importance. Before the session began, a highly sympathetic history of the State Bank of Springfield appeared in the *Sangamo Journal*. It was signed "A Looker-on."[64] In view of Lincoln's interest in the State Bank, and the fact that the initials of the signature are his initials, it is probable that he wrote the history.

The Governor, in his message to the legislature, revealed an attitude critical of the State Bank. He did not favor paper money, and he wanted a state investigation because the State Bank refused to extend loans, demanded payment of obligations due, and declined to pay some of its own bills. Governor Carlin wanted "a rigid and impartial investigation."[65]

When a motion passed to investigate the Bank of Illinois at Shawneetown, Lincoln joined the majority in killing the move 55–24. Lincoln, however, had Springfield on his mind, not Shawneetown. There already was one investigation of the State Bank at Springfield in progress, and things were going well there. The measure authorizing the investigation passed the second day of the

63 February 19, 1840.   64 November 8, 1839.   65 *HJ*, 1839–40, p. 23.

scssion—sooner than the Governor called for it in his message. Lincoln's Sangamon colleague Edward D. Baker was named to the committee. The following day Baker withdrew, and Lincoln received the appointment. Obviously, Lincoln was guiding a movement in defense of the State Bank. He did not want to cover up anything scandalous, but he wanted to save the State Bank.

The State Bank Investigating Committee is the only committee on which Lincoln served whose records are on file. Here is the record:

> December 26, 1839—Letter to the State Bank president signed by all members of the committee, including Lincoln
> Dec. 28—Lincoln present
> Dec. 30—Lincoln present. "On motion of Mr. Lincoln, the committee went into an election, by ballot, of a chairman and clerk...."
> Dec. 31—Lincoln present
> Jan.　1—Lincoln present. "On motion of Mr. Lincoln, Mr. Divine [an officer of the Branch Bank at Galena] was now sworn to the facts and statements contained in the paper, submitted by him and to such answers as are thereto attached."
> Jan.　2—Lincoln absent
> Jan.　4—"Committee met pursuant to adjournment. All the members present except Mr. Lincoln."
> Jan.　6—Lincoln absent
> Jan.　7—Lincoln absent
> Jan.　8—Lincoln present
> Jan.　9—Lincoln present
> Jan. 10—Lincoln absent
> Jan. 11—Lincoln present
> Jan. 13—Lincoln absent
> Jan. 14—Lincoln present
> Jan. 15—Lincoln present in the morning and evening, absent in the afternoon
> Jan. 16—Lincoln present
> Jan. 17—Lincoln absent
> Jan. 18—Lincoln present
> Jan. 20—Lincoln present[66]

[66] *Reports of Session, State of Illinois*, 1839–40, pp. 339–48.

That makes a total of twelve committee sessions when he was present and eight when he was absent. The record of questions asked, motions made, and time present and absent does not give Lincoln a particularly impressive committee record. As Whig floor leader he could not spend too much time with the committee and relied on other members on the committee.

Lincoln followed the State Bank matter closely and his votes on amendments which are contrary to his expressed views were designed to save the State Bank. One which falls in this category—since it is contrary to the Lincoln record generally—was an amendment that "no member of the General Assembly shall be a director, agent, cashier, clerk or director, of the parent bank or branches, shall become indebted to said bank or branches, either on bills of discount or exchange in a greater sum than $10,000."[67] The amendment carried 47–36, with Lincoln against it. Later that same day the sponsor of the amendment withdrew it. Lincoln opposed it because he knew that many of the legislators were involved in the banking operation in one way or another, and with this particular amendment on the bill, the entire measure might go down to defeat—the State Bank at Springfield with it. In addition, it was known by some of the legislators that one of their colleagues owed considerably more than $10,000 to the State Bank branch in Alton. He was John Hogan, a popular member and a friend of Lincoln. Lincoln did not want to lose his vote or his good will. There were twenty-one members who had loans, either as "payers" or "as endorsers," from the State Bank.

The bill which finally passed stated that the State Bank "is hereby revived, and the forfeiture of its charter for refusing to pay for its notes, or other evidences of debt, in specie, is hereby set aside."[68]

A move to make "each Stockholder in said Bank" liable for the obligations of the State Bank was defeated, Lincoln voting to protect the stockholders.[69] Lincoln voted for the removal of the Chicago branch of the State Bank. This carried 47–36. At that time Chicago was smaller than Springfield, Jacksonville, and Alton. Chicago had a population of 4,853 in 1840.

[67] *HJ*, 1839–40, p. 284.　　[68] *LIll*, 1839–40, p. 15.　　[69] *HJ*, 1839–40, p. 229.

Lincoln was able to keep the State Bank alive during this session, although at times it looked to him that it would be buried "without benefit of clergy."[70] The Governor's request that the State Bank be forced to pay in actual metal was not passed. In its report to the legislature, the State Bank pleaded its cause. Paying in specie caused "large amounts of the precious metals" to leave the country; besides that, the other banks in the country were not doing it, so the State Bank had to suspend payments in specie also.[71]

The final compromise was a measure permitting the State Bank to refuse payment in specie until the end of the next session of the legislature, a provision that would make the next session a lively one. This was a victory for Lincoln since most had agreed with a newspaper comment at the beginning of the session: "The State Bank is dead for all purposes."[72]

However, one of the Gallatin legislators wrote to an editor, "The Bank will not go down. The leaders of the Van Buren party are too much in debt to it to suffer such a result."[73] In the end that observation turned out to be the correct analysis. There were enough Democrats who joined with the Whigs to save the State Bank.

Not connected with the Bank, but in the field of finances, was a measure relating to promissory notes. In line with his thinking in other sessions Lincoln introduced an amendment: "Provided, that nothing herein shall be construed to legalize the taking of more than twelve per cent per annum, in any case whatever."[74] The amendment was adopted, but the bill lost.

On the second day of the legislative session the Democrats held a state convention, and the following day the Whigs had a meeting at which they adopted a resolution drawn by Lincoln which challenged the Democrats to debate: "*Resolved*, that every member of that Convention, who introduced any such resolution or resolutions, or any amendment thereto, be respectfully requested to bring the same, or a correct copy thereof, into this Hall, and to attempt

[70] *CW*, I, 159.

[71] *Reports of Session, State of Illinois*, 1839–40, p. 309.

[72] *Peoria Register and Northwestern Gazetteer*, December 28, 1839.

[73] Samuel D. Marshall to Henry Eddy, December 19, 1839, IHL.

[74] *HJ*, 1839–40, p. 296.

to sustain it by facts and arguments. *Resolved,* that on the discussion of said resolution, we will meet their authors, man for man, and speech for speech, in order that the public may see with whom are the facts, and with whom are the arguments."[75]

The Whig challenge resulted from earlier three-day debates held in November. The Whigs felt the debates were successful and worth trying again when the legislature was in session, since then the crowds would be greater.

The debates were held, and Lincoln opened for the Whigs. Newspaper reaction to his talk reflected their political bias. The pro-Whig *Sangamo Journal* found Lincoln's talk "characterized by that great force and point for which he is so justly admired"; the debates centered on the Van Buren administration, and Lincoln sustained his argument "not by rant, declamation and assertion, but by an array of documentary evidence, which could not be disputed."[76] The *Quincy Whig* called Lincoln's performance "a speech which no man can answer, but Calhoun will try Saturday evening."[77] The *Illinois State Register* took a different view—though moderate for them—of Lincoln's performance:

> Mr. Lincoln's speech . . . is in the main a temperate and argumentative address. . . . It is pleasant to find a man among them who occasionally is able to . . . deal in sober reason. . . . We derive great pleasure from the fact, that powerful as it is thought to be by them, that it can be answered with so much ease and effect.[78]

The same issue noted that Lincoln objected to everything Van Buren suggested, right or wrong: "Like one of old who said doubtingly, 'Can any good come out of Nazareth?' Mr. Lincoln will say, 'Can any truth come out of Van Buren?' No! And if he should hear that gentleman say the sun sets in the West, doubtless he would disbelieve the evidence of his senses rather than believe Van Buren." This began a series of *Illinois State Register* editorials analyzing Lincoln's address, a real tribute to the seriousness with

[75] *CW*, I, 155.
[76] January 3, 1840.
[77] January 4, 1840.
[78] February 8, 1840.

which the opposition considered it. The editorials began to hit a little harder. They expressed astonishment that Lincoln "may be a believer in the practicability, and usefulness of an inconvertible paper currency."[79] They added, "We are in courtesy bound to suppose that Mr. Lincoln really believes it. How much credit such an opinion does to the intelligence of any gentleman, we leave our readers to judge."

The day after Christmas, Lincoln concluded the debate for the Whigs before a small crowd. His speech was later printed in pamphlet form and became a Whig campaign document. In his opening remarks he admitted that the small attendance "casts a damp upon my spirits." Douglas had been the chief debater for the Democrats, and Lincoln's remarks were directed toward Douglas's support for Van Buren's proposal for a sub-treasury system. One of Lincoln's main points against the plan was that it would "reduce the quantity of money in circulation." The picture he painted of the sub-treasury system was frightening indeed. It would double or treble the difficulties faced by the poor. It would result in abuses; "Judas carried the bag—was the Sub-Treasurer of the Savior and his disciples. . . . A Sub-Treasurer has in his hands $100,000 of public money. . . . Who that knows anything of human nature, doubts that, in many instances, interest will prevail over duty, and that the Sub-Treasurer will prefer opulent knavery in a foreign land, to honest poverty at home?"[80]

In the same speech he contrasted the "astounding" expenses of the Jackson and Van Buren administrations with their predecessors: "The last 10 years under Gen. Jackson and Mr. Van Buren cost more money than the first twenty-seven did, (including the heavy expenses of the late British War) under Washington, Adams, Jefferson, and Madison." The legislator who seemed unconcerned about the internal improvements fiasco that cost the state of Illinois well over $10,000,000 was shocked by a Van Buren federal administration which in a year spent "forty millions, being about two dollars and fifty cents to each soul."

Joshua Speed years later recalled that Lincoln made this lengthy

[79] February 14, 1840.
[80] *CW*, I, 159–79.

speech "without manuscript or notes. . . . He had a wonderful faculty in that way."[81]

A future Illinois governor heard him and recalled:

> Mr. Lincoln . . . surprised me by his ability and by his apparent logical frankness. He seemed to concede to his adversary almost everything he could claim, but I observed that he always found means to escape the effect of his own concessions. His language was simple but exact. His statements were clear and his arguments must have given great satisfaction to the party he represented. He asserted his propositions with firmness and supported them in the most effective manner.[82]

Lincoln commented on his speech in typical manner in a letter to Stuart in Washington, "Well, I made a big speech, which is in progress of printing in pamphlet form. To enlighten you and the rest of the world, I shall send you a copy when it is finished."[83] The Democratic *Illinois State Register*, a few months after publication, noted that it was "recognized by the [Whig] party as its text book in this State."[84]

Much more significant than anything Lincoln said in these debates was the fact that he emerged as a man who knew the issues on the national scene. Here spoke a state legislator whose vision clearly was not bounded by the state of Illinois.

An unusual matter which came before this legislative session was a petition to impeach John Pearson, a circuit judge. The Judiciary Committee recommended public hearings on the charges, and this carried 64–23, Lincoln voting for the hearings and in reality for consideration of impeachment.

The *Chicago American* commented, "Judge Pearson says . . . that he accepted the appointment of Judge on account of an 'affection of the lungs.' Since his acceptance, however, much as his lungs may have been diseased, he has exhibited a remarkable affection of the brain."[85] The newspaper also noted that in Scripture "the ass

[81] Wilson, *Intimate Memories*, 20.

[82] John M. Palmer, *Bench and Bar of Illinois* (2 vols., Chicago, 1899), II, 752.

[83] *CW*, I, 184.   [84] May 8, 1840.   [85] January 29, 1840.

opened his mouth and spake," and Judge Pearson "in humble im-
mitation" does the same.

David Davis commented in a letter to relatives, "A more grossly
ignorant, corrupt, and tyrranical Judge never disgraced the bench,
since the day of Jeffries."[86] The *Galena Advertiser* thought Judge
Pearson "totally incompetent to discharge the duties of his judicial
office."[87]

The House met as a body to hear the charges and witnesses. This
took several days of their time. The House finally voted 45–40
that they did not have evidence sufficient to impeach Judge Pearson. However, Lincoln and many of the better legislators voted
for impeachment. The next day thirty of the House members filed a
protest stating that Judge Pearson should have been impeached,
that he had "violated the right of trial by jury . . . has prevented
an appeal from his decision to a higher tribunal," and that he had
disregarded some state laws as nothing "but a legislative flour-
ish."[88] Lincoln signed the protest but after his signature added the
words "true as I believe." No other legislator added anything or
in any way qualified his protest.

No evidence of bribery or corruption appeared, and the case
was of such a nature that in later years corrective measures would
have been handled differently. Even those opposed to the judge
admitted that he was "in feeble health."[89] In Chicago the impeachment action brought forward much sympathy for the judge and a
meeting in support of him brought out "the largest meeting of the
citizens, ever known in Chicago."[90] The *Illinois State Register* pro-
claimed the judge's innocence "evident to every man of common
discernment."[91] That overstated the case. A sick man who had become autocratic on the bench, Judge Pearson needed hospitaliza-
tion or retirement. Impeachment was too severe a remedy.

In the field of education Lincoln again this session provided no
leadership. He did assist in speeding the bill authorizing the school

[86] David Davis to unnamed relatives, January 19, 1840, IHL.
[87] January 22, 1840.
[88] *HJ*, 1839–40, pp. 150–51.
[89] *SgJ*, January 14, 1840.
[90] *ISR*, January 4, 1840.
[91] January 15, 1840.

commissioner of Sangamon County to turn over the school funds to the three counties created from Sangamon County, but this was merely an administration matter for an equitable but already accomplished division of funds; it could not be considered an indication of any great interest in the field of education.

On a House measure to make school commissioners elective, thus giving the office greater emphasis, a motion to kill the bill was defeated 53–25, with Lincoln one of the twenty-five voting to kill it. In this he again lined up in opposition to the legislators who were trying to push the cause of education in Illinois. Late during the session the measure passed 54–27; Lincoln again opposed it.

The major education bill of the session—a lengthy bill "making provision for organizing and maintaining Common Schools"—did not pass the House until the next to the last day of the session, with no roll calls and virtually no consideration by the House.[92] There is no record of any Lincoln support or opposition.

Early in the session the House agreed 36–34 to consider an "act to distribute the school fund to the several counties in the state," Lincoln opposing consideration of the measure.[93] On this measure the education supporters were divided, so Lincoln's vote cannot be considered an anti-school vote. The state's financial needs had to be balanced against the state's educational needs—and both were great. Senator Orville H. Browning pointed to the dilemma faced by the General Assembly when he stated, "Deficits existed year after year in the treasury, which were supplied by borrowing from the School Fund."[94]

On one education bill Lincoln presented an amendment, but apparently it did not meet the approval of the House. He withdrew the proposal. There is no record of its introduction in the *House Journal* and no known copy of the amendment which might give a clue to its contents. The only information is a newspaper statement that he "withdrew his amendment to the bill in relation to common schools."[95]

[92] *LIll*, 1839–40, pp. 259–87, and *HJ*, 1838–39, p. 326.
[93] *HJ*, 1839–40, pp. 105–106.
[94] *SgJ*, January 17, 1840.
[95] *Ibid.*, February 7, 1840.

By this time, 1839–40, the legislature was no longer taking up matters of divorce, leaving these to the courts. The one exception came from Lincoln, who presented a "petition of Mrs. Sarah Martin for a divorce."[96] A committee was appointed to consider the matter, Lincoln serving as chairman of the three-member committee. The committee reported favorably and presented a bill which the House passed. In the Senate it was never considered and died a quiet death.

During the session Peter Cartwright, a prominent political and religious figure, was present. One member wrote, "Cartwright is here inquiring of the Members whether his daughter can obtain at our hands the justice of a divorce. . . . Cartwright has no proof that his daughter was abused and for this reason a divorce cannot be obtained by court. My own opinion is that the girl had no right to marry contrary to law and I am not willing to punish her all the days of her life for a wrong committed in her youth. I shall vote in favor of a divorce."[97] The divorce was not granted by the legislature. The Judiciary Committee of the House reported that granting legislative divorces would be "unwise, injudicious and improper."[98]

There is an indication of public recognition of Lincoln's leadership in the number of petitions he presented to the House. The average for legislators this session was 1.2 petitions. Lincoln handled five petitons, a total exceeded by only two other House members; another also presented five. Too much significance should not be attached to petitions, but their number does show some increasing awareness of Lincoln by the public.

One of the major issues during the session concerned the seating of a member from Pike County, Richard Kerr and Oscar Love contesting for the seat. The House of Representatives makes all decisions as to seating. The issue was whether Kerr had vacated his seat.

Kerr was a Whig, Love a Democrat, and the issue divided along

---

[96] *HJ*, 1839–40, p. 184.

[97] Fern Nance Pond, "Letters of an Illinois Legislator, 1839–40," *Abraham Lincoln Quarterly*, September, 1949.

[98] "Report on Divorces," House Judiciary Committee, February 28, 1839, 2.

party lines. Kerr left Pike County for Iowa "to open a farm under a contract from an Indian agent, for one year."[99] The Whigs said he kept all his property in Illinois and that he had no intention of changing his residence. The Democrats said he had moved to Iowa, vacating the seat. When the Governor called a special session, the county clerk of Pike County notified the Governor that the seat had been vacated. An election was held and Love won the election in a small turnout.

Lincoln took an active part in adjudicating this affair, which saw the leadership of both parties fighting for a vote in a closely divided House. The battle went back and forth, and the outcome depended to a great extent on how many Whigs or Democrats would be absent from the floor at voting time.

Kerr showed up the fourth day of the session and stated, "I understand that another person is occupying my seat, and as I believe I am alone entitled to it, I ask the speedy action of the House on the subject."[100] The next day Lincoln moved "that until this contest be determined, neither of the contesting parties be entitled to a seat in this House."[101] The House agreed to his amendment, but the next day it reversed that decision. The House then sat as a body to hear testimony on the Kerr-Love fight. Kerr finally won 44–43 on Christmas Eve, a victory for Lincoln and his Whig colleagues. Two Democrats voted with them.

On the second day of the session, Lincoln introduced a measure to clear up a matter concerning which there was confusion—whether a small area should have gone into Sangamon County or into Menard County. Lincoln introduced a bill "to authorize the Collector of ——— County to Collect Taxes."[102] He left the name of the county blank. Appointed chairman of the committee to take care of the bill, he became so involved in other things that he did not report the bill out of committee until four days before the session ended. It came out of the committee in the same form it entered, the name still blank. It was amended in other ways in

[99] *SgJ*, December 17, 1839, quoting from the report of the House Committee on Election.

[100] *HJ*, 1839–40, p. 25.

[101] *Ibid.*, 39.

[102] *Ibid.*, 6, and *CW*, I, 155.

the House, but passed the House with the county name still not entered. It did not receive consideration in the Senate.

During the course of the session, Lincoln's Sangamon colleague Ninian W. Edwards offered a strange resolution—"that the support of any measure or law . . . ought not to operate to the prejudice of any member of the Legislature, in any suit to which he is a party, in any courts of this State, and more especially if such law is unconstitutional."[103] Lincoln supported Edwards, and the House accepted the resolution after some modification. What caused this resolution is not known.

Lincoln presented the petition for incorporation of the Mechanics Union of Springfield. He served as chairman of the committee to consider the petition, and the three-man committee reported favorably. While he did not write the bill, an amendment to it is in his handwriting, mentioning the names of the incorporators. The purpose of the corporation was to afford "relief to the sick and disabled members thereof, and to the widows and orphans of deceased members; for the establishment of a common school and a public library, and for the promotion of literature, science and the mechanic arts; and for no other purpose whatsoever."[104] The Mechanics Union actually was a sort of insurance society. It was "limited to mechanics of good moral character, free from all bodily infirmities."[105] There was an initiation fee of one dollar and payments of twenty-five cents per month. Members in good standing for six months could, during illness, draw three dollars a week sick benefit, "until such disability shall terminate in health or death: Provided that such disability has not arisen from drunkenness, horse racing, voluntary fighting, or any other vicious, improper or immoral act."[106] In addition, twenty dollars was to be given toward funeral expenses, and widows were to receive, "should they need it," twenty to fifty dollars.

Another petition Lincoln handled was for adding some territory to the town of Petersburg in the newly created county of Menard.

[103] *HJ*, 1839–40, p. 27–28.

[104] *LIll*, 1839–40, p. 74.

[105] Harry E. Pratt, "The Springfield Mechanics Union, 1839–48," *ISHSJ*, March, 1941.

[106] *LIll*, 1839–40, p. 74.

He headed the committee appointed to take care of the matter. Lincoln not only wrote the bill which was introduced but also had written the petition requesting the measure.[107] The proposal passed the House but failed to become law because of difficulty over a lengthy Senate amendment.

Lincoln was keeping his eye on the local voters in many ways. The House was meeting in the Second Presbyterian Church in Springfield, and when one of the members had a resolution reserving the hall for "every night in the week" for committee meetings, Lincoln successfully amended the resolution to read that the hall would be reserved by the House on Mondays, Wednesdays and Fridays.[108] The resolution came four days before Christmas, and the Presbyterians of the town probably appreciated Lincoln's consideration.

Some of the legislators were not too sympathetic to the needs of the Presbyterians or any other Sangamon County residents. In spite of the citizens' promise to pay $50,000 to bring the seat of government to Springfield, the statehouse commissioners from Springfield now reported that there was "no reasonable expectation" of Springfield citizens meeting their obligations during the coming year, "owing to the present deranged state of their finances."[109] One legislator wanted to start "a suit against certain citizens of Springfield for the balance due . . . on the building of the State House in Springfield."[110] The fight was over the method of payment, and the House tabled the resolution 43–38, Lincoln, of course, favoring the tabling.

Newton Cloud, a Methodist minister from Morgan County, who in an earlier session had been Lincoln's choice for speaker, introduced a resolution "that a joint committee of two on the part of the House, and one on the part of the Senate, be appointed to invite the Rev., the Clergy [sic] of Springfield to officiate alternately . . . to open the daily sessions of the two Houses during the present session by prayer to Almighty God."[111] This lost in a Saturday session. On Monday, as the first item of business, Lincoln moved

107 *CW*, I, 179–80.   108 *HJ*, 1839–40, p. 74.
109 *Reports of Session, State of Illinois*, 1839–40, p. 410.
110 *HJ*, 1839–40, p. 223.   111 *Ibid.*, 72.

the vote on the Cloud resolution be reconsidered. It was agreed to reconsider the matter. One legislator wanted to pay each clergyman five dollars "for each day they give their attendance." That lost. Another unsuccessfully moved "that the prayer known as the 'Lord's Prayer' be used only."[112] Then the resolution to have daily prayer carried 50–37, Lincoln supporting the resolution. The Senate killed it.[113] This caused a reader of the *Illinois State Register* to call the attention of the legislature to Benjamin Franklin who had called for prayer at the national level. The writer hoped that Franklin's example "may not be lost upon those legislators who, in the consideration of political questions, may forget that the Most High liveth among men."[114]

On a measure regulating businesses selling less than a quart of liquor, Lincoln amended it in the House so that the power to license would not be delegated to the trustees of incorporated towns but to the county. Lincoln told the House that either the towns "should have nothing to do with the matter, or if burthened with it, that they should have the proceeds of the Licenses they granted."[115] At a Christmas Eve meeting of the Springfield town board, Lincoln and the other trustees had just voted to charge twenty-five dollars for a two-month license within the town of Springfield. Lincoln, then serving on the Springfield town board, did not want to be plagued with decisions on which place to license. Perhaps he also felt that licensing within a larger area made more sense, since if Springfield refused to license anyone, the applicant could move outside the city limits and still keep most of his business.

A Vermilion County legislator introduced an amendment on the tavern regulation bill that said that if a majority of qualified voters of an incorporated town or other government unit would petition against granting a license, that the license should not be granted. This was a form of "local option." The amendment lost when it received a 39–39 vote, Lincoln voting against it. The same amendment came up again a few weeks later, this time losing 42–34, Lincoln again voting against it. The anti-liquor leaders in the state were most unhappy. One minister wrote, "From all the facts that I

112 *Ibid.*, 1839–40, p. 75.
113 *SgJ*, January 3, 1840.
114 January 18, 1840.
115 *SgJ*, December 31, 1839.

can collect on the subject, I conclude that most of the Temperance Men who leave the East for the West leave their temperance principles behind."[116]

A House bill passed that was a little less hard on businesses selling liquor than the act of the previous session. Lincoln supported the House bill, but it died in the Senate.

A Lincoln amendment to a revenue measure permitted "all Revolutionary pensioners within this State . . . to loan all or any part of the money which they may have acquired exclusively by means of their pensions without paying any tax whatever."[117] His amendment was adopted. The entire bill, including Lincoln's amendment, was later buried in a committee. This illustrated Lincoln's growing skills in legislative procedure, even though he did not win. This amendment Lincoln had originally drafted as a separate bill, and as such it would have had only a slim chance of passage. When a revenue measure came along, Lincoln saw his opportunity and quickly changed his bill to an amendment, and the amendment was adopted. In this way his amendment could "ride" on someone else's bill. In this instance, however, he failed, for the bill did not carry.

One day the *House Journal* records simply stated that "Mr. Lincoln presented the petition of a Farmer." The *Sangamo Journal* added that Lincoln presented the petition of an "Old Farmer" complaining "most bitterly of the destruction of his rights, real and sacred, by the Internal Improvement System."[118]

Lincoln supported a proposal to require all males between the ages of twenty-one and fifty to "labour one day on the public roads . . . and that all further road labor shall be by assessment on property."[119] It failed 41–40.

Lincoln was the House sponsor of a Senate bill to incorporate the Clinton Steam Mill Company. There was no controversy, and the measure became law.

Lincoln wrote a bill for his colleague Edward D. Baker, "legal-

[116] Rev. John Prinless to Milton Badger, quoted by Clyde E. Buckingham in "Early Settlers of Rock River Valley," *ISHSJ*, September, 1942.

[117] *HJ*, 1839–40, pp. 116–17.

[118] January 7, 1840.

[119] *HJ*, 1839–40, p. 120.

izing the Survey and plat of the town of Mount Auburn in the county of Dane."[120]

Lincoln was named on a committee to check into the possibility of the state paying Fayette County "for the charges and expenses of keeping the State prisoner, Antony Gikoski, in the jail of Clinton County."[121]

Lincoln served as chairman of a committee to which was referred a petition for a road from Petersburg to the town of Waverly in neighboring Morgan County. He drafted the bill which, with some amendments, became law.

He voted in favor of electing tax collectors and assessors in the counties.

A move to give Wisconsin fourteen of the northern counties of the state was defeated 70–11. Lincoln voted with the majority. Had the minority position carried, Chicago would now be in Wisconsin.

Hankins of Vandalia moved to suspend for five years work on the new capitol, so that the seat of government might be brought back to Vandalia for ten years. Lincoln was absent at the time, but the Hankins motion was quickly disposed of, 55–27.

Lincoln introduced a bill "to amend several acts in relation to Constables."[122] The measure was unusual because Lincoln did not write it. It was common for Lincoln to write proposals for others, but seldom did he introduce bills not written by himself. This measure, calling for the bonding of constables, died in committee.

In the regular session of 1838–39, the legislature had postponed the congressional election of 1840 for one year because of the 1840 census. Under the new proposal, it was to be held as originally scheduled. Lincoln opposed the measure but was not sure he was doing right. He had written Stuart, who was then serving in Congress, for advice, but Stuart did not reply in time. In a letter to Stuart, Lincoln predicted the bill which had just passed the House "will also pass the Senate." [123] It did not.

---

[120] *CW*, I, 183.
[121] *HJ*, 1839–40, p. 135.
[122] *Ibid.*, 215.
[123] *CW*, I, 195.

Acting in behalf of the Finance Committee, Lincoln introduced a bill "authorizing the purchase of a house for the use of the Governor . . . provided the same shall not cost more than eight thousand dollars."[124] Also, one month after its readiness for occupancy, "no allowance for house rent or traveling expenses shall be made to the Governor." Lincoln wrote the bill himself, but it failed to even reach the Senate.

Once during the session, John Dawson of the Sangamon delegation walked onto the floor while they were voting and asked his colleagues how to vote. A lengthy letter in the *Illinois State Register* described the incident: "Mr. Edwards answered him from across the house that he was going to vote against the bill; Lincoln informed him that he should vote for it. . . . The House was not a little amused by the perplexity of the Sangamon delegation."[125] In the letter describing this incident all the legislators were referred to with the title "Mr." prefixed to their names except the future President. The letter simply called him "Lincoln."

On Lincoln's motion the appropriations bill went to a Committee of the Whole House and then passed. It appropriated, among other things, $31.50 for "making a coffin, and other services rendered in the burial of Hon. James Copeland," a House member who had died during the session; $5.00 to Thomas Maffit for swearing in the new members of the House; and $200.00 to the Second Presbyterian Church for the use of their building as the hall for the House of Representatives, with the understanding that "the trustees of the Second Presbyterian Church may retain the four stoves now in the same, for the use of said church, until said stoves be required for the use of the State."[126]

Lincoln served as House sponsor of the bill "to incorporate the city of Springfield."[127] Named chairman of a three-member committee to check over the bill, he helped the lengthy bill pass. It went into great detail as to what powers the city had, e.g., "to license, tax and regulate hacking, carriages, wagons, carts and drays . . . to provide for and regulate the inspection . . . of whisky in barrels . . . to tax, restrain, prohibit and suppress, tipling houses,

---

[124] *CW*, I, 197.
[126] *LIll*, 1839–40, pp. 82–84.

[125] February 5, 1840.
[127] *HJ*, 1839–40, p. 252.

dram shops, gaming houses, bawdy and other disorderly houses."[128] Lincoln added an amendment: "The citizens of Springfield shall be exempted from any taxes for county purposes, except upon real estate."[129]

At the time Springfield was given its charter, only three cities in the state had been chartered: Chicago, Cairo, and Alton—all getting their charters in 1837. Significantly, the Springfield charter permitted only United States citizens to vote. The state constitution gave aliens the right to vote. Opinion in Springfield and among the Sangamon legislators divided on the matter. When it came to a vote in the House, Ninian W. Edwards and John Dawson of Sangamon County voted against it, but the measure carried.

During the month of January, while the legislature met in Springfield, Lincoln attended none of the meetings of the Board of Trustees of Springfield.

In another attempt to help the residents of towns, Lincoln placed an amendment on a measure in the Finance Committee which called for one-half the real estate and personal property tax collected by the county to be paid over "to the President and Trustees of each incorporated town" within the county.[130] The measure, together with the amendment, was tabled.

Lincoln was the House sponsor of a Senate bill providing the procedure for a change of venue from one circuit court to another. The measure became law.

Lincoln supported a move to decrease the speaker's pay from seven dollars to six dollars—three days before the end of the session. This was a reversal of the position he took in the regular session a year earlier. The speaker during this session automatically was William L. D. Ewing, who had defeated Lincoln at the regular session. Once during the sessions the hot-tempered Ewing and another legislator "came very near fighting a duel."[131] Just prior to the end of the session Ewing stepped aside. "Circumstances of a most afflicting character impel me to leave my place

[128] *LIll*, 1839–40, pp. 6–15.
[129] *ISR*, February 5, 1840.
[130] *CW*, I, 183.
[131] T. J. Nance to Catharine Nance, January 9, 1840, quoted by Fern Nance Pond, "Letters of an Illinois Legislator."

in the House of Representatives for the remainder of the session," Ewing said in his message to the House.[132] Newspapers explained that his absence was caused "by the distressing intelligence of the death of his infant son."[133] Newton Cloud of Jacksonville—rather than Lincoln—took over the speaker's chair for the last three days. Cloud was a Democrat, but unobjectionable to the Whigs, who made no attempt to stop the naming of Cloud, even though they had a 46–45 majority.

A dispute arose within the Sangamon delegation as to whether $2,000 should be spent to improve navigation on the Sangamon. Nance, the Democratic member of the delegation, favored it, but Dawson headed the Whig attempt to kill it, arguing that $2,000 could not do anything and would be just a waste of money. The House joined Dawson, Lincoln and the other Sangamon Whigs in killing the appropriation.

Lincoln supported a move to limit the length of time the secretary of state could hold office. That same day Governor Carlin sent a message to the Senate: "I nominate Stephen A. Douglas to be Secretary of State."[134] Whether Lincoln knew of the Governor's nomination at the time of his vote is not known. He did know that his friend and client A. P. Field had resigned after winning court assurance that he did not have to and that the Governor would make a Democratic appointment to that office.

Lincoln handled the bill setting up the time for holding courts in the Eighth Judicial Circuit. The bill was not written by him, but probably by one of the judges; Lincoln introduced it as a courtesy.

On the last day, motions which would have delayed the closing of the special sessions were opposed by Lincoln. He was anxious to get back to his law practice. About this time David Davis wrote to a friend, "No State has been as badly governed as ours save Mississippi. . . . Legislation with us is as unstable as the winds. The grand object seems to be to provide offices for partisans. . . . The good of the people is not thought of."[135]

---

[132] *HJ*, 1839–40, p. 304.

[133] *ISR*, February 8, 1840.

[134] *Senate Journal*, 1839–40, p. 236.

[135] David Davis to Julius Rockwell, February 10, 1841, IHL.

About a week before Christmas, word reached Springfield that the Whigs had nominated William Henry Harrison for President and John Tyler for Vice-President. The Whigs received this news "with great enthusiasm."[136]

There is no known recognition by Lincoln of this until a month later, when he wrote to Stuart in Washington, asking for "as many copies of the life of Harrison, as you can spare from other uses. . . . The nomination of Harrison takes first rate. You know I am never sanguine; but I believe we will carry the state. The chance for doing so, appears to me 25 per cent better than it did for you to beat Douglas. A great many of the grocery [tavern] sort of Van Buren men, as formerly, are out for Harrison. Our Irish Blacksmith Gregory, is for Harrison. I believe I may say that all our friends think the chance of carrying the state, very good."[137] Nine days later he wrote to Stuart that Harrison was "going ahead."[138] Lincoln turned out to be a poor prophet. Van Buren carried the state 47,443 to 45,576 for Harrison. As one of the five Whig candidates for presidential elector in Illinois, Lincoln's name appeared regularly in the Whig papers, always the last of the five electors mentioned. Most listed him as "A. Lincoln of Sangamon," but the *Alton Telegraph* called him "Ab'm Lincoln of Sangamon."[139]

The *Illinois State Register* was positive Harrison did not have a chance: "Will Harrison be our next President? You have the answer by spelling his name backwards—No Sirrah."[140]

In voting on individuals during the session, Lincoln followed his usual pattern of voting generally for Whigs but sometimes jumping the party line to vote for Democrats. When Democrat John Calhoun was up for election as clerk of the House, Lincoln voted for his Whig opponent.

For the first time in any session Lincoln voted on fewer roll calls than the average House member. He missed the roll call

---

136 *SgJ*, December 24, 1839.
137 *CW*, I, 184.
138 *Ibid.*, I, 200.
139 January 18, 1840.
140 February 28, 1840.

twenty-three times, while the average House member missed 12.2 times. Committee work accounts for most of his absences, and the record shows he was an active legislator, one of the leaders. This session concluded his third term in office, in which he showed more leadership than in any other term.

Toward the end of the session, one of Lincoln's colleagues wrote to his wife, "We have 10 lawyers that take up more time than all the other members. There is Lincoln, Baker, Hardin, Webb, Ficklin, Williams, Walker, Fisk and others."[141]

In addition to his service on two standing committees, Lincoln served on fourteen special committees. Seven times he served as chairman. Abraham Lincoln clearly had become one of the leaders of the House of Representatives. If there was appreciation in Sangamon County for what he had done, it did not show itself in his race for a fourth House term, a race that started soon after the legislature adjourned.

During this special session the House met on forty-seven days, but Lincoln and the other legislators received a day's pay for fifty-seven days. They were paid for all Sundays and for the Christmas and New Year holidays, when they were not in session. Lincoln's total pay for the session was $228, with no travel pay because he lived in Springfield.

For several issues before adjournment, the *Sangamo Journal* announced that a new publication, the *Old Soldier*, would be published in behalf of the Whigs. Lincoln was one of the five responsible for its appearance. Two of the others were his House colleague E. D. Baker and his long-time friend, Joshua Speed. The *Alton Telegraph*, a Whig newspaper, commented, "We have reason to know that it will be conducted with great ability."[142]

With "tongue in cheek," the *Illinois State Register* said they would start a new publication too and call it "The High-Comb Cock."[143] They mentioned the various types of poultry that would be featured, clearly referring to leading Whigs; among them was "the Lincoln-shire cock, who runs himself down to look for his

[141] Fern Nance Pond, "Letters of an Illinois Legislator."
[142] January 11, 1840.
[143] January 1, 1840.

own friends at the late Nance election." (The reference was to the House special election, where Nance beat the Whig candidate Lincoln was supporting.)

Other things of interest to Lincoln, but not yet connected with the legislature, were happening.

A "strange new sect," the Mormons, were moving into the state.

A Roman Catholic church was being built in Springfield.

The law partnership of S. A. Douglas and John D. Urquhart dissolved.

A nineteen-year-old girl, Mary Todd, was staying in Springfield with relatives.

Also, unknown to Lincoln 1839–40 was a seventeen-year-old West Point cadet, U. S. Grant, who wrote to his cousin about the wonders of the school he had just entered—and about a personal problem: "My pants sit as tight to my skin as the bark to a tree and if I do not walk military, that is if I bend over quickly or run, they are very apt to crack with a report as loud as a pistol."[144]

---

[144] Letter from Grant to his cousin McKinstrey Griffith, September 22, 1839, quoted in Carl Sandburg, *Lincoln Collector* (New York, Harcourt, Brace and Company, 1950), 302.

10

The 1840 Campaign

We have lost the legislature in consequence of the Great Majorities against us in the southern part of the State. . . . Baker (ed), Lincoln, Gov. Duncan, and myself are going to spend all our time in the southern counties to discuss the principles of our party in every neighborhood. . . . Tomorrow Lincoln and my Self leave for Belleville.—Letter of Secretary of State A. P. Field, August 17, 1840[1]

His FREQUENT VISITS with Miss Mary Todd were not the only thing on Lincoln's mind between legislative sessions. The practice of law took most of his time, and there was the matter of increasing Whig strength in Sangamon County and in the state.

Between sessions Lincoln received the only known legal fee growing out of internal improvements. Other legislators profited greatly in many ways from schemes that were passed, but Lincoln did not abuse his office in this way. This lone instance may have been an emergency bit of help Lincoln provided. And even in this case the bill for fifty dollars for services rendered was in the handwriting of another attorney, Schuyler Strong.

The day after the session adjourned on February 4, 1840, the Whigs mailed around the state a circular written by Lincoln. He and four other members of the Whig state central committee signed it. The circular outlined in detail how to carry the state for the

[1] Field to Henry Eddy, IHL.

Whigs. County captains, precinct captains, and section captains were to be set up throughout the state. The circular also pushed the new Illinois Whig publication, the *Old Soldier*, to be "published until after the Presidential election. It will be superintended by ourselves, and every Whig in the State MUST have it. . . . Copies will be forwarded to you for distribution among our political opponents. The paper will be devoted exclusively to the great cause in which we are engaged."[2]

The circular was sent out with the heading "Confidential" to the Whig leaders in the state. The *State Register* of Springfield followed its usual anti-Whig line and condemned the "secret circular." This calls, it charged, for "appointing spies" and is "an improvement on the Spanish Inquisition." The *Register* quoted the Bible against Lincoln and his friends. "They prefer darkness to light, because their deeds are evil."[3] Lincoln and the other *Old Soldier* editors retaliated by accusing the Democrats of "robbing the mail" to get the "confidential" circular.[4]

The *Old Soldier* was trying to transfer the personal popularity of one "old soldier"—Andrew Jackson—to William H. Harrison, another "old soldier." This led the *Illinois State Register* to comment, "In their speeches throughout the country, Mr. Baker and Mr. Lincoln denounce Gen. Jackson, and in unmeasured terms pronounce his administration of the Government corrupt. In their recent editorials, they say that 'a man always acts safer when he casts his vote for men of tried patriotism like Gen. Jackson.' "[5] The *Alton Gazette* said, "It would be much more appropriate if the Springfield Junto would call their paper 'The Petticoat' instead of the 'Old Soldier.' "[6] All this talk and criticism boosted the subscription list and by the end of February there were eight thousand subscribers for the *Old Soldier*.[7]

When Lincoln's old enemies and the new ones created by the

---

[2] *CW*, I, 202–203.

[3] February 4, 1840.

[4] *CW*, I, 204.

[5] February 14, 1840.

[6] *Alton Gazette*, quoted in *Old Hickory*, Democratic organ published in Springfield, March 16, 1840.

[7] Thomas C. Browne to Henry Eddy, February 25, 1840, IHL.

stir over the *Old Soldier* combined, Lincoln wrote to Stuart in Washington that he did not think his "prospects individually are very flattering, for I think it is probable I shall not be permitted to be a candidate."[8] But at the convention the Whigs again nominated Lincoln for the House. His House colleague Ninian W. Edwards was left out, and Edwards felt hurt by it. Lincoln shared that feeling. "I was much, very much, wounded myself at his being left out," he wrote.[9] Lincoln may have felt somewhat hurt also by the fact that Edward D. Baker, who did not have his legislative experience, was slated for advancement to the State Senate while Lincoln stayed a House candidate.

The Democrats meanwhile had nominated Douglas, who was now living in Springfield, for state representative from Sangamon County. Douglas declined. "Considerations of a private nature ... constrain me to decline the nomination," he said.[10]

About this same time the *State Register* under the heading "The Tribune," carried this small item: "We have received the first number of a paper, under the above title, published at Chicago. . . . It raised the Van Buren and Johnson flag." The *Register* also noted that the *Chicago Tribune* has a "suspicious appearance."[11]

During the 1840 campaign, the *Sangamo Journal* advertised "Lincoln's Speech and Tippecanoe Almanacs."[12] The speech was his attack on Van Buren's sub-treasury policies. In August the *National Intelligencer* quoted from it, the first national attention Lincoln had ever received.

Around the state the name of Lincoln was becoming better known. He spent as much time outside his district as in it. In Peoria the *Peoria Register* praised him for leadership on national issues. However, their reporter observed that "no sketch from memory" about Lincoln's remarks could do him justice, "and none is therefore attempted."[13] But while the reporter failed to mention any-

---

[8] *CW*, I, 206.

[9] *Ibid.*, I, 208.

[10] *ISR*, April 24, 1840.

[11] April 17, 1840.

[12] April 10, 1840, and other issues.

[13] Ernest E. East, *Abraham Lincoln Sees Peoria* (Peoria, 1939), 3, quoting the *Peoria Register and Northwestern Gazetteer*.

thing Lincoln said, he did record the menu for the dinner meeting: "Roast beef, roast mutton, roast venison, roast veal, boiled mutton, boiled ham, pickled tongue, roast turkey, boiled turkey, roast chicken, roast quail, quail pie, stewed prairie chicken. Dessert in addition."

What was Lincoln like as a speaker? A close friend of these years reminisces:

> Lincoln was in no sense bound by artificial patterns of bodily motion or gesture, though it could be said he followed a measure of characteristic routine. When he first rose to speak, he seemed uneasy. At times he was awkward. His head, sometimes his shoulders, tilted forward. As he warmed to his subject, the uneasiness lifted and he would use one hand or the other for emphasis, the idle hand usually resting behind his back. He often stressed points by inclining his head [in] one direction or another. Sometimes a leveled finger accentuated them.
>
> As emotions grew, his towering figure straightened. He was given to raising both arms high, as if to embrace a spiritual presence. A climax reached, he would stand, one hand grasping his coat, the other behind him as corroborative logic flowed.
>
> In the earlier stages of an address, Lincoln's voice was pitched very high. As conviction waxed, it modulated, though remaining in an upper middle register.[14]

Whatever limitations he may have had as a speaker, he was effective, and the Whigs were using him more.

Lincoln not only hit on issues; one circular which he signed referred to President Van Buren as "effeminate and luxury-loving."[15] Lincoln did everything he could to promote the candidacy of Van Buren's opponent, General William Henry Harrison. He regularly reported to Stuart in Washington the newest recruits for the Harrison forces. One postscript stated, "Jalp. Ball has come out for Harrison. Ain't that a caution?"[16]

Lincoln's candidate was the military hero of Tippecanoe, but

[14] Earle Benjamin Searcy, "The Lincoln Voice," quoting Dr. William Jayne, from a newspaper interview in the *Lincoln Herald*, October, 1949.

[15] *CW*, I, 205.

[16] *Ibid.*, I, 208.

no one knew where he stood on issues, other than that he opposed Van Buren. It was a campaign of the log cabin (in which Harrison was born) against the fancy clothes of Van Buren. Other issues were secondary. Nevertheless, the election seemed to arouse everyone. Governor John Palmer recalled in 1886: "It seems to me now, for I had but the year before become a voter, that after the nomination of General Harrison for the presidency, every man, woman, and child who could speak plainly enough to be understood, became a vociferous screaming partisan."[17]

Lincoln and Douglas met occasionally during this campaign and had formal and informal debates. One of the issues used against Van Buren was that in New York he had given free Negroes owning property the right to vote. A widely circulated Van Buren biography mentioned this. Lincoln used this against Van Buren. Douglas simply denied the truth of the statement in the biography. Some Whigs then secretly wrote to Van Buren and asked him whether the biography stated the fact correctly. Van Buren replied that it did. Armed with this letter, Lincoln waited until Douglas used the "untrue" charge again. Then Lincoln read the letter and made Douglas so furious that he took the book and threw it into the audience.[18]

When Lincoln spoke in Tremont, Douglas sat in the audience. The *Sangamo Journal* reported, "During the whole of Lincoln's address Douglas manifested the utmost petulancy and want of gentlemanly decorum frequently interrupting the speaker, and reminding one forcibly of 'a tempest in a teapot.' At the close of Lincoln's speech, which was responded to by three hearty cheers, the 'little giant' ascended the rostrum, but it was no go. . . . He only raved incoherently." Lincoln spoke to "frequent and spontaneous bursts of applause"; it was also recorded that he told "many highly amusing anecdotes which convulsed the house with laughter."[19]

Not all reaction to his speeches was favorable. One Democratic

[17] John M. Palmer, *Life and Services of Hon. Joseph Gillespie* (Illinois Bar Association, 1886), 9.

[18] There are several sources for this incident, including Herndon in Hertz, *The Hidden Lincoln*, 435.

[19] May 15, 1840.

newspaper stated that "from outward appearance" it looked as if he came "originally from Liberia"—not considered a compliment in 1840.[20] Replying to the Liberia charge, the *Sangamo Journal* said it "comes with bad grace" from the party whose head [Van Buren] "smells rank with devotion to the cause of Africa's sons." The newspaper spoke of Lincoln's "able and forcible manner. . . . Upon the whole, his speech was a sound and sensible one—did much honor to himself and great justice to the cause. . . . At the close of Mr. L's speech a Van Buren gentleman of the legal profession who sometimes sports on the political arena, stept forward and demanded to be heard . . . and held forth for some time in a warm and boisterous manner. . . . Mr. Lincoln was then invited to remain in tow and see himself used up the next day. He accepted the invitation and remained. At the designated hour the next day, the wood and the lamp were ready but the high priest came not to the sacrifice. At length the gentleman who had given the challenge appeared and gave notice that there would be no debate unless Mr. Lincoln would get the people together, which he refused . . . and thus the farce ended."[21]

A future leader of the German voters in Illinois, Gustave Koerner, heard Lincoln for the first time when he spoke for Harrison. Koerner wrote:

> In point of melody of voice and graceful delivery, though not in argument, most all other speakers surpassed him. His appearance was not very prepossessing. His exceedingly tall and very angular form made his movements rather awkward. Nor were his features, when he was not animated, pleasant, owing principally to his high cheek-bones. His complexion had no roseate hue of health, but was then rather billious, and when not speaking, his face seemed to be overshadowed by melancholy thoughts. I observed him closely, thought I saw a good deal of intellect in him, while his looks were genial and kind. . . . No one in the crowd would have dreamed that he was one day to be their President, and finally lead his people

[20] Miers, *Lincoln Day by Day*, I, 134, quotes *Register*, but it is not clear whether it is from Carlinville or Springfield. Evidently picked up from the *Alton Telegraph*, April 11, 1840, and/or the *Sangamo Journal*, April 10, 1840.

[21] *SgJ*, May 8, 1840.

through the greatest crisis it had seen since the Revolutionary War.[22]

Koerner also recalled that Lincoln, in his speech in Belleville that year, appeared "rather depressed and . . . less happy in his remarks than usual. He sought to make much of the point that he had seen in Belleville that morning a fine horse sold by a constable for the price of twenty-seven dollars, all due to the hard times produced by the Democrats. He was somewhat nonplussed by the constable, who was in the crowd, crying out that the horse had but one eye."

Lincoln felt that the only reason the Whigs of Sangamon County reslated him for nomination for state representative was his ability to make a speech; that ability was being recognized more and more around the state. His candidacy for presidential elector—to cast a vote at the electoral college—gave Whigs a good excuse to invite him. And there were many more people to speak to in the state; from an 1830 population of 157,000 the state had grown to a population of 476,000 by 1840.

The *State Register* remarked, "The Junto have determined in secret conclave to revolutionize the southern part of the State, and have appointed A. P. Field and A. Lincoln missionaries to . . . the benighted region."[23]

The term "missionary" spread among the opposition, and when Lincoln and Field spoke in Waterloo, the Democratic *Belleville Advocate* reported that "one of these said traveling missionaries (Lincoln) held forth . . . to a large gathering of Democratic sinners. . . . But there happened to be present an advocate of the Democratic doctrines (Adam W. Snyder) who, when Missionary Lincoln had finished his incontrovertible sermon, got up and in a plain unvarnished discourse, left the poor missionary in an extremely pitiable predicament."[24] During the campaign he spoke at Alton ("highly argumentative and logical . . . enlivened with numerous anecdotes");[25] at Belleville—"lucid, forcible, and effec-

[22] *Memoirs of Gustave Koerner* (2 vols., Cedar Rapids, Torch Press, 1909), I, 443–44.

[23] August 18, 1840.   [24] August 29, 1840.   [25] *Alton Telegraph*, April 11, 1840.

tive"[26] was the verdict in a sympathetic newspaper account; "weak, puerile, and feeble"[27] reads the report of another analysis, which added, "He should have rested his fame upon his printed speech, going the rounds in the federal papers . . ."; at Decatur (the opposition forces "have not been able to start a man that can hold a candle to him in political debate. All their crack nags . . . have come off the field crippled or broken down");[28] at Shelbyville ("a very able address delivered us by General Ewing; he was followed by Lincoln. Mr. Lincoln had but a thin audience");[29] at Waterloo (Lincoln "seemed like a man travelling over unknown ground");[30] at Equality ("listened to with so much patience that the Whigs were in extacies [*sic*]");[31] at Salem ("completely done up, even his anecdotes failed to command attention");[32] at Mt. Vernon ("listened to with attention; possessing much urbanity and suavity of manner, he is well calculated for a public debater; as he seldom loses his temper, and always replies jocosely and in good humor—the evident marks of disapprobation which greet many of his assertions do not discompose him, and he is therefore hard to foil");[33] at Mt. Vernon Lincoln and McClernand debated in a Methodist church, not yet completed, which "consisted only of walls, roof, floor"; the debate was "spirited";[34] at Albion, where he debated a former legislator, Isaac Walker, whose long flowing beard was in stark contrast with the youthful Lincoln, Lincoln was "remarkably direct and forcible";[35] and at other cities and villages in the state, some of which no longer exist.

[26] *Missouri Republican*, April 13, 1840.

[27] *Belleville Advocate*, April 13, 1840.

[28] *Quincy Whig*, May 25, 1840.

[29] *ISR*, July 10, 1840.

[30] *Ibid.*, September 4, 1840.

[31] *Ibid.*, October 16, 1840.

[32] *Ibid.*

[33] *Ibid.*

[34] *Recollections of the Rev. John Johnson* (Nashville, Southern Methodist Publishing House, 1869), 259.

[35] Gibson William Harris, a law student in Lincoln and Herndon's office from 1845–47, "My Recollections of Abraham Lincoln," *Farm and Fireside*, December 1, 1904.

The *State Register* commented that Lincoln's speeches were so bad they "will place Van Buren in the majority."[36]

The *Sangamo Journal* noted: "Mr. Lincoln is still in the lower part of the State, addressing the People. Mr. McClernand having found that he was not the man to meet him has sent for . . . Lamborn to assist him. Lamborn though well disposed to earn something in laboring for the party, had succeeded but little better than his friend McClernand. Nothing has been heard from Mr. Snyder [who debated Lincoln at Waterloo] since his 'Waterloo defeat.' "[37]

When Lamborn and Lincoln debated in Equality, the official Illinois Van Buren newspaper reported that Lincoln made a speech "without alluding to the name of the Federalists once. He entered into an elaborate defence of Federal principles under the name of Whiggery, and when he had concluded, his venerable grey-haired friend [Lamborn] advanced and gave him his hand, saying, 'Well done, my young friend; our canoe is safe in your hands.' "[38]

At Lawrenceville, Lincoln had some strong words with a former Democratic legislator, William G. Anderson. After Lincoln had been there, Anderson wrote the kind of letter which frequently led to duels of honor:

> On our first meeting on Wednesday last, a difficulty in words ensued between us, which I deem it my duty to notice further. I think you were the aggressor. Your words imported insult; and whether you meant them as such is for you to say. You will therefore please inform me on this point and if you designed to offend me, please communicate to me your present feelings on the subject, and whether you persist in the stand you took.[39]

Lincoln replied:

> Your note of yesterday is received. In the difficulty between us, of which you speak, you say you think I was the aggressor. I do not think I was. You say my "words imported insult." I meant them as a fair set-off to your own statements, and not otherwise; and in that light alone I now wish you to understand them. You ask for my

[36] May 29, 1840.
[38] *Old Hickory*, October 5, 1840.
[37] September 25, 1840.
[39] *CW*, I, 211.

"present" feelings on the subject. I entertain no unkind feeling to you, and none of any sort upon the subject, except a sincere regret that I permitted myself to get into such an altercation.[40]

There was no further correspondence between the two. Typical of Lincoln is his ability to tactfully minimize personal friction without retreating from a position.

But on another occasion during this campaign of 1840 Lincoln responded to an opponent in such a way as to cause harm to his personal relationships. It became known as "the skinning of Thomas"—something his friends boasted about but he himself always regretted. In a speech for the Democrats at the Sangamon County courthouse, Jesse B. Thomas cast slurs upon the Long Nine. Lincoln was not present when the talk began, but when notified he came quickly. Lincoln became momentarily angry by what he heard. He at first "wanted to whip" Thomas.[41] As was customary, Lincoln called for and was given the platform to answer his political opponent. Lincoln then mimicked Thomas's gestures and voice so mercilessly that Thomas actually started crying. The next day Lincoln apologized to Thomas, but what he had done "was the talk of the town."[42] Twenty-five-year-old David Davis was present and reported that Lincoln was "terrific in his denunciation" and "had no mercy" on Thomas.[43] This was unlike Lincoln, however. Ordinarily while disagreeing vigorously, he managed to keep the good will of his opponents.

He spoke for the Whigs at Mt. Carmel. An observer recalls: "His first address was delivered in the courthouse in the afternoon when there were a number of women in the audience. He was tall and rather ungainly in appearance but dignified and eloquent in his own particular style in the use of forceful Saxon monosyllables. His speech in the evening was made to a houseful of men and boys when he seemed to let himself down to their level, pouring forth a torrent of witticisms and anecdotes which aroused the wildest

---

[40] *Ibid.*

[41] Stephen T. Logan, "Stephen T. Logan Talks About Lincoln," *Abraham Lincoln Association Bulletin*, September 1, 1928.

[42] Angle, *Herndon's Lincoln*, 159.

[43] King, *Lincoln's Manager*, 38.

bursts of applause. I could not but admire the skill, humor and fairness of his platitudes."[44]

By serving as one of the main speakers for the Whigs in the state, Lincoln took a long step forward in his political career. Whether a person agreed with a letter in the Democratic *Register* of Springfield that Lincoln was being thoroughly defeated in debate, or whether one believed the *Sangamo Journal* which called it "a lie,"[45] Lincoln received a great deal of publicity.

One of the major Whig rallies in Illinois was held in Springfield, attracting people from throughout the state and from neighboring states. Estimates of the crowd varied from fifteen to twenty thousand. The *Hard Cider Press*, published weekly by the *Chicago American* and named after one of the symbols of Harrison, reported: "The number of Delegates present was not less than FIFTEEN THOUSAND! The encampment covered SEVENTY-TWO ACRES OF GROUND!"[46] Another observer noted "twenty thousand people . . . present, a great number indeed, when it is considered that there were then no railroads . . . and that Springfield had then hardly more than three or four thousand people in it."[47] The number of people attending is impressive in view of the fact that it represented approximately 5 per cent of the state's population.

Democrat John M. Palmer tells his experience:

> Early in the morning of the day before the meeting was to be held, Judge Douglas and I left this city for Carlinville. After crossing Sugar Creek, we met the head of the column of advancing Whigs. In the lead was an immense team of some eight yoke of oxen attached to a wagon upon which was a canoe forty feet long. Other teams were drawing log cabins ornamented with living coons, coon skins and gourds and other "backwoods" articles. . . . Near where the prosperous city of Girard now is, we met "Jo Gillespie" as we then called him.
>
> As soon as he saw Douglas and me, he proposed three cheers for

[44] A. J. Galloway, *Chicago Tribune*, February 12, 1900.
[45] October 23, 1840.
[46] June 13, 1840, copies at Chicago Historical Society Library.
[47] *Memoirs of Gustave Koerner*, vol. 1, 442.

"Tippecanoe and Tyler too," which were given and taken up by the column; and then he called for three groans for Douglas and Palmer. This call met with a prompt response, and the groans were taken up by the column, and it seemed to me for miles across the open prairie this wave of groans followed . . . until it appeared as if it would never cease.[48]

Lincoln was one of a long list of speakers at the meeting, and one witness recalls that "none of them [were] greater" than Lincoln.[49] But one observer sympathetic to him recalled that Lincoln was by no means the outstanding orator. "The palm of eloquence was conceded to a young Chicago lawyer, S. Lisle Smith."[50]

The *Illinois State Register* (referred to by the *Missouri Republican* as the "receptacle of all things vile upon earth")[51] reacted to the big Harrison rally by quoting this from a Democratic statement: "Our opponents selected for the day and hour of their celebration, the birthday of George III, him from whom our ancestors wrested our liberties."[52] The preceding issue stated, "We write . . . surrounded by log cabins on wheels, hard-cider barrels, canoes, brigs and every description of painted device, which, if a sober Turk were to drop among us would induce him to believe we were a community of lunatics or men run mad."[53]

Illinois cast five electoral votes, and all five went to Van Buren. Of special interest was the state-wide balloting for electors. There were some Abolition electors also—the top man getting only 160 votes in the entire state—but here is the vote for the major electors:

Van Buren Electors		*Harrison Electors*	
Adam W. Snyder	47,441	Buckner S. Morris	45,574
Isaac P. Walker	47,442	Samuel D. Marshall	45,571
John W. Eldridge	47,440	Edwin B. Webb	45,573
John A. McClernand	47,440	Cyrus Walker	45,573
James H. Ralston	47,631	Abraham Lincoln	45,385

[48] Palmer, *Life and Services of Gillespie*, 10.

[49] Tarbell, *Life of Lincoln*, 165, quoting Gen. T. J. Henderson, then fifteen years old.

[50] Isaac Arnold, *Reminiscences of the Illinois Bar Forty Years Ago* (Chicago, Fergus, 1881), 5.

[51] December 21, 1840.   [52] *ISR*, June 12, 1840.   [53] *Ibid.*, June 5, 1840.

This gave Van Buren a victory in Illinois, even though the nation went for Harrison. Lincoln must have been unhappy because, for all his campaign activities in much of the state, he ran last.

Lincoln himself was not able to vote. In the southeastern part of the state he campaigned for Harrison right up to election day, November 2. He brought the election returns from Lawrence County to Springfield. For this he received nineteen dollars—the only known emolument he received for spending several weeks on the road for the Illinois Whigs.[54]

Lincoln also ran last among the winners in the race for state representative in Sangamon County, but topped the leading loser, Calhoun, by almost six hundred votes. Lincoln would have done better had he devoted less time to campaigning around the state and more to campaigning in Sangamon County. Moreover, the routine duties of his growing law practice kept him busy when at home and also kept him on the legal circuit and away from home much of the time.

The steady pounding that the Democrats dealt Lincoln for his part in trying to run the Whigs in the county and the state also helped to diminish his vote total. Nevertheless, he received a majority, and he won. He was ready to take his seat in the House of Representatives for the last time, a hectic time that included the "fatal first."

[54] Pratt, *Personal Finances*, 99.

11

A Special Session—And an Important Jump

Their leader (Mr. Lincoln) then made an assault upon unoffending window, through which he *broke* his way and made his escape, followed by two of his faithful adherents (Gillespie and Gridley), who slipt gracefully out of the window, and piled themselves beneath it upon the body of their *chivalrous* leader.—*Belleville Advocate*, December 12, 1840

PRIOR TO the regular session of the legislature, set for December 7, 1840, Governor Carlin called a special session to convene on November 23, 1840. Its purpose was to meet the problem of the mounting internal improvements debt with which the young state had been saddled by Lincoln and his legislative colleagues in 1837.

Among the distinguished members in the House and Senate in this session (including the full session which immediately followed the special session) were Pierre Menard, the first lieutenant governor of the state, who spoke English with a heavy French accent but had much common sense; Cyrus Edwards, the former Whig senator and former candidate for governor; Lyman Trumbull, a new House member who made a distinguished record in later years in the United States Senate; Adam W. Snyder, former congressman and Democratic candidate for governor; and many others who soon became well known on the national scene.

Of the House members, forty-five were farmers, twenty-three lawyers, eleven merchants, seven doctors, a mechanic, a shoemaker, a manufacturer, and a tavern keeper. Only three were born in Illinois. Twenty-four were born in Kentucky and thirteen in Virginia. Two were born in Ireland. In the Senate not a member was a native of Illinois.

On the session's first day the clerk marked "Abram" Lincoln present. The misspelling of his first name was not uncommon. He was called "Lincoln," and he signed his letters simply "A. Lincoln."

On the second day of the session voting was held for speaker, with the outcome known in advance. William L. D. Ewing, Lincoln's longtime opponent, won over Lincoln, 46–36. The other House officers were not chosen along strictly partisan lines. Hardin nominated Lincoln for speaker. When Ewing was elected, Lincoln graciously consented to serve on the committee to escort his successful opponent to the speaker's chair.

A resolution passed quickly asking the Senate to trade places with the House. The new capitol not yet completed, the House was meeting in the Methodist Church. The exchange was called for "on account of the impossibility of the House discharging its business in so small a place as the small frame Methodist church."[1] The *Missouri Republican* commented, "The Church is very small, and the members are crowded together . . . without any means whatever for writing."[2]

The Senate, meeting in the Second Presbyterian Church, readily agreed. The Second Presbyterian Church was built "at a cost of fourteen thousand dollars. . . . It was of brick and was forty-five by seventy feet. On top was a square belfry. . . . The building was heated by wood-stoves. . . . Its seating capacity was about three hundred persons."[3] One of Lincoln's friends reported that it was "completed very handsomely."[4] Within three weeks both houses were able to meet in the new state capitol.

Prior to the Governor's message, the House received a remarkable report from former Attorney General Wickliffe Kitchell. It is amazing that he anticipated problems Illinois would face in future years and that his solutions sound more like those of a twentieth

[1] *HJ*, 1840–41, p. 7.

[2] November 27, 1840.

[3] "Descriptive Sketch of the Different Houses of Worship," *Brotherhood Messenger* of the Second Presbyterian Church, Springfield, February, 1913.

[4] James C. Conkling to Mercy Levering, January 24, 1841, photostat at IHL.

century sociologist than a pioneer attorney general. He called for flexibility in prison sentences, a fairer and more modern court structure, greater protection for the poor by attorneys, and for the abolition of the death penalty. At that time the death penalty was common, not only for murder but for other crimes ranging from arson to perjury. Attorney General Kitchell wrote, "While life remains, the most wicked may repent, the most abandoned may be brought to a sense of moral duty to God and his fellow man. . . . Life being given by God alone, it is believed that it ought not to be taken away by man, unless the safety of society most absolutely demands the sacrifice."[5]

Kitchell resigned as attorney general in order to become a member of the House. He was replaced as attorney general by story-telling Josiah Lamborn, a tall, fluent lawyer who was conspicuous on sight because of a badly deformed foot. However, what made his election as attorney general so unusual is that he had just been up for disbarment before the Supreme Court. While the court did not disbar him, it warned him "to guard his reputation with jealous watchfulness, that the indiscretions which have been committed may not be repeated."[6] Lincoln did not vote for Lamborn, but since Lamborn was not a Whig, the matter did not test his conscience.

The House approved an additional rule presented by nonsmoker Lincoln and the other Rules Committee members "that no smoking be allowed in the Hall during the hours of session."[7]

Then the legislature heard Governor Carlin give his message— a message which places him in the category of one of the state's weak governors. It started strongly, telling the legislators about the difficulties to be faced because of the internal improvements debt— now $13,643,601.83. Governor Carlin said that the "state is measurably overwhelmed with pecuniary embarrassments. . . . High sense of honor and justice imperiously forbid delinquency in its payments." He then came to the climax of his address: "It ought

---

[5] *HJ*, 1840–41, p. 11.

[6] Cornelius J. Doyle, "Josiah Lamborn, Attorney-General of Illinois, 1840–43, *ISHSJ*, July, 1927.

[7] *HJ*, 1840–41, p. 17.

not to be concealed that if the vast debt which has been incurred on account of our Internal Improvements is ever paid, it must be done through resort to direct taxation. I am clearly of [the] opinion that it would be better to postpone the adoption of this policy for the ensuing two years."[8]

Governor Carlin did not have the courage to take the course his own message demanded had to be taken. He suggested that the January interest payment be met through the sale of lands or bonds—and so it was met—but because the Governor failed to follow the logic of his own message on taxes, the state soon defaulted. While the Governor procrastinated, financial interests in the East holding the Illinois bonds gave much better advice: "There is an apprehension that [the legislature], under some misguided policy, may lack the moral firmness to levy taxes; and this we think entirely indispensable in your State."[9]

Regarding the banking issues of the day, the Governor took the traditional Jacksonian stand. He urged the state's banks to issue payments in specie for their notes as soon as possible. Before the end of this short special session this became the big issue.

Lincoln headed the opposition to printing eight thousand copies of the Governor's message, possibly because of its statements on banking, and a compromise printing of five thousand copies was worked out. Lincoln was told that the cost of printing eight thousand copies was thirty or forty dollars and "not worth quarreling about." Lincoln replied that once this precedent was set, "hereafter, many sums will be allowed without a quarrel, and without objection." He added that he doubted that one-half of the copies were ever distributed. He said they could be found "in places namable and unnamable—in short, everywhere, but amongst the people."[10]

Hardin introduced an amendment which would have repealed the Internal Improvements Act, but he made it clear that the state intended to pay its just debts. The motion lost, but Lincoln supported Hardin. But a few days later, when a bill passed which

[8] *Ibid.*, 18–24.
[9] Senate Reports, *Illinois Reports*, 1840–41, 260.
[10] *SgJ*, November 27, 1840.

stopped all payments to personnel on internal improvements, Lincoln was one of the eleven who voted against the bill; seventy-seven voted for it, so it carried easily. This bill, in effect, repealed the act, the only step the state could possibly take. Lincoln may have voted against it because the act did not say specifically, as had Hardin's amendment, that the state would meet its obligations.

One morning when Lincoln was absent, a resolution was quietly introduced which called for a committee to "enquire into the expediency of repealing all laws providing for the removal of the seat of government from Vandalia to Springfield."[11] It further called for the study of removal of the capital back to Vandalia "until the State debt is paid"—a considerable period of time in view of the size of the internal improvements debt. The speaker and presiding officer was William L. D. Ewing of Vandalia. He had planned this and had Representative Richard Bentley of Vandalia's neighboring Bond County introduce the resolution. It passed the House before anyone even had time to ask for a roll call. It called for the House to appoint a committee of three and for the Senate to appoint two. Ewing appointed Bentley, the man who sponsored the resolution and favored Vandalia; James M. Bradford, a freshman member from Sangamon County; and William J. Hankins, who represented the Vandalia territory along with the speaker, but who had not even been present at any of the sessions. When the resolution reached the Senate, that body defeated it, but amazingly Springfield's Senator Edward D. Baker voted for it. Ironically, Baker was the main speaker when the cornerstone was laid for the new capitol. The other Springfield senator, Archer G. Herndon, more understandably voted against it.

What Lincoln is most remembered for in this special session was an episode he wanted people to forget in later years—a jump out the window to prevent a quorum.

Illinois law provided that the banks in the state did not have to renew payment in the actual metal—"in specie"—until the end of the next session of the legislature. Since the two-week special session was held prior to the regular session, the Democrats, who disliked the Whig-controlled banks, decided to put these state

11 *HJ*, 1840–41, p. 38.

banks on the spot by adjourning the special session *sine die* (the final adjournment motion) on Saturday afternoon, even though everyone knew they would be meeting in the regular session on the following Monday. A letter from the president of the State Bank, Thomas Mather, added to the difficulty of the position Lincoln and the State Bank's defenders faced. It stated that the bank "has been for some time ready to resume payments in specie."[12] The statement was intended to instill a false sense of security in the State Bank, with no idea that an adjournment might force the issue immediately.

Representative Joseph Gillespie of Madison County, the man who jumped out the window with Lincoln, related that the Whigs "got wind of the thing on the morning of the day when the adjournment was to take place, [actually they learned of it at least the day before] and then instantly resolved that they would absent themselves and thus break up a quorum, but, as the Constitution of 1818 would allow such a vote to be taken without a call of the ayes and noes, it was necessary that two Whigs should be in the House to call for them. . . . Lincoln and I were selected . . . and the Whigs promised to keep out of the way. When the motion was put, we called for the ayes and noes, and there was no quorum voting."[13]

The speaker sent out the sergeant-at-arms, a man by the name of William Murphy, to bring members in. In performing this office Murphy had police powers. Murphy told the House that one member threatened him with a cane, but others were more co-operative, and soon Murphy had enough additional men there to provide a quorum. Lincoln and Gillespie surveyed the situation quickly and asked the two other Whigs who had been brought in to ask for the roll call, the procedure which forces an actual quorum to be present. The doors were blocked by assistants to the sergeant-at-arms, so Lincoln and thirty-one-year-old Gillespie—and perhaps a third man—hastily took the only other possible course; they jumped out of the window of the Second Presbyterian Church, where the House was meeting.

It did them no good, however, for the speaker counted them as

[12] Senate Reports, *Illinois Reports*, 1840–41, p. 248.
[13] Gillespie, *Recollections*, 25.

present and voting. So the immediate battle was lost. A quorum was sixty-one votes, and Lincoln's recorded vote made the sixty-first. The incident proved highly embarrassing to Lincoln.

The *Illinois State Register* said that Baker in the Senate was the mastermind behind the Whig action, but the *Register* was not kind to Lincoln either:

> Mr. Lincoln, of Sangamon, who was present during the whole scene, and who appeared to enjoy the embarrassment of the House, suddenly looked very grave after the Speaker announced that a quorum was present. The conspiracy having failed, Mr. Lincoln, came under great excitement, and having attempted and failed to get out at the door, very unceremoniously raised the window and jumped out, followed by one or two other members. This gymnastic performance of Mr. Lincoln and his flying brethren did not occur until after they had voted and consequently the House did not interfere with their extraordinary feat. We have not learned whether these flying members got hurt in their adventure, and we think it probable that at least one of them came off without damage, as it was noticed that his legs reached nearly from the window to the ground! By his extraordinary performance on this occasion, Mr. Lincoln will doubtless become . . . famous. We learn that a resolution will probably be introduced into the House this week to inquire into the expedience of raising the State House one story higher, in order to set in the third story so as to prevent members from jumping out of windows! If such a resolution passes, Mr. Lincoln in [the] future will have to climb down the spout.[14]

In a more serious vein the *Register* concluded its story with a call for the defeat of the Whig legislators involved. If their action is not repudiated by the people, the *Register* intoned, "we may bid farewell to our boasted liberties." They found the end result of Lincoln's action would be "anarchy which may lead to Monarchy!" Lincoln's friends at the *Sangamo Journal* did not mention it in their publication, nor did the Whig *Alton Telegraph* breathe a word of it.

The *Peoria Democratic Press* thought the jumping terrible. "Every body condemns and despises the course pursued by the

14 December 12, 1840.

Whig party in this affair. Such a course of proceeding, if successful, would amount to revolution; but as it turned out otherwise, it is only a petty revolt."[15]

It was not just in later years that Lincoln was sensitive to the "jumping issue." Early in January—about two months later—it was referred to in debate, and Lincoln replied in a heated manner and the speaker called him to order. The issue came up when the Whigs objected to taking a day off from sessions to honor Jackson's victory at New Orleans. W. H. Bissell, future Illinois governor, with a square chin, a large Roman nose, and a close-clipped mustache, rose and said that the Whig objections to taking off one day "came with an ill grace from a party who had deserted the House and some of whom had leaped out of windows on a memorable occasion." The *Register* reported that after being called to order, Lincoln "said that as to jumping, he would jump when he pleased and no one would hinder him." Later, Lincoln "endeavored to quiet the storm."[16]

The *Peoria Register* called the adjournment action against the bank "the act of destroying our state faith and our state credit."[17]

In this short special session, Lincoln took an active part in a contested election, a Gallatin Saline bill, and other matters of little general interest. But the thing he was to be remembered for in this special session was a short trip from a window to the ground. The jump did not hurt him physically, for two days later he was in his seat for the start of the regular session.

Humiliating Lincoln and the Whigs further, when the regular session met on Monday, the legislature voted to take all measures as they were left when the special session ended. This meant, in effect, that the special session and the regular session were continuous with the exception of this one adjournment. All this had only one purpose—to embarrass the Whigs and the banks. Lincoln fought the move to continue the bills on the House calendar as if there had been no adjournment, but he lost 42–40.

Lincoln and the Whigs were not winning many battles.

[15] December 9, 1840.
[16] *ISR*, January 15, 1841.
[17] December 11, 1840.

12

"The Fatal First"—And a Final Session

Abraham Lincoln of Sangamon is emphatically a man of high standing, being about six feet four in his stockings, slender, and loosely built. He is, I suppose, over 30 years old, has been in the legislature repeatedly, and was run as one of the Whig electors in the late election. Mr. L. is a self-made man, and one of the ablest, whether a lawyer or legislator, in the State. As a speaker, he is characterized by a sincerity, frankness and evident honesty calculated to win attention and gain the confidence of the hearer. —*Quincy Whig*, appearing in the issue of the "Fatal First."[1]

THE FINAL Lincoln term in the House of Representatives was the strangest. He appeared to be losing some interest in the state's legislative battles. This may have been partly due to his growing law practice, but mostly to complications caused by his interest in the opposite sex.

Little did Lincoln dream in the early part of 1840 that in four years he would buy the home recently built by the Episcopal rector, Rev. Charles Dresser, and that in two years this same clergyman would perform Lincoln's marriage ceremony.

Lincoln, never particularly a "ladies' man," experienced something during his final term that made him unusually despondent. His health, both mental and physical, suffered. Before this period of 1840–41 he had experienced some unhappiness in courtship, but never had it affected him so much.

[1] January 1, 1841.

In 1837, Lincoln met the girl he eventually married—Mary Todd, a cultured girl with soft brown hair and blue-grey eyes. She was a cousin of Stuart and a sister-in-law of Ninian W. Edwards. Mary was a Kentucky girl who could not get along with her stepmother and so spent three months in 1837 with her sister in Springfield. Two years later she returned to Springfield to reside permanently.

Short and somewhat plump, she was a contrast to Lincoln in more than height. While his education was limited, she was well educated for the times and spoke fluent French. Nine years younger than Lincoln, she tended to be quick-tempered and vivacious. Lincoln's anger rose slowly, and he had a more plodding personality. But whatever their differences, they were interested in each other.

Before their marriage, however, something happened that affected Lincoln's performance during this final session of the legislature. It came to be known by Lincoln and his friends as the "fatal first of January."

The regular session began December 7, 1840. Its first concern was to provide payment for the interest on the huge internal improvements debt. The interest would come due January 1.

During this session Lincoln had his most responsible record on internal improvements. He favored the state paying every penny it owed, including obligations incurred by its agents. Not all legislators took this position. Some felt that the debt was too huge to pay and that it would be best to forget it and start anew with a clean ledger sheet. Others had special projects they still wanted to see completed, believing they would help the state's financial situation. One resolution called for the rejection of any proposal looking to "abolishing any State road whatever."[2] Lincoln quickly moved to table this resolution, and it was killed. The majority of legislators realized that something had to be done.

Ewing appointed a majority of Democrats to all committees, but the Internal Improvements Committee he packed with Whigs be-

[2] *HJ*, 1840–41, p. 108.

cause "he thought the subject had become odious to the people, and he would throw the responsibility on the Whigs."[3]

What finally passed, with Lincoln's support, was authorization for issuing $300,000 in additional bonds to "pay the interest which will legally fall due on the Internal Improvement debt" at a rate not to exceed 7 per cent.[4]

Lincoln introduced an amendment with his own plan for taking care of the interest payment. The *Peoria Register* immediately denounced it as "a mere gull trap."[5] Lincoln's proposal was referred to the Finance Committee, on which Lincoln served, but the measure did not get any further. It had some deficiencies, but constituted a more realistic appraisal of the total situation than the feeble measures passed. Lincoln wanted to authorize the governor to issue "Illinois Interest Bonds" with details about interest and time of redemption left out. Lincoln's bill added that the state's portion of taxes on all newly owned land should be set aside for paying the interest on the bonds. In addition, he provided that "hereafter the sum of thirty cents for each hundred dollars' worth of all taxable property shall be paid into the State Treasury."[6]

In debating his measure Lincoln acknowledged that "the details of the bill might be imperfect" but that he believed in "the correctness of its general features." It would be good "as a permanent measure" responded Murphy of Cook County, but it "would not answer the present emergency."[7] The debate continued for two days, some supporting Lincoln, more opposing him.

Lincoln's proposal failed to carry. The measure which passed permitted the state to issue bonds, but since it provided much less additional state income, soon Illinois did not pay interest on its bonds. Whether even Lincoln's proposals would have met the need is doubtful, but it would have come closer to reality. Lincoln told the House that he had "no pride in its success, as a measure of his own, but submitted it to the wisdom of the House" for possible

[3] *Missouri Republican*, December 2, 1840.

[4] *LIll*, 1840–41, p. 167.

[5] December 11, 1840.

[6] *CW*, I, 216.

[7] *SgJ*, December 11, 1840.

changes.[8] Lincoln hoped his proposal would "carry us on till the next Legislature."[9] The House had struggled over the matter, but was unable to agree on anything. On December 10—twenty days before the interest was due—the Senate prodded the House by resolution, noting that the Senate would "remain in session, if necessary, until 12 o'clock this evening, in hopes of paying the January interest on the public debt."[10] Piqued, the House passed a resolution that the Senate "need not incommode themselves longer than half past eleven o'clock this evening in waiting for the action of the House on the subject of the January interest."[11] Then the House took no further action that day on the question. But the legislature did, on December 16, pass the authorization for bonds for the interest due on January 1.

There was also the sensitive question: Must the bonds to take over care of this interest be sold at par value? It wounded Illinois pride to sell them under par, but Lincoln argued correctly that "to restrict them to be sold at par value only was tantamount to prohibiting their sale."[12] Actually, some were eventually sold for as little as "fifteen to twenty cents on the dollar."[13]

Taking care of the long-term indebtedness was a more vexing problem and became the center of many legislative fights. Three days after Lincoln made his unsuccessful proposal for taxation, he introduced a separate bill which probably said essentially the same thing. No copy of this bill exists. Called "an Act to provide for the payment of interest on the State debt," it was tossed from committee to House and back again for several weeks before it was finally defeated.

By this time in his legislative career, Lincoln no longer gave up after two defeats. When another frequently amended bill on the same general subject was being contested, Lincoln offered an amendment that was, in fact, a totally new bill. The House accepted this with one amendment. The Senate acted quickly on

[8] *Ibid.*
[9] *ISR*, December 11, 1840.
[10] *Senate Journal*, 1840–41, p. 67.
[11] *HJ*, 1840–41, p. 102.
[12] *ISR*, February 26, 1841.
[13] Krenkel, *Illinois Internal Improvements*, footnote on 170.

the bill received by it only four days before adjournment. With one amendment adopted by the House, the bill became law. How much of the final bill was the work of Lincoln? Probably a major part. It called for an additional tax of ten cents on each $100 worth of property, the money to be "set apart exclusively for the payment of interest on the state indebtedness."[14] It also established a minimum valuation of three dollars an acre for all land in the state.

But the ten cents per $100 worth of property was far from enough to meet the need. This brought the maximum tax in Illinois to eighty cents on $100 of assessed property, while in other states in the surrounding area it ran much higher. Ohio also had a substantial debt, but it had a rate of two dollars per $100 of assessed property, and at that time it was a much wealthier state.

The *Chicago Weekly Tribune*, the *Chicago American*, and a few other newspapers favored adequate taxation to meet the problem, but other newspapers warned against it. The *Tribune* advised, "Let us pay now and our credit will rise."[15] But this advice was not heeded. A Madison County legislator correctly predicted what was to come. He wrote to a friend, "If a public *debt* is a public *blessing*, Illinois is certainly a *blessed* state. It is possible the *January* interest may be paid, but look out for July."[16]

The end result was that in July, 1841, four months after the legislature adjourned, Illinois defaulted on interest payments, and *all* Illinois bonds "fell to 14 and 15 cents on the dollar."[17] The next year—1842—the state collected only $98,546.14 "for the general expenses of government, while interest charges on the state debt amounted to nearly $800,000 annually."[18]

The *Sparta Democrat* commented near the end of the session, "No state could be in much worse condition than ours at present. All its officers are unpaid—even the members of the Legislature

[14] *LIll*, 1840–41, p. 165. It should be added here that this account differs somewhat from references in otherwise usually reliable sources. There were several bills with similar titles, and the errors appear to be caused by confusing the bills with titles very much the same, an easy error to make.

[15] December 5, 1840.

[16] George Churchill to Gershom Flagg, January 2, 1841, IHL.

[17] Krenkel, *Illinois Internal Improvements*, 172.

[18] *Ibid.*, 149.

are unable to pay their boarding bills, except with Auditor's warrants—and no provision made or likely, I fear, to be made to meet the interest on the state debt. Unless something is done wisely and promptly our very government will fall asunder."[19]

The legislature had also abolished the Board of Public Works, prohibited the issuance of script, and called for completion of only the Northern Cross Railroad from Springfield to Meredosia. But all these actions, supported by Lincoln, were taken far too late.

One Springfield observer, who had originally come from the eastern section of the country, expressed astonishment at the loose practices in spending money on internal improvements. Illinois does not spend "half as much time and consideration upon . . . voting away millions of dollars, as the legislature of Connecticut would in the appropriation of $1000."[20]

In less than a year after the last Lincoln session, the debt totaled more than $15,000,000. It was a chapter in his legislative life he was probably glad to leave behind.

In the middle of Lincoln's final session in the legislature occurred one of the strangest episodes in his life. He referred to it later as "the fatal first of January."[21]

What happened cannot be fully documented, but a highly reliable team of scholars state that this is "the date on which Lincoln asked to be released from his engagement to Mary Todd."[22] The leading biographer of Mrs. Lincoln, Ruth Randall, believes that a broken engagement was the cause. Among Lincoln's contemporaries this seems to have been an accepted fact. Mary or Lincoln may have broken the engagement or they may have agreed to break off relations.

The engagement was frowned upon by the Ninian Edwards family with whom Mary was staying. Perhaps the aristocratic Ninian W. Edwards told Mary and Lincoln that the match was not a good one. Ninian and his wife had seen Lincoln and Mary sitting together on the sofa with the black, horse-hair covering at

[19] February 12, 1841.

[20] David Davis to William P. Walker, letters of 1839 and 1840, quoted in King, *Lincoln's Manager*, 36.

[21] Letter to Speed, *CW*, I, 282. [22] *CW*, I, footnote on 282.

their home and agreed that in so many respects the two seemed opposites. This was true, yet Lincoln and Mary Todd also had much in common. A son of the Edwards later said, "My mother and my father at that time didn't want Mary to marry Mr. Lincoln. . . . When my mother saw that things were becoming serious between Lincoln and Mary, she treated him rather coldly. . . . During 1841 and 1842 my mother did what she could to break up the match."[23]

Perhaps part of the difficulty was due to the strange character of Ninian W. Edwards, an unpopular man with his legislative colleagues, and a man embittered by the Whigs in Sangamon County who had slated Lincoln for re-election to the House while unceremoniously dropping Edwards. It would be in line with the somewhat warped Edwards' personality to harbor a grudge.

A month before the "fatal first" Mary wrote a friend about "the crime of matrimony," probably with family opposition to a proposed marriage with Lincoln in mind.[24] Whatever the cause of the break, the highly emotional Mary "could understand without being personally offended."[25] One of Mary's close friends wrote a month after the "fatal first," "Poor A—I fear his is a blighted heart. Perhaps if he was so persevering as Mr. W—he might finally be successful."[26]

The various accounts contradict each somewhat, but this much is clear: Lincoln for a while was unusually depressed, so much so that he temporarily lost interest in everything. His physical appearance revealed a sick man. And all of it was traceable to Mary Todd, the socially prominent young lady he had been courting.

Some citizens in the pioneer society reported simply that he "went crazy."[27] On January 22, a friend wrote to Lincoln's colleague Hardin, "We have been very much distressed, on Mr. Lincoln's account; hearing that he had two Cat fits and a Duck fit since we left."[28] On January 22, the Galena newspaper had this to

[23] Stevens, *A Reporter's Lincoln*, 75–76.

[24] Mary Todd to Mercy Levering, December, 1840. Copy at IHL.

[25] Ruth Painter Randall, *Mary Lincoln* (Boston, Little Brown, 1953), 57.

[26] Mercy Levering to James C. Conkling, February 7, 1841, photostat at IHL.

[27] Mrs. N. W. Edwards to Herndon, *The Hidden Lincoln*, 374.

[28] Martin McKee to John J. Hardin, January 22, 1841, Chicago Historical Society Library.

say: "Mr. Snyder of the Senate and Mr. Lincoln of the House are ill. Each party is thus deprived at present of one of its leaders."[29]

Lyman Trumbull, after Lincoln's death, recalled: "Mr. Lincoln took very little part in the legislation of that session. It was the period when . . . he was engaged in love affairs which some of his friends feared had well-nigh unsettled his mental faculties. I recall but one speech he made during the session. In that he told a story which convulsed the House to the great discomfiture of the member at whom it was aimed."[30]

A colleague of Lincoln in the House in an earlier session—with no reference to "the fatal first"—considered Lincoln "the victim of terrible melancholy. . . . When by himself, he told me that he was so overcome with mental depression, that he never dared carry a knife in his pocket."[31] The source for that statement was Robert Wilson, one of the Long Nine, and sometimes not too reliable a witness, but a man who knew Lincoln well. Another close political friend, Orville H. Browning, recalled that after "the fatal first" Lincoln was "incoherent and distraught" for about a week; "I think it was only an intensification of his constitutional melancholy."[32]

He was almost thirty-two years old and not married, when most men at that period were married before twenty-one. He did have eleven unmarried colleagues in the House, but Lincoln may have felt this was his last chance to get a wife.

He himself referred to months of despondency following January 1, 1841. On January 20, he wrote to Stuart recommending that Dr. Anson G. Henry be appointed Springfield postmaster. "I have, within the last few days," Lincoln added, "been making a most discreditable exhibition of myself in the way of hypochondriasm and thereby got an impression that Dr. Henry is necessary to my existence. Unless he gets that place he leaves Springfield. You therefore see how much I am interested in the matter."[33]

[29] *Northwestern Gazette and Galena Advertiser*, January 22, 1841.

[30] Horace White, *Life of Lyman Trumbull* (New York, Houghton Mifflin, 1913), 426–27.

[31] Wilson, *Intimate Memories*, 32.

[32] Nicolay and Hay, *Lincoln*, I, 187.

[33] *CW*, I, 228.

Three days later he wrote and mentioned "the deplorable state of my mind at this time."[34] Eleven days later Lincoln wrote Stuart, "You see by this that I am neither dead nor quite crazy yet."[35]

Years later, Lincoln's friend Joshua F. Speed gave lectures about Lincoln and recalled: "In the winter of 1841 a gloom came over him till his friends were alarmed for his life. Though a member of the Legislature, he rarely attended its sessions. In his deepest gloom, and when I told him he would die unless he rallied, he said, 'I am not afraid, and would be more than willing. But I have an irrepressible desire to live till I can be assured that the world is a little better for my having lived in it.' "[36] The Lincoln quotation and facts have been gilded with age, but it shows the importance Lincoln's close friend placed on the event.

As to being "rarely" in sessions, it was not that bad. On the "fatal first," Lincoln voted on the only recorded roll call. The next day, January 2, a number of votes were taken, but Lincoln is recorded only on the motion to adjourn. That was Saturday. No sessions were held on Sunday; Monday he missed entirely. Tuesday he was there for the opening but missed the rest of the session; that afternoon he filed divorce papers in the circuit court for Ann McDaniel versus Patrick McDaniel. Wednesday he again attended. Thursday he was there for the opening of the session, left, then returned in the afternoon and actually took part in debate. After that he attended with some degree of regularity, with the exception of one full week beginning January 13. During that week he missed all roll calls and was not present at any time except for one unimportant roll call which changed the name of a county from "Orange" to "Kendall." From January 20 on, he was usually in attendance. So the accounts that he missed the entire session, or that he "rarely attended" during this session because of his gloom are greatly exaggerated.

One Springfield resident wrote to his fiancee that Lincoln was having some "painful" experiences in his romantic life. Because

[34] *Ibid.*, I, 229.

[35] Lincoln to Stuart, National Archives, copy at IHL, unpublished.

[36] Joshua Speed, *Reminiscences of Abraham Lincoln and Notes of a Visit to California* (Louisville, John P. Norton, 1884), 39.

of these Lincoln was "confined about a week, but though he now appears again he is reduced and emaciated in appearance and seems scarcely to speak above a whisper. His case at present is truly deplorable but what prospects there may be for ultimate relief I can not pretend to say."[37]

Months later, in June, Mary Todd wrote to a friend that Lincoln "deems me unworthy of notice," that she had "not met him in the gay world for months." She added that even if he did not pay attention to her, it would give her "much, much happiness" if he "should be himself again."[38]

Twenty-three months after the "fatal first," on November 4, 1842, Lincoln and Mary Todd were married by the local Episcopal minister. They were married in the Edwards home, where there were "hurried preparations for the wedding supper."[39]

Before Mary Todd married him, Lincoln went through this period of melancholy. On January 23, 1841—more than three weeks after the "fatal first"—Lincoln wrote to his law partner, "I am now the most miserable man living. If what I feel were equally distributed to the whole human family there would not be one cheerful face on the earth. Whether I shall ever be better I cannot tell: I awfully forbode I shall not. To remain as I am is impossible; I must die or be better, it appears to me."[40]

Obviously such an attitude would tell on his work in the remaining weeks of his final session. As late as a week after this 1840–41 legislative session was completed, a young Springfield lawyer wrote to his fiancee, "I fear . . . he [Lincoln] will withdraw himself from the society of us inferior mortals."[41]

From the viewpoint of Lincoln's health, it probably was a good thing that there was a session of the legislature at this time, for

[37] James C. Conkling to Mercy Levering, quoted by Logan Hay in "Lincoln in 1841–1842," *Abraham Lincoln Quarterly*, September, 1942. Location of original letter is not indicated.

[38] Letter to Mercy Levering, quoted by Hay in "Lincoln in 1841–1842." Location of original letter is not indicated.

[39] Octavia Roberts, "We All Knew Ab'ham," *Abraham Lincoln Quarterly*, March, 1846, from an interview with the bridesmaid.

[40] *CW*, I, 229.

[41] Carl Sandburg and Paul Angle, *Mary Lincoln, Wife and Widow* (New York, Harcourt, Brace, 1932), 181, quoting Conkling to Mercy Levering, March 7, 1841.

it gave him something to think about instead of brooding on his
personal difficulties.

Lincoln had been fighting for the Illinois secretary of state,
Alexander P. Field, who was able to have the Whig majority on the
Illinois Supreme Court say that Governor Carlin could not dismiss him. But since the issue had stirred some anti-Whig talk,
Field resigned shortly after the session started. Governor Carlin
then appointed Stephen A. Douglas to the post. A Peoria newspaper
reported, "A jollification was had on the occasion of the elevation
of the little giant to the secretaryship, which of course was a most
splendid affair, there being nothing drank but sparkling champaign."[42]

Ten days later the House was considering a resolution to permit
the Governor, the justices of the Supreme Court, and the secretary
of state "to take seats within the bar of this House whenever it
may suit their convenience during the present session."[43] But an
amendment was adopted removing the secreary of state from that
invitation, a direct slap at Douglas. Two months later Douglas
had "mended his fences" enough, so that he was elected to the
Illinois Supreme Court.

Lincoln served on a number of committees during the special
and regular sessions, in addition to his service on the two standing
committees of Finance, and Canals and Canal Lands. Other committees on which he served: Rules; Joint Rules (for joint meetings of the House and Senate); committee to study the Senate bill
"to vacate the town plat of the town of Livingston" (Lincoln was
chairman);[44] committee to confer with the bank of the state of
Illinois "to ascertain whether and upon what terms" a loan could
be secured for the interest on the internal improvements debt;[45]
committee to investigate the "causes which have produced the
very large expenditure for the item of public printing" (Lincoln
was chairman);[46] committee to study "An Act providing for the

[42] *Peoria Register and Northwestern Gazetteer*, December 11, 1840.
[43] *HJ*, 1840–41, p. 94.
[44] *Ibid.*
[45] *Ibid.*, 47.
[46] *Ibid.*, 137.

election of a public Binder";[47] committee to study "An Act regulating the sale of Property";[48] committee to make a recommendation regarding the petition "to authorize Richard C. Norred to erect a mill-dam across the Sangamon River" (Lincoln was chairman);[49] committee to consider "the best means of further providing for the payments of interest on the State debt";[50] committee "on the petition of John Stuart" (Lincoln was chairman);[51] and the committee "on unfinished business."[52]

The committee to look into the state printing expenses was suggested by Lincoln as a way to get at the Democratic *Illinois State Register* which was doing the printing, and a chance to help his friend Simeon Francis, who ran the rival *Journal*. Also, there were charges that printing costs were double what they should be.

The *Register* ran a surprisingly objective account of Lincoln's request, including the fact that Lincoln stated that he "intended no attack on any individual."[53] Attempts to amend Lincoln's proposal for a select committee to look into the matter failed, and the committee of three was appointed with Lincoln serving as chairman and two Democrats, Lyman Trumbull and Joseph Ormsbee, as the other members of the committee. This gave Lincoln the committee he wanted, but the Democrats had two-to-one control of it. When the committee reported—Trumbull reporting for the committee— they said that nothing was wrong with the expenditure for public printing. Lincoln did not file a minority report. The *State Register* noted: "Mr. Lincoln has recovered from his indisposition and has attended the House for more than a week past, during which time he made no minority report, although he attended every meeting of the committee of Investigation. Now, we ask any man of either political party, whether Mr. Lincoln is a man who would have re-

---

[47] *Ibid.*, 343, 355. Lincoln was not originally appointed to this committee, but he apparently was added later to take the place of one of the other members who stepped aside.

[48] *Ibid.*, 411.

[49] *Ibid.*, 295.

[50] *Ibid.*, 455.

[51] *Ibid.*, 517.

[52] *Ibid.*, 553.

[53] January 1, 1841.

fused to speak out, if he had anything to tell?"[54] A previous issue stated: "Mr. Lincoln attended every meeting of the committee, summoned the witnesses, all of whom were Whigs, and did not stop the investigation until he was thoroughly satisfied."[55]

If Lincoln had been in completely good health, it is doubtful he would have let the occasion pass without some comment. After the committee made its report, the *Sangamo Journal* commented, "The health of Mr. Lincoln did not permit him to examine the Report, and he did not read it until several days after it made its appearance."[56] Hardin called it "a whitewash."[57] The *St. Louis Era* offered to do the printing for Illinois for half the price the state had been charged—either an indication of excessive prices or that the St. Louis newspaper knew it would not get Illinois printing.[58] The *Peoria Democratic Press* was pleased with the committee action: "When it is considered that Mr. Lincoln, a leading Whig member of the House, was the chairman of the committee . . . it must be conceded that Mr. Walters [of the *Register*] has come off most triumphant."[59]

One of the problems faced by the legislature during this session was that of redistricting. Lincoln favored a small number of legislators to facilitate the transaction of state business. He told the House that when he first came (in 1834) there were fifty-five members instead of ninety-one and "business was conducted with twice the facility." The issue was finally resolved by saying that "each twelve thousand white inhabitants shall be entitled to one Senator" and that "each four thousand white inhabitants shall be entitled to one Representative."[60] Lincoln voted for it.

In the Governor's message to the legislature, Carlin stated that he had had reports of fraudulent voting along the rivers, in which some people had traveled by boat and voted in one place after another. The Governor made it clear that he had no knowledge as

[54] January 29, 1841.
[55] January 22, 1841.
[56] January 26, 1841.
[57] *Chicago American*, January 23, 1841.
[58] Quoted in *Chicago American*, December 30, 1840.
[59] January 20, 1841.
[60] *LIll*, 1840–41, p. 23.

to the truth of the charge, but that the legislature should set up penalties for "rigid punishment of offenders."[61] Lincoln introduced a resolution to refer the matter to the Committee on Elections to report an act which would "afford the greatest possible protection of the elective franchise against frauds of all sorts whatsoever."[62] A St. Louis newspaper reported: "The resolution of Mr. Lincoln proposes the enactment of a law with the severest penalty for the abuse of the elective franchise."[63]

John A. McClernand of Gallatin County offered a substitute resolution which called for five members from the House and three from the Senate to compose a special committee to look into the matter. The difference between the two proposals was that Lincoln's would have been referred to a committee in which the Democrats outnumbered the Whigs five to four; McClernand's proposal would give the Democrats a five to three advantage. Lincoln was unhappy with what was happening. He had "every reason to believe that all this hue and cry about frauds was entirely groundless, and raised for other than honest purposes."[64] McClernand's amendment to Lincoln's resolution—which in reality made it a new resolution—passed by a straight party vote. Lincoln then voted against the passage of the resolution which he had introduced but which had been changed to give the Democrats a greater edge.

The Democrats charged that "frauds to the number of 500 votes perpetuated in Sangamon County at the last August election have just been discovered. . . . There were 3,100 votes polled at the last August election in this county. The returns of the marshal, who has just completed the census of this county, show but 2,656 male persons in Sangamon county of 20 years old and upwards."[65] The Democrats were embarrassed when the Whigs showed that their figures were incorrect and that no fraudulent voting had taken place in Sangamon County.

The bill which resulted from this became a matter of major controversy. The Lincoln record is one of favoring both prison and

[61] *HJ*, 1840–41, p. 28.
[62] *Ibid.*, 34.
[63] *Missouri Republican*, December 2, 1840.
[64] *Quincy Whig*, December 12, 1840.
[65] *SgJ*, December 11, 1840, quoting Democratic handbill.

a heavy fine for fraudulent voting. The majority of the House (39–34) favored a heavy fine only. But the senators agreed with Lincoln and passed a separate bill calling for prison "not exceeding thirty days."[66] The House finally accepted this solution.

When the Senate bill came over, one forward-looking House member wanted to amend the election procedure so that citizens could vote by secret ballot, which would be "deposited in boxes kept for that purpose, which shall not be opened, or the vote counted until the closing of the polls."[67] To vote at this time, a person walked up to the clerk and the judge at the polling place, told them for whom he wanted to vote, and they would then write it down. The 1818 Illinois constitution said, "All votes shall be given *vive voce* until altered by the general assembly." Those who wanted a secret ballot were called advocates of a "keep dark system" and Governor Ford in 1854 said that moves to have a secret ballot would destroy "all manly independence and frankness."[68] The proposal for a secret ballot lost 50–27, Lincoln being among the majority killing it.

Petitions of an unusual nature were presented to the legislature by a group of people in Randolph and Washington counties who called themselves the Reformed Presbyterian Church. The Senate Judiciary Committee report explained the background and made recommendations:

[The petitioners] represent, in substance, that . . . because the existence of God is not recognized as the source of civil rule in the national constitution, and because His law is not acknowledged as the supreme law of the land, they cannot become incorporated with the national society and be made component parts of the body politic. They allege that they cannot be compelled into citizenship. . . . They therefore ask to be relieved from serving on juries, and from paying the usual fines for nonattendance. . . .

We do not see that the Legislature can, upon principle, grant the indulgence asked for in this case. . . . The committee also deny the authority of the Legislature to meddle with matters of religion.

[66] *LIll*, 1840–41, p. 112.
[67] *HJ*, 1840–41, p. 392.
[68] Ford, *History of Illinois*, 86–87.

It is our only proper sphere to make laws for civil government, universal in their application, and operating equally upon all, and let religion alone. We can give no one sect a preference over another without violating these principles, which we deem sacred and fundamental in a free and just government.[69]

Early in the session occurred one of the few examples of Lincoln's leadership in the field of education during his four terms in the legislature. He introduced a resolution "that the Committee on Education be instructed to enquire into the expediency of providing by law for the examination, as to their qualifications, of persons offering themselves as school teachers, and that no teacher shall receive any part of the Public School Funds, who shall not have successfully passed such examination."[70] A move to kill Lincoln's resolution lost 49–40. It was referred to the Education Committee, and the final result included a section in a lengthy new school bill which stated that the trustees of a school district "shall examine any person proposing to teach a school in their vicinity, in relation to the qualifications of such person as a teacher. . . . And no person shall be entitled to receive any compensation from the school fund until he shall have been examined and received a certificate of qualification."[71] It was a very loose arrangement for determining qualifications, but better than nothing.

A bill to make sure that the school districts received the money due them from the various counties passed 80–3, with Lincoln part of the overwhelming majority.

When the Senate measure came to the House calling for the reorganization and speed-up in public education, Lincoln voted with the majority, 42–37, to send the matter to a select committee. Some of the supporters of the measure believed this a delaying tactic designed to kill the bill. Two weeks later the committee reported this important education bill, and when a motion was made to lay the bill on the table, it lost 57–17, Lincoln one of seventeen who wanted to table the measure. When it came near passage stage, Lincoln voted against moving the bill ahead, but again, he was

[69] Senate Reports, *Illinois Reports*, 1840–41, 143–44.
[70] *HJ*, 1840–41, p. 46.
[71] *LIll*, 1840–41, p. 279.

outvoted, this time 54–24. The bill then passed—and Illinois took a major step forward in encouraging public schools. While the lengthy bill helped Illinois education greatly, it "did not bring about free public schools, because there was no provision for local taxation."[72]

Even though less effective in this session than in the two sessions of his third term, Lincoln took an active part, despite his melancholy. He could cast but a single vote, but his word carried weight because he had experience, was at least nominally the Whig leader, and hailed from the second most densely populated county in the state. The 1840 census figures showed Morgan County, in the central part of the state, the largest county, with 19,154 people; Sangamon County second with 14,716; and Cook County tenth with 10,201.[73]

It is significant that the Galena newspaper, in listing the ten men who spoke most frequently on issues during the session, did not include Lincoln.[74]

Internal improvements was the most important controversy, but changing the judicial structure in the state was the most hotly debated matter between the two parties. As the Whig candidate for speaker, Lincoln served as their chief spokesman in the House and would have been expected to be an active participant in any proposals about changes in the judiciary, particularly since he was a lawyer and had taken part in some of the pre-session disputes in which the matter centered. But Lincoln is not reported in the newspapers as having taken part in this debate at any time. This is additional evidence that Lincoln was not in good health. As it turned out, Lincoln's mental depression probably was decisive in the bill's passage, for a change of one vote would have killed the measure, and Lincoln was both skilled and respected enough to contrive the defeat had he been well.

The Illinois Supreme Court had rendered some decisions along strictly partisan lines, including one case in which Lincoln helped

[72] Robert Gehlmann Bone, "Education in Illinois Before 1857," *ISHSJ*, Summer, 1957.

[73] *Sparta Democrat*, January 8, 1841.

[74] *Northwestern Gazette and Galena Advertiser*, January 13, 1841.

the Whig, A. P. Field, keep his position as secretary of state. The Supreme Court overturned a lower court decision that the Governor had the authority to remove Field. The vote was strictly on party lines; since the Whigs had the majority on the Court, Field who was described by the *Chicago Democrat* as "the raw head and bloody bones of the opposition," was retained.[75] This type of action caused resentment among the Democrats, and with some justification.

A more important issue soon resulted in the complete revision of the Supreme Court structure and personnel. That issue was the foreign vote. The state constitution of 1818 stated only that to be eligible to vote, a person must be a free male, twenty-one years old, and a resident of the state for at least six months. Nothing was said about citizenship, and both parties were fighting hard for the foreign vote. But the Whigs were losing it. At least one expert observer calculated the foreign vote as more than 90 per cent Democratic.[76] Of about ten thousand foreign votes cast in Illinois in 1840, more than nine thousand went to the Democrats. That was enough to be decisive in the close elections Illinois was having. If there had been no foreign vote, the Whigs reasoned, Democratic Governor Carlin, who won by less than a thousand votes, would not be the chief executive but a Whig would be occupying that position. Van Buren defeated Harrison by only 1,867 votes in Illinois, the alien vote being the decisive factor.

David Davis wrote after the election to a relative in the East, "We think that if the *Irish* did not vote more than *3 times* we could easily carry the State. . . . The Irish vote along the line of the Canal increased most wonderfully, and in nearly every other county of the State, the Whig vote has enlarged greatly."[77]

A check of the poll books in Springfield in 1838 showed that there was "a unanimous vote for the Democratic ticket among the aliens."[78]

The Whigs brought this matter before a court at Galena—before

75 December 30, 1835.

76 Ford, *History of Illinois*, 214–15.

77 David Davis to William P. Walker, November 16, 1840, IHL.

78 Harry Pratt, "Lincoln—Trustee of the Town of Springfield," *Bulletin of the Abraham Lincoln Association*, June, 1937.

Judge Daniel Stone, Lincoln's old Whig legislative colleague, and he not surprisingly decided that an alien could not vote. The Democrats immediately entered the legal battle, and action was finally postponed by the Illinois Supreme Court from the June term until December of 1840—after the presidential election. Then the Illinois Supreme Court was supposed to act on it, and by then a Democratic legislature with a Democratic governor was in session. Rumors were circulated—spread by the lone Democrat on the four-man Supreme Court—that the Whig justices were going to rule that aliens could not vote.

Douglas handled the case before the Supreme Court for the Democrats. He wrote a friend to tell what happened when the matter was brought up in June before the election: "The Hon. T. W. Smith, one of the judges of the court, informed me that the decision was to be three against one . . . in favor of cutting off the alien votes. . . . When the appointed hour arrived for making the decision, the judges appeared upon the bench and laid their papers before them . . . about to deliver opinions. I rose and moved to dismiss the cause in consequence of a defect in the record. . . . I then filed the reasons for my motion, and after argument the cause was continued until the present term of court."[79] Because Douglas could anticipate the Illinois Supreme Court decision, he was able to postpone the judicial decision until after the election— and until the legislature was in session, giving the Democrats one more election by means of the foreign vote. But then the Supreme Court, controlled by the Whigs three to one, was expected to rule that aliens could not vote.

There was furious objection from the Democrats to such a ruling and they controlled the law-making process. Perhaps out of fear of Democratic legislative action, the court finally ruled that the aliens could vote. But it was too late. The Democrats were angry at the Illinois Supreme Court and anxious to take charge.

Their proposal to do it was simple—add five more members to the Illinois Supreme Court, to be chosen by the Democratic legislature. There was already one Democratic member on the court (the able and thoroughly dishonest Theophilus W. Smith), and

[79] To John A. McClernand, January 29, 1841, *Letters of Stephen A. Douglas*, 95.

three Whigs. If the plan carried, it would give the Democrats a 6–3 edge on the court.

The fact that the lone Democrat on the Supreme Court was a man of such low character aroused great reaction to any court packing. The Democrat, Theophilus W. Smith, less than a month before the session started, had been in Chicago leading a mob which wanted to lynch a man. The judge was carrying a pistol, but the sheriff of Cook County successfully resisted the mob and the Supreme Court Justice.[80] Whig reaction to more Democrats on the Supreme Court was the same as Hardin's: "A beautiful set of scoundrels they will elect to these offices."[81]

Raising doubts for many people was the fact that Illinois had a far from illustrious history of Supreme Court Justices. Governor Ford tells about one of the first justices, William P. Foster:

> He was a great rascal, but no one knew it then, he having been a citizen of the State only for about three weeks before he was elected. He was no lawyer.... He was believed to be a clever fellow. ... He was assigned to hold courts in the circuit on the Wabash; but being fearful of exposing his utter incompetency, he never went near any of them. In the course of one year he resigned his high office, but took care first to pocket his salary, and then removed out of the State. He afterwards became a noted swindler, moving from city to city, and living by swindling strangers and prostituting his daughters, who were very beautiful.[82]

The *Chicago American* commented, "Men with whom you would not trust your dinner are now seeking situation on the bench of the Supreme Court."[83]

Debate on the judicial proposal was long and bitter. A Democratic senator wrote, "The debates on the subject have been vehement & exciting partaking much of party abuse & personal crimination. Should the measure fail, Judges . . . may be expected to display the malignity of their hearts against all those lawyers

[80] *Northwestern Gazette and Galena Advertiser*, November 20, 1840.

[81] Hardin to Stuart, January 20, 1841, letter at the Chicago Historical Society Library.

[82] Ford, *History of Illinois*, 28–29.   [83] February 16, 1841.

who have with manly firmness advocated this bill. I have heard many gentlemen of the bar of the first respectability declare that they could not again appear before the supreme court unless that court should be reorganized."[84] Newspapers were just as violent in their beliefs as legislators. The *Quincy Argus* reported that after Baker spoke against the bill he "sat down foaming and raging like a mad man."[85]

The measure passed on February 1 by a vote of 45–43. Since the party makeup was 50–40, Democrats outnumbering the Whigs (one member had no party affiliation), this meant that the Whigs were receiving some Democratic support. "Packing the court" was not an issue on which Democrats would be united—as a Democratic President discovered almost one hundred years after this Illinois incident. But the 45–43 vote showed that if one more Democrat had switched, the measure would have been defeated.

Thirty-five members filed a protest, setting forth why they felt passage of the judicial change was not good policy. One of these was Abraham Lincoln. The author of the protest appears to have been Hardin. Had Lincoln been in better health, he probably would have authored the protest, as he did most other Whig documents.

Because the judges would be Democratic, Lincoln opposed the move to make the clerks of the circuit courts appointive rather than elective.

The men elected to the Illinois Supreme Court—all Democrats—actually were men of ability. They included Thomas Ford, soon to be governor; Sidney Breese, soon to be a United States Senator; and Stephen A Douglas, who was twenty-seven years old—the youngest man ever to serve on the Illinois Supreme Court either before or since that time. Supreme Court judges received only $800 a year, so that those elected "accepted the judgeships merely as stepping stones to something better. Consequently, the judges, with very few exceptions, were active politicians, constantly scheming and electioneering for promotion to higher or more lucrative positions."[86]

---

[84] J. H. Ralston, January 30, 1841, IHL. Signature of person to whom his letter is addressed is not legible.

[85] February 20, 1841.

[86] Snyder, *Selected Writings*, 143.

Douglas took a "deep interest" in the measure and actively lobbied for it. One of the members described what happened: "One man from Southern Illinois was brought in sick and laid on a pallet in the north end of the Hall. The member from Champaign County, Mr. Busy [Busey] with the sick man was our 'forlorn hope' to carry the bill."[87] Douglas held Matthew W. Busey around the neck until the roll call was completed, then Busey stepped forward and announced his vote for the bill. The sick man and Busey gave the court plan the majority it needed.

One newspaper explained the story of the "sick" man:

> He went into the House drunk, gave the vote in the same condition, and in retiring from the House FELL off the stair steps and injured himself so badly that he was carried to his place of boarding. . . . Being unable to walk to the House, he provided his party friends to pack him up stairs and lay him on a couch in one corner of the House, and in this position he voted the second time for the bill.[88]

The *Missouri Republican*, which called Douglas

> *That Little chief—that ruthless man,*
> *That head of a Republican clan,*

noted that Douglas made a speech for the bill in the lobby that was "most violent and Cataline."[89] Douglas received the smallest number of votes of any of the men elected to the court. One unhappy anti-Douglas man wrote to a friend, "But Dug a great *Supreme Squire*. I tell you we're a great people."[90] The sponsor of the measure to elect the judges was not enthusiastic about the selection of the Little Giant: "Douglas is talented but too young for the office. On the whole, however, we could not do much better than to have elected him."[91]

[87] A. Cavarly to Lincoln, September 10, 1858, RTL.

[88] *Illinoian*, March 27, 1841.

[89] January 30 and February 1, 1841.

[90] M. McConnell to George T. M. Davis, February 17, 1841, Missouri State Historical Library.

[91] A. W. Snyder to Gustave P. Koerner, February 14, 1841, IHL.

An interesting sidelight is that Dan Stone, the member of the Long Nine who joined Lincoln in his antislavery protest in Lincoln's second term, received fourteen votes for one of the judgeships. It took a majority of the members of the House and Senate to secure election.

One of the men elected to the Supreme Court, Thomas Ford, later called the law "confessedly a violent and somewhat revolutionary measure."[92] The fight was an important one in Illinois history, but it was a fight in which Lincoln did little but vote.

In this session there was once again an election contest, Lincoln prominent in trying to decide it, particularly prior to "the fatal first." William J. Phelps, a Whig from Peoria County who was seated when the session began, voted for Lincoln for speaker. Democrat Norman H. Purple contested his seat. Lincoln urged early action on the question because "the heat of party would be augmented by delay."[93] The speaker declared these remarks out of order since there had been no mention of partisan heat. Lincoln also suggested that the two contestants "agree as to the voters about which there was no dispute, and that the committee should then take up the disputed votes and decide upon them one by one."[94] This was agreed to.

The Democratic majority of the committee favored seating the Democrat; the Whig minority was for seating the Whig. Because at this time all votes were public, the committee could and did determine the legality or illegality of the ballots cast. One voter was rejected because his father "does not recollect whether his son is 21 years of age or not."[95] About a month after the session began, the Whig won by a 48–33 vote, a number of Democrats having crossed over to support the Whig.

Toward the end of the session O. H. Browning, former state senator from Adams County, was approached about running as the Whig candidate for governor. He replied that he could not run, but he mentioned five whom he thought good prospects: Baker, Webb, Eddy, Jenkins, and Cyrus Walker. He added, "If the nomi-

[92] Ford, *History of Illinois*, 217.
[93] *ISR*, December 11, 1840.
[94] *Peoria Register and Northwestern Gazetteer*, December 11, 1840.
[95] *HJ*, 1840–41, p. 64.

nation is made without reference to the Internal Improvements system, Cyrus Edwards, Lincoln, Ninian Edwards, and others may be added to the list, and I will, with great pleasure, and in good faith, support any one of the gentlemen above named."[96]

"Hardin was the most active Whig member in the House," recalls an observer, "but Lincoln was more popular because of his uniform courtesy. While Douglas, then Secretary of State, was extremely positive in all his assertions of facts, Lincoln always used the subjunctive. He would say: 'If you will examine the record of such a date or on such a page, I think you will find this to be true,' never closing the door, so that an opponent could contest his position without questioning his veracity."[97]

But not all was business during the session.

"Some senators prefer a seat in the *gal*lery to one in the Senate Chamber. Why is this?" inquired the *Springfield Courier*.[98] The *Peoria Register* commented, "The number of chickens, turkeys, oysters, &c., that has disappeared since the meeting of the legislature is incalculable. . . . The number of gallons of Irish whisky manufactured into hot punch and punished, would if collected in one grand reservoir at the head of the Sangamon River and let loose, overflow the whole region."[99]

Lincoln was handling his share of measures of a purely local nature. As chairman of the committee "to vacate the town plat of Livingston," he added certain amendments which he drew up as a favor to colleagues, taking care of property problems in a small Sangamon County community, in Putnam County, and in St. Clair County. The St. Clair amendment—concerning "the south end of Charles Street" in Belleville—was rejected by the Council of Revision (the governor and Supreme Court justices, who as a group could veto bills), but finally the bill passed without the Belleville amendment.[100]

[96] Browning to Hardin, January 14, 1841, letter at Chicago Historical Society Library.

[97] *Chicago Tribune*, February 12, 1900, quoting A. J. Galloway, assistant enrolling clerk of the Senate.

[98] Quoted in *Chicago American*, January 19, 1841.

[99] December 11, 1840.

[100] *CW*, I, 220.

Another measure of local interest that Lincoln worked on was the "manufacturing of salt at the Gallatin Saline." Lincoln originally handled it in the House for the Senate sponsor, but voted against it when amended.[101] He said he could "go for the bill if he could be satisfied that we were not making a bad bargain."[102] He introduced a bill "to establish a ferry across the Illinois River." This ferry was to operate at Peoria, and the law specified that William L. May, the former Democratic candidate for Congress, was to run it.[103] This act also specified what the rates should be: "Man, six and one-fourth cents; man and horse, twelve and a half cents; gig, buggy, sulkey, or one-horse wagon, twenty-five cents."[104] Lincoln also introduced a measure "for the relief of the creditors of the late William Wernwag."[105] A bridge was to be constructed across the Sangamon River, and Wernwag, in charge of construction, had ordered certain materials and had some work done. Then he died. Lincoln's bill set up a procedure for going into the circuit court to receive the money from Sangamon County for Wernwag's obligations on the bridge project.

When residents of the new Menard County—which included Lincoln's old home of New Salem—wanted to change the boundaries of their county, Lincoln favored sending the measure to committee. His only comment on the controversial measure was that he "would obey the will of his constituents."[106]

Lincoln voted on a host of local measures. Examples include his opposition to extending the limits of Bond County; he voted against incorporating the Peoria Marine and Fire Insurance Company and the Exeter Manufacturing Company; and he voted to vacate the plat of the town of Iowa in Perry County. In most cases it is impossible to determine the reason Lincoln voted for or against a local measure. He probably relied on the counsel of colleagues whom he trusted in unfamiliar cases.

For other measures on which Lincoln voted, no roll call is re-

101 *HJ*, 1840–41, p. 86.
102 *ISR*, December 11, 1840.
103 *HJ*, 1840–41, p. 161.
104 *LIll*, 1840–41, p. 113.
105 *HJ*, 1840–41, p. 161.
106 *SgJ*, February 26, 1841.

corded. These included many of considerably less than state-wide importance which became law: a bill "to incorporate the Philomathean Society of Mount Carmel, Illinois";[107] to change the name of Mary E. Brown "to that of Mary E. Stribling";[108] to change the name of Catharine Marshall to Catherine Van Wagener, and of Adelia A. Scott to Adelia A. Trumble;[109] and to incorporate "the LeRoy Manual Labor University."[110]

At one point Lincoln received petitions both for and against Richard C. Norred's building a mill-dam across the Sangamon River. The final solution was a compromise bill presented by the three-member committee, probably worked out by Lincoln, that called for John Primm, Sr., "to build and maintain a mill-dam across the Sangamon River" and further allowed William Carpenter "to build a mill-dam across the Sangamon River at or near where he now keeps a ferry."[111]

In this session for the first time, Lincoln supported a move to have a new state constitution drafted. In earlier years he may have opposed it for fear that a new constitution would revive the question of whether Illinois was a slave state or a free state. Indicative of its citizens' acceptance of Illinois as a free state is that during this session a bill passed which made it easier for free Negroes to register as being free at any county courthouse. The measure went through both the House and Senate so easily that not even a roll call was required. The measure was introduced by a new legislator who was doing an effective job, twenty-seven-year-old Lyman Trumbull. Trumbull was "tall, well proportioned, with a slight stoop, probably owing to his great short-sightedness, and had rather light hair and blue eyes. His complexion was very pale."[112]

For United States senator, Lincoln cast his ballot for Cyrus Edwards, the Whig candidate for governor who had been narrowly defeated by Carlin and who was now serving in the House of Representatives. Democrat Samuel A. McRoberts was elected

107 *LIll*, 1840–41, pp. 126–27.
108 *Ibid.*, 206.
109 *Ibid.*, 211.
110 *Ibid.*, 298–300.
111 *Ibid.*, 189.
112 *Memoirs of Gustave Koerner*, Vol. I, 425.

77–50, with one vote—cast by Cyrus Edwards—going to Edward D. Baker. The Baker vote was another indication that many Whigs regarded Baker as a man of greater ability than Lincoln, even though Baker was Lincoln's junior both in age and in years of legislative service. This vote electing McRoberts took place on December 16, two weeks before the "fatal first." The *Alton Telegraph* said of McRoberts, "Public report does not speak very highly, either of his talents, or of his political honesty."[113]

Lincoln nominated Simeon Francis of the *Sangamo Journal* for public printer, but Francis was defeated as Lincoln knew he would be. Lincoln's other votes for individuals in this session were not particularly noteworthy; he generally voted for the Whig.

By December 17, 1840, it was cold enough for Richard Murphy of Perry County to move "that the Door-keeper of this House cause to be put up two additional Franklin stoves, that this House may be rendered more comfortable."[114] The motion carried.

When a matter regarding the control of liquor sales came up, one legislator moved "that after the passage of this act, no person shall be licensed to sell vinous or spiritous liquors in this State, and that any person who violates this act by selling such liquors shall be fined the sum of one thousand dollars, to be recovered before any court having competent jurisdiction."[115] It was an all-out prohibition on the sale of liquor in Illinois, and Lincoln, who did not drink, moved to table the amendment. The hard-drinking legislators supported Lincoln's motion 75–8.

When a motion was made by Hardin to adjourn from Christmas Eve, December 24, a Thursday, until the following Monday, the motion lost 51–28, Lincoln among those voting that there should be sessions on Christmas Day and on the Saturday following Christmas. While the vote to adjourn for those days failed, neither on Christmas Day nor the next day was a quorum present, so that on both days the speaker ruled that for lack of a quorum, the House would not meet. Lincoln is not recorded as present on the only roll call on December 24, the day before Hardin wanted to adjourn.

[113] December 19, 1840.
[114] *HJ*, 1840–41, p. 129.
[115] *Ibid.*, 136.

When a woman in Vermilion County wanted to give some property to the controversial Society of Friends (Quakers), a law to make this possible lost by a 50–23 vote, but Lincoln was one of those who wanted to give her that right.

Another strange, though less oppressive, piece of legislation came to the House from the Senate. It changed an appropriation for a library for the Supreme Court and legislature and—in the same bill—repealed the state premium on wolf scalps. The latter part of this "momentous" legislation became a matter of heated controversy during the session, provoking debate on several occasions. Lincoln's vote favored keeping the wolf bounty, but the measure changed from repealing the bounty on wolves to increasing it. Lincoln voted against the increase.

Lincoln supported a resolution which condemned the "monarchial financial experiments of Martin Van Buren," but the Democrats killed the strongly partisan resolution on a straight party vote.[116] On another occasion Lincoln supported a resolution praising Andrew Jackson's military accomplishments, but voted against a move to praise his presidential administration.

Toward the end of the session, the appropriation for the new capitol became a concern to Lincoln. Moves to relieve the citizens of Springfield from their obligation and commitment for the structure were defeated 50–33 and 69–15. Lincoln supported the effort to eliminate this obligation, not a surprising position for a Springfield legislator to take, but inconsistent with Lincoln's previous pledges to see that the money was raised. The state's appropriation in the original bill was for $20,000 to complete the work, and Lincoln successfully moved to change that figure to $30,000. He argued that many of the workers had not been paid and that their needs were "most urgent."[117] Then on Lincoln's motion the bill passed.

Lincoln headed the fight to pass a bill permitting the Springfield citizens, who had made the pledge of $50,000 for the capitol, to pay in internal improvements scrip, which meant a substantial reduction in the amount owed to the state, since the scrip sold for

[116] *Ibid.*, 170.
[117] *ISR*, February 5, 1841.

much less than par. That this would have been a dangerous principle, had it been applied to anything else, can be seen from the fact that in 1839, $616,870.70 was issued in scrip and in 1840, $1,342,-372.82. This in a state which had a balance in the bank of $33.91 as of December 1, 1840; the auditor estimated that for the year 1840 expenditures would exceed income by $112,040.81—not counting the tremendous internal improvements debt and expenditure. Taking any money in scrip under these circumstances was not wise, for Illinois needed all the cash it could get.

Some legislators were not happy with the job being done by two state House Commissioners, A. G. Henry and William Herndon, both friends of Lincoln, in supervising construction of the new capitol. Douglas and James Shields were authorized to examine the books, and they reported to the legislature that the books were not kept properly and laws were violated. Nevertheless, they recommended approval of the appropriation request; otherwise a "great injustice will be done mechanics, laborers," and others who have worked on the building.[118] It is difficult to determine how much in the various reports was political and how much fact. Henry and Herndon were Whigs, Shields and Douglas Democrats. But Shields and Douglas were not the only ones to issue criticism.

More serious criticism came from the Committee on Public Accounts and Expenditures, with the minority of Whigs on the committee agreeing. They pointed out that Henry and Herndon had been allowed three dollars per day in pay during the construction period, and that the two took this all days, including Sundays, when they did nothing to earn their pay. They said that the whole thing "evinces a determination on their part to compel the Legislature to sanction the expenditure of near another hundred thousand dollars in Springfield, the accomplishment of an object which the people of the State had a right to believe would have been accomplished by the promised donation of the citizens of Springfield."[119]

There were three state House Commissioners, and the third com-

[118] Senate Reports, *Illinois Reports*, 1840–41, p. 140.
[119] *Ibid.*, 238.

missioner also disagreed with Henry and Herndon, and added that money to be disbursed was placed with a Mr. Webster and sometimes "disbursed by him . . . in merchandise, instead of money."[120]

At one point during the session a legislator complained that "better accommodations were promised as an inducement to the removal of the seat of Government to this place."[121] Lincoln replied that "in common with the rest of the community, the citizens of Springfield felt the severity of the times." He stressed that no special promises were made to get the capital in Springfield. Lincoln added, "If the gentleman from Fulton thought he was paying too high for his bread and meat, let him go home and invite his constituents to come and set up a competition in this line of business."

The legislature added to "the severity of the times" by passing a bill "regulating the Sale of Property."[122] It provided a way of appraising property that favored the man who owed the debt, and said that unless two-thirds of this appraised value was bid at execution of the sale, the sale would be invalid. To his credit, Lincoln voted against it. The practical effect was to suspend the collection of debts, causing even more economic chaos. Ten legislators of both parties signed a protest to the passage of this measure, but Lincoln was not among them. The United States Supreme Court finally threw out the statute as "unconstitutional and void on the ground that they [the laws] impaired the obligation of contracts."[123]

The House passed, without even a roll call, an amendment to the Militia Act to the effect that, in the event of a call, those "who may volunteer or be drafted shall have the right of electing their own officers."[124] Lincoln, elected a captain in the Black Hawk War by his own men, perhaps was sympathetic.

Toward the end of the session, Lincoln introduced a bill "supplemental to the charter of the Springfield and Alton Turnpike

---

[120] House Reports, *Illinois Reports*, 1840–41, p. 126.

[121] *SgJ*, January 29, 1841.

[122] *LIll*, 1840–41, pp. 172–73.

[123] Arnold, *Reminiscences of the Illinois Bar*, 17.

[124] *HJ*, 1840–41, p. 319.

Company.''[125] The committee to which it was assigned reported it back with an amendment which permitted the railroad line to use state property. A legislator far from the area to be served by the railroad objected to the use of state land because it was being used to help one section of the state and not another. Lincoln replied that state property "would all be lost and go to ruin, if the principle be adopted that no one shall have any, for fear all shall not have some.''[126]

The measure had a strange history. It was referred to committee twice. The second time, the committee had additional amendments, and Lincoln at that point moved to table his own bill. Then it was revived and amendments placed on the bill; then it failed to get enough votes to make passage stage in the House; the next day the bill was brought to life again by a 55–19 vote, Lincoln not even voting on his own measure. Finally it was tabled; a few days later Lincoln again revived it and the measure passed by a 48–23 vote. It provided that the company could build a railroad from Alton to the Springfield area, and it had the usual provision that the state could buy the railroad after fifteen years.

Lincoln supported a move to order completion of the Central Railroad, but it lost 58–23. He favored chartering a company to build a railroad from LaSalle to Dixon. In line with his other votes to promote railroads and navigation, Lincoln supported moves to complete the Northern Cross Railroad from Springfield to Jacksonville.

When a measure came up "to authorize John Wilson to keep a ferry across the Mississippi River," Lincoln favored an amendment: "Provided that such rates be reasonable.''[127]

Lincoln worked hard, both in committee and on the floor, to support moves to complete the Illinois and Michigan Canal. Much of the final language of this bill was probably Lincoln's.[128] At one point Lincoln offered an amendment allowing the state to spend an additional $3,000,000 in bonds for completion of the canal.

---

[125] *Ibid.*, 325.

[126] *ISR*, February 19, 1841.

[127] *HJ*, 1840–41, p. 440.

[128] *Ibid.*, references throughout the proceedings.

Bissell moved to cut that figure in half, and Lincoln accepted the lesser figure without debate.[129] Wickliffe Kitchell, former attorney general who had resigned to become a House member, expressed amazement that with the state "already prostrated by debt . . . that gentleman [Lincoln] thought it would be for the interest of the State to go still deeper." Kitchell then ridiculed Lincoln.

Lincoln "begged leave to tell an anecdote. The gentleman's course the past winter reminded him of an eccentric old bachelor who lived in the Hoosier State. Like the gentleman from Montgomery [Kitchell], he was very famous for seeing big bugaboos in everything. He lived with an older brother and one day he went out hunting. His brother heard him firing back of the field and went out to see what was the matter. He found him loading and firing as fast as possible in the top of a tree. Not being able to discover anything in the tree, he asked him what he was firing at. He replied a squirrel—and kept on firing. His brother believing there was some humbug about the matter, examined his person and found on one of his eye lashes a big louse crawling about. It is so with the gentleman from Montgomery. He imagined he could see squirrels every day, when they are nothing but lice."[130]

The newspaper noted that after Lincoln's story the House "was convulsed with laughter." One observer related that laughter was so hearty that "all business was at once suspended. In vain the Speaker rapped with his gavel. Members of all parties, without distinction, were compelled to laugh. They not only laughed, but they screamed and yelled; they thumped upon the floor with their canes; they clapped their hands; they threw up their hats. . . . For the remainder of the session he [Kitchell] lapsed into profound obscurity."[131]

On the measure to authorize the sale of more bonds for the

---

129 *HJ*, 518–21, does not mention the amendment to the Lincoln proposal, but the *SgJ* of March 5, 1841, does. Since the amendment was one agreed to by all, the clerk of the House apparently included it in Lincoln's original amendment, rather than do the extra stenographic work involved in reporting an amendment to an amendment.

130 *SgJ*, March 5, 1841.

131 Francis F. Browne, *The Everyday Life of Abraham Lincoln* (New York, Thompson, 1886), 171, quoting James C. Conkling.

Illinois and Michigan Canal, Lincoln argued that "to prosecute the work now was in fact the most economical plan that could be adopted: to stop it, would involve the State in much more debt and ruin."[132] The debt-heavy legislators did not accept his argument, although the canal was ultimately completed.

When a lengthy bill came up which established a public highway system for the state, Lincoln was in the minority in voting against it. The measure carried 44–36.

Again in this session, the State Bank became a major item of business, and Lincoln upheld the interest of the bank in Springfield. By this time the banks in the state were hopelessly enmeshed with internal improvements, and the legislative attempts to save the banks without adequate attention to the internal improvements debt were destined to failure.

Some legislators were convinced the banks were somehow responsible for all the economic chaos in the state. A Pope County representative wrote to a friend, "J. A. McClernand has commenced an uncompromising War against all the Banks in the World."[133] Other legislators were doing the same. Chances of saving the State Bank did not look good.

Making the situation worse was the requirement for payment in specie. The president of the State Bank sent a communication to the legislature that "no resumption has taken place west of Pennsylvania." As the only bank to pay in specie it was placed "in a position of much difficulty."[134]

Lincoln wrote a State Bank bill introduced by Peter Green from Clay County. Lincoln probably felt the bill had better chances of passing if Green introduced it. Or he may not have felt up to the task of introducing it himself and going through the struggles of passage. It permitted the State Bank to charge interest up to 8 per cent on loans of less duration than seven months, and it permitted the State Bank to circulate bills of less than five dollars' denomination. When the measure ran into opposition, Lincoln added an amendment, hoping to make it more acceptable, but the

[132] *ISR*, March 12, 1841.
[133] George W. Waters to Henry Eddy, December 22, 1840, IHL.
[134] Senate Reports, *Illinois Reports*, 1840–41, p. 416.

bill was so drastically amended by others that Lincoln ended up voting against the measure he had originally drafted. Yet, strangely, he voted for the amendments. Amendments by others reduced the interest the State Bank could receive and increased requirement by the State Bank for loans to the state to take care of internal improvements interest.

Why did Lincoln support certain amendments on a bill he had drafted and then vote against the bill? There are three possibilities: (1) he was not feeling well; (2) he voted for the amendments not fully understanding them and when he did discover their tenor, he voted against the bill; or (3) he checked with one of the officials of the State Bank he consulted on these matters after the amendments were adopted and was advised that the changes would do more harm than good. We can only guess at the correct answer.

Those who disagreed with him, Lincoln felt, were trying to "crush the Bank" while he was trying to save "both it and the state."[135] At one point during the sessions, Lincoln and McClernand had a "peculiarly sharp and personal" debate of some length about the State Bank. Should the State Bank be the fiscal agent for the state? The Democrats were giving the Whigs trouble on this issue. Lincoln replied with some heat that he was "tired of this business. If there was to be this continual warfare against the Institutions of the State, the sooner it was brought to an end the better."[136]

In the final days of the session, Lincoln prevented an amendment which would have required the State Bank to pay the state 3 per cent on its capital stock each year; he also made the motion which killed an attempt to close the bank automatically if there were "any violations" of a proposed statute.

On State Bank matters, Lincoln's views frequently failed to carry and the final result was legislation he considered undesirable. Within one year the State Bank had to close its doors. It would have been even rougher in the legislature for the State Bank but for its branches in Galena, Quincy, Jacksonville, Vandalia, Alton, Belleville, Mount Carmel, Danville, and Lockport, the last branch

135 *ISR*, March 5, 1841.
136 *Northwestern Gazette and Galena Advertiser*, February 17, 1841.

established as a result of a move from Chicago. In each of these areas people had some obligations to the bank and contacted their legislators.

A minor but much-discussed matter concerning the State Bank was the "Bill for the Relief of William Dormady," a measure introduced by Richard Murphy of Cook County.[137] Dormady had alleged in court that certain State Bank notes he had were burned. When the jury ruled against him, he tried to get a bill through the legislature. Murphy felt the State Bank was using illegal means to avoid paying the bill. Lincoln spoke on the matter at least twice. He declared that Murphy "without investigation . . . charged fraud and dishonesty upon the Bank."[138] He also stressed the importance of the legislature's abiding by court decisions. The measure, introduced early in the session, under Lincoln's leadership was defeated 45–30 in the final week.

One Springfield observer wrote to a friend, "I have no doubt but the bank will get any kind of a suspension law or almost any other law its friends will ask."[139] He charged that the State Bank has "bought up enough to defeat any bill they wanted, or to pass what they wanted."

This was not the case, although unethical conduct on the part of the bank is not difficult to imagine. The State Bank did not get all it wanted, but the legislature was not unkind either. Probably one reason was that Lincoln's sub-treasury speech of the previous session had "astutely allied the Whigs and a faction of the Democrats in support of the State Bank."[140]

A somewhat unusual resolution was introduced calling on Congress "to vote against all further appropriations for the military academy at West Point."[141] Lincoln supported the resolution, but it was buried in a committee. Feeling existed around the nation that West Point had become something other than what it was thought to be intended for, to be of assistance to the states.

[137] *HJ*, 1840–41, p. 138.

[138] *SgJ*, December 25, 1840.

[139] M. McConnell to George T. M. Davis, February 17, 1841, Missouri State Historical Society Library.

[140] Harry E. Pratt, *Lincoln in the Legislature* (Madison, Fellowship of Wisconsin, 1947), 10.

[141] *HJ*, 1840–41, p. 353.

The Whigs and a minority of Democrats voted 45–33 to urge passage of a national bankruptcy act by Congress, a matter of bitter national dispute. Lincoln voted with the Whigs in favor of a bankruptcy act. A motion to add corporations to those who could go into bankruptcy lost 42–38, Lincoln siding with the majority.

Lincoln supported a measure "confining Justices of the Peace and Constables to their districts."[142]

Lincoln drew up an amendment appropriating eighty-one dollars for William W. Watson of Springfield "for the use of a room for the Supreme Court twenty-seven days at their June term 1840."[143] But rather than risk opposition because of his Whig connections and his work for Springfield, which some resented, Lincoln had his friend Ebenezer Peck, a Democrat, introduce it and it carried.

A matter that caused much discussion in Illinois and beyond the state's borders was legislation to assist the Mormons, who had recently been moving into Hancock County, Illinois, from Missouri, where public officials had not been sympathetic to their "strange" religion. An act to incorporate the city of Nauvoo passed the House so easily that it needed no roll call, but soon legislators were being questioned about what they had done. Two of the unusual features were the authorization to establish a university, to be called "The University of the City of Nauvoo," and the authority to "organize the inhabitants of said city . . . into a body of independent military men, to be called the 'Nauvoo Legion.' "[144] Actually this legion was subject to all other state and federal laws and to the call of the governor, but this did not halt widespread talk about an "independent military force" which the legislature had authorized the Mormons to organize.

It was easy to secure this legislation because the Mormons were not solidly aligned with either party. They had been voting Democratic under the leadership of Joseph Smith, but then the Democrats in Washington turned down a Smith request. Congressman John Reynolds tells of bringing Smith to the President: "When we were about to enter the apartment of Mr. Van Buren, the prophet asked me to introduce him as a 'Latter-Day-Saint.' It was

[142] *Ibid.*, 400–401.   [143] *CW*, I, 239.   [144] *LIll*, 1840–41, pp. 52–57.

so unexpected and so strange to me, the 'Latter-Day-Saints', that I could scarcely believe he would urge such nonsense on this occasion to the President. But he repeated the request, when I asked him if I understood him. I introduced him as a 'Latter-Day Saint', which made the President smile."[145] Smith asked for money for damages done to the Mormons in the state of Missouri, but Missouri's two Democratic senators resisted such a move.

In August of 1840, the Mormons supported the Whigs. This meant that both political parties were anxious to please the independent-voting Mormons, and getting several bills through the legislature, including the militia proposal, was not difficult. Less than a year after the legislature adjourned, Smith wrote an open letter: "In the next canvass, we shall be influenced by no party consideration. . . . We care not a fig for Whig or Democrat; they are both alike to us, but we shall go for our friends, our tried friends, and the cause of human liberty, which is the cause of God. . . . [Stephen A.] Douglas is a master spirit, and his friends are our friends."[146]

Initially, much sympathy existed for the Mormon's plight. The *Sangamo Journal* referred to them as "that persecuted people" and protested "the outrages committed upon them" in Missouri.[147] But this sentiment gradually changed.

There was some reason for the Mormons to organize a military force. Led by Smith, the Mormons had settled in Missouri but had been forced to move from place to place. As their numbers grew, so did their Missouri neighbors' fear of them. Finally Governor Boggs—in 1838—ordered the Mormons to "be exterminated or driven from the state."[148] They fled across the Mississippi into Quincy, Illinois, where the residents gave them a warm welcome, regarding them as poor people who were being persecuted for their religious beliefs. From Quincy the Mormons moved to nearby Hancock County, where they settled in a small village called Com-

[145] Reynolds, *My Own Times*, 367.

[146] George R. Gaylor, "The Mormons and Politics in Illinois, 1839–1844," *ISHSJ*, Spring, 1956.

[147] January 19, 1841.

[148] Clyde E. Buckingham, "Mormonism in Illinois," *ISHSJ*, June, 1939.

merce City. Smith changed the name to Nauvoo. Mormonism flourished and so did Nauvoo, which soon became the largest city in Illinois.

But the flow of people with different religious beliefs unsettled the older residents of the area. In addition, the Mormons "vastly outvoted the southern settlers in Hancock County, who, of course, bitterly resented abolitionist domination."[149] Soon anything that went wrong was blamed on the Mormons. Some division within the ranks of the Mormons added "fuel to the fire."

Mormon records for 1842 describe Nauvoo as "a city of 10,000 inhabitants with thousands more settled in the immediate vicinity."[150] This was obviously becoming a powerful political force in the state, and any individual or party that lost the Mormon vote added his voice to their other critics.

The climax came in 1844 when Smith and his brother were killed by a mob while they awaited trial. This last session of Lincoln's in the legislature, 1840–41, was only three years before Smith's death. Legislation enacted by Lincoln and his colleagues helped the Mormons temporarily, but in the long run it created more antagonism toward the misunderstood people.

Besides the act incorporating the city and authorizing the university and the militia, a separate act was passed authorizing "a public house of entertainment to be called Nauvoo House." In accordance with Mormon teaching, "spiritous liquors of every description" were forever prohibited from the establishment. Of great interest was the next to last paragraph of the act: "And whereas Joseph Smith has furnished the said association with the ground whereon to erect said house, it is further declared that the said Joseph Smith and his heirs shall hold by perpetual succession a suite of rooms in the said house, to be set apart and conveyed in due form of law, to him and his heirs by the said trustees as soon as the same are completed."[151]

Also passed was the incorporation of the "Nauvoo Agricultural

---

[149] Herbert Spencer Salisbury, "The Mormon War in Hancock County," *ISHSJ*, July, 1915.
[150] Buckingham, "Mormonism in Illinois."
[151] *LIll*, 1840–41, pp. 131–32.

and Manufacturing Association," which had as its purposes "the promotion of agriculture and husbandry in all its branches, and for the manufacture of flour, lumber and such other useful articles as are necessary for the ordinary purposes of life."[152] Named as one of the commissioners for the corporation was Joseph Smith.

That the somewhat unusual protective measures taken by the Mormons were thought necessary is understandable, because even in the courts they seldom received justice. Judges tended to follow public opinion—and public opinion was not with the Mormons. The *Missouri Republican* of St. Louis noted: "Judge King lately presided at an anti-Mormon meeting in Ray County. He is the Judge of that Circuit, and the Mormon prisoners, now in jail, are to be tried before him. Truly, they have an excellent chance for a fair and impartial trial!"[153]

Nauvoo was but one of many cities Lincoln and the other legislators helped. Lincoln took special interest in a minor amendment to the city charter of Springfield, a Senate bill, which he helped guide through the House.

When there was debate over salaries for public officials, in this session Lincoln generally voted for the lower figure. For example, the attorney general's salary Lincoln voted to lower from $1,600 to $1,000. He also voted to reduce the pay of legislators from four to three dollars a day.

For each day of the session all members received four dollars. There were ninety-eight days, for which members were paid a total of $392.00. Since Lincoln lived in Springfield, there was no allowance for travel for him. Included in the ninety-eight days were thirteen Sundays on which the General Assembly did no business. Lincoln also was paid fully for all sessions he missed during this final term.

Lincoln voted against a bill to license "merchants, auctioneers, money brokers and others."[154]

There was much discussion about taxing ("licensing," a better sounding word, was frequently used) doctors and lawyers. Hardin, a handsome man popular with the women, wanted to exclude from

[152] *Ibid.*, 139–41.   [153] January 8, 1839.   [154] *HJ*, 1840–41, p. 446.

any tax "female Practitioners of the healing art"; Hardin won, but Lincoln voted to tax them.[155] Lincoln and a 41–28 majority voted against a move to tax lawyers ten dollars in each county in which they practiced. Later, the matter came up again—only this time it was fifteen dollars—and Lincoln made the motion which killed the idea.

One of the House members—probably in jest—suggested a tax of ten dollars on House members and twenty dollars on Senators. Along with all other moves to tax legislators, it failed. Wickliffe Kitchell, the former attorney general who was serving in the House, moved to tax all legislators five dollars. Lincoln told the House that there was an unwritten rule preventing members "from voting in cases in which they were interested and it appeared to him they were interested in this case."[156] The newspaper account reported that Lincoln's reply drew laughter—and the proposed tax failed.

With five days to go in the session and with work piled high, the House voted to limit each legislator to ten minutes debate on any topic.

On one of the final days a resolution passed by a 57–15 vote calling for a constitutional amendment limiting the President of the United States to one term. Lincoln voted for it. Had it passed the other states and Congress, it might have prolonged his life. The *Rock River Express* spoke for many Illinois citizens when it said, "For obvious important reasons, a President of the United States should hold his office for only one term."[157]

Newspaper comments on the legislature were generally most unsympathetic. "We anticipate that the state will derive no benefit from its labors," said the *North Western Gazette and Galena Advertiser*.[158] The *Alton Telegraph* called the session "disgraceful and disastrous."[159] A citizen went even further and characterized them as "outcast Devils down at Springfield."[160]

[155] *Ibid.*, 446–47.

[156] *ISR*, March 12, 1841.

[157] January 23, 1841.

[158] December 14, 1840.

[159] February 12, 1841.

[160] Henry A. Griswold of Chicago to Lt. John W. Phelps, January 15, 1841, Chicago Historical Society Library.

Lincoln opposed a rule change which would have required a member to vote if present. In legislative bodies there are times when the individual legislator considers it politically wise not to vote, and there are times when he cannot agree with either opponent or proponent. The proposed rule change lost 61–22.

Toward the end of the session a motion was passed that whenever there was a "call of the House" the absentees should be listed. The "call of the House" is a parliamentary device used early in a legislative session simply as a stalling device, but later in the session as a means to insure a quorum. Whenever a legislator who has a measure coming up sees attendance lag or sees few present when he is about to make an important speech, he can demand a "call of the House," which means that House members off the floor are rounded up—sometimes by police—and then the roll is taken. The motion to record the absentees carried 54–14, Lincoln one of the fourteen opposing it.

On four occasions during the last three weeks a "call of the House" was requested, and each time Lincoln was absent. Lincoln may have absented himself frequently during the session with instructions to a page to inform him immediately at his law office— just across the street—when there was a roll call. Ordinarily, this would have protected him because "Lincoln" is half way through the alphabetical roll call, and it was common for a legislator to "explain his vote" as his name was reached. But the "call of the House" is a quick, simple roll call where the only response is "Present." In all four instances when Lincoln was absent for the "call of the House," he was present for the roll calls immediately preceding and following the quick "call of the House." This would indicate a plan to be present at roll calls, but frequently absent otherwise.

On the recorded roll calls during the session (including the short special session), Lincoln voted 397 times and did not vote ninety-two times, a much higher absentee record than at any previous session. Lincoln's ninety-two absences compares with an average of 53.7 absences by his House colleagues. Lincoln voted with the majority 188 times, with the minority 106 times. Procedural motions—tending to be somewhat partisan since usually no issues are

271

involved—found Lincoln with the majority thirty-two times and with the minority forty-one times.

But regardless of all the voting records and statistics, it was evident that Lincoln was somewhat tired of life as a state representative. He had had trouble with people in his own party in Sangamon County, and on the two elections in 1840, when his name was on the ballot, he trailed the rest of his party in votes.

Lincoln did not run again in 1842. He wanted a change of scenery.

After the session, things started to get back to normal in Illinois. Within a week the *Alton Telegraph* had switched from political advice to admonitions to mothers on rearing children: "Do not give them hot food. . . . Hot food will injure the teeth and stomach."[161]

Within a week Stuart wrote to Daniel Webster, the designated United States secretary of state:

> The post of Charge d'Affaires at Bogota, New Granada, is at present occupied by James Semple, a citizen of the State of Illinois. The Whigs of that State, believing that, if a vacancy should occur in that office, by resignation or otherwise, it would, as a matter of course, be filled by a Citizen of the same State, have requested me to present the name of Abraham Lincoln, as one well qualified to fill such vacancy. Mr. Lincoln possesses talents of a very high order, his personal character is without reproach, he is a favorite with the people and his appointment would be regarded as a compliment to the State.
>
> Believing him honest and capable, I would add my own earnest wish to that of my friends at home, that the New Administration may bestow that appointment upon him, and shall be happy to acknowledge it, as a favor shown to my State, to my friends, and to myself.[162]

[161] March 6, 1841.

[162] F. Lauriston Bullard, "When John T. Stuart Sought to Send Lincoln to South America," *Lincoln Herald*, October–December, 1945.

13

Lincoln and the Issues

The true rule in determing to embrace, or reject anything is not whether it have any *evil* in it; but whether it have more of evil than of good. There are few things *wholly* evil, or *wholly* good. Almost everything, especially of governmental policy, is an inseparable compound of the two; so that our best judgment of the preponderance between them is continually demanded.—ABRAHAM LINCOLN, six years after retirement from the Illinois House of Representatives[1]

WHAT WAS Lincoln's overall record on the major issues in four terms in the legislature?

While the significance of his votes is not apparent in every case, the overall picture of the stand he took on issues is rather clear.

In this chapter no attempt is made to analyze his position on internal improvements, already dealt with in considerable detail in several chapters, or on the slavery issue, discussed in Chapter VI. The main issues, together with Lincoln's judgment and action with regard to them, follow in alphabetical order.

Agriculture

In his first session Lincoln voted for the incorporation of agricultural societies. His strong support of internal improvements can also be considered a vote favorable to agriculture. One of his beliefs was that better transportation facilities would mean a greater

[1] *CW*, I, 484, from a speech delivered in the U. S. House of Representatives, June 20, 1848.

demand for Illinois farm products and therefore higher prices for the farmers. He generally favored measures he considered helpful to the small farmer.

Banks

One of Lincoln's great interests was supporting the State Bank in Springfield, which he consistently worked for in all four terms. He was generally sympathetic to other banking interests also. He voted once against extending the charter of the Bank of Kaskaskia, but this may have been because he thought Kaskaskia a dying community. Later he changed his mind and voted for continuing the charter. He regularly supported the Shawneetown Bank of Illinois. He opposed measures which he felt would be harmful to banks, such as legislative investigations, prohibition against issuing bank notes of less than five dollars, and proposals for making bank stockholders responsible for bank debts. On proposals to investigate loans to legislators, and relations of the legislature to the State Bank, he had a mixed record. He was not averse to such investigations, but feared their effect on the State Bank.

Business

An unsuccessful businessman himself, Lincoln was sympathetic to the problems that business faced. His record, with few exceptions, must be considered good. The major exception is internal improvements, which ultimately did damage to business in Illinois, although Lincoln's intent was good.

In voting on the many corporations the legislature had to approve or disapprove, it is not always clear why he voted favorably or unfavorably. Sometimes the directors named in these various bills belonged, or did not belong, to his political party. It was common for many of these corporations to be well supplied with legislative names, but Lincoln was not involved in this type of "conflict of interest."

He consistently opposed amendments which would make stockholders responsible for the debts of the corporation. He almost always voted against giving future legislators the power to "alter, amend or repeal" the corporation charter.

He favored limited partnership; he voted for mechanic's liens; he supported measures to apprehend horse thieves. When proposals were made to license businesses, he generally opposed them. On the four occasions when he favored licensing, he leaned toward small license fees.

Church and State

Lincoln consistently opposed adjourning on Christmas Day, perhaps because legislators were paid for working on holidays and Sundays.

Some interrelationship between church and state was assumed. It caused little comment, for example, when the warden of the state penitentiary, whom Lincoln had helped into office, reported that of the thirty men in confinement, "but three have ever attended Sabbath School and but one has been a member of a Temperance society. The Sabbath, by all, has been disregarded since they came to the west."[2]

In his first term he supported a bill giving all religious societies certain basic freedoms; the measure passed 35–15. In his third term he revived a motion to have the sessions open with prayer. In his final term he unsuccessfully supported a person's right to give property to the controversial Society of Friends (Quakers).

Convention System for Political Parties

At first he strongly opposed the convention system brought to Illinois by Stephen A. Douglas. As the Democrats grew stronger by using the system, Lincoln changed his opinion. A year after he retired as state representative, Lincoln wrote to a friend in Petersburg, "I am sorry to hear that any of the Whigs of your county, or indeed of any county, should longer be against conventions."[3]

A New State Constitution

Lincoln at first opposed the writing of a new state constitution. This opposition may have been rooted in the fear of seeing the

2 *HJ*, 1838–39, December 6, 1838, report of B. S. Enloe.
3 *CW*, I, 318.

slavery issue revived. In later years, however, so many people had come to Illinois because it was a free state that slavery supporters no longer nourished hopes of making Illinois a slave state, so that he ceased opposing a new constitution.

Even in 1841 there were "some fearful apprehensions" about the proposed convention to alter the constitution. An Illinois newspaper editor wrote to a friend, "It has been publicly stated here that many of the members of the Legislature voted for that measure (calling a convention) with the intention of making an attempt to introduce Slavery into our State —and that *this* is one of the objects of the proposed convention. It is further stated—and that too, by those who have opportunities of knowing, that many of our leading politicians are warmly in favor ot if."[4] If Lincoln had fears about slavery in connection with a new state constitution, those fears were shared by others. But he must have gradually seen the need for a new state constitution; this need became more urgent over the years.

Counties

No clear pattern emerges as to Lincoln's views of state relationships with counties except that he was far-sighted in opposing the creation of small counties.

Courts

Lincoln opposed the major court change which occurred during his last term, the addition of five members to the Illinois Supreme Court, thus making a Democratic court out of a Whig court. He consistently voted for the restriction of the authority of the justices of the peace and the constables. He supported legislation to permit the assignment of judges with light loads to areas with crowded dockets. He consistently voted for the right of legislators as well as the courts to grant divorce. He favored the election of the clerks of the courts, so long, at least, as party interests were not adversely affected. He supported the licensing of lawyers, but opposed the proposal to charge lawyers ten dollars for each county in which they practiced.

[4] Th. Gregg, editor of the *Carthaginian*, to John Russell, August 5, 1841, IHL.

Economy

His record in economy might have been a good one except for one issue—internal improvements. But since this blunder, in which Lincoln shared illusions with many others, was so monumental, his record must be classified as poor by any gauge. Throughout his service he voted for the scheme that saddled the state with a debt it did not ever pay completely. Illinois did not even pay the face value of the debt (in the form of bonds and scrip) until years after Lincoln's death. It was an unbelievably chaotic project foisted on the state by some of the most brilliant men ever to serve in its legislative halls.

Anything else in this field must be considered minor compared with this ill-conceived venture, but in other fiscal matters Lincoln tended to be conservative. Whether a room he considered unnecessary was to be rented or salaries were to be kept down, he carefully weighed the cost—with this one tremendous exception of internal improvements.

Education

Somewhat surprisingly, Lincoln's record in the field of education was not particularly good. In a state which badly needed a system of free public schools, he generally voted against legislation which would have moved the schools ahead.

His record shows that he was concerned about the poor quality of teachers. The first school journal of Illinois, published in 1837, was able to survive only one year "because the teachers were unable to understand its methods. . . . We could expect little of teachers because little was expected of them by the people."[5]

In many schools there was much discipline but little learning. This may have influenced Lincoln. One of Lincoln's legislative colleagues was a teacher, and rules like this one in his fellow legislator's school were typical in the schools of those days: "No school boy shall converse with or write to any school girl, unless such communication be strictly in reference to their studies."[6] To the easy-

[5] "The Common School—The Movement of 1835," *ISHSJ*, January 3, 1919.
[6] Ledger of Thomas J. Nance for the "Farmers Point School House," IHL.

going Lincoln the unnecessarily harsh rules of the academically weak schools must have been offensive.

But an even greater influence may have been the fact that in Sangamon County schools were flourishing. An 1837 state report showed seventy-eight schools in Sangamon County, more than in any other county. There were five thousand students (a remarkably high figure), more than twice as many as in any other county. Cook County (which includes Chicago) had only three hundred students in the same report. Six counties had no schools.[7] One prominent Sangamon County leader, George Forquer, probably summed up the thinking of the majority when he wrote that he doubted the "practicability of . . . any coercive system of common schools."[8]

The unpopularity of the education tax levy passed in 1825 may have affected Lincoln. Public reaction to this tax was so severe that the law was repealed.

But whatever the cause, the record is there. Generally he did not vote in support of the educational program. Yet whenever votes were needed for training the handicapped, he could be counted on, or for incorporating private colleges and academies. The state's financial dilemma, largely due to internal improvements, may have been responsible for his not too enlightened record in the field of public education. At no time did he serve on the Education Committee. Educational matters which effected Sangamon County were usually handled by other legislators.

Executive Authority

Lincoln generally favored increasing the governor's authority in Illinois. At this time legislative power was at its height in the state, and the executive power was weak. Lincoln favored giving the governor authority to name state's attorneys rather than have the legislature do it; he favored giving the governor greater administrative authority over appointed officials. But when some legislators did not want to pass resolutions unless they had guber-

[7] "Letter to the Auditor of Public Accounts . . . showing the condition of the schools for the year 1837," submitted to the Senate January 7, 1839, 2–3.

[8] *SgJ*, July 12, 1832.

natorial approval, he defended the legislature's right to pass resolutions independently of the state's chief executive.

Federal Government

With the exception of the slavery issue, Lincoln followed Whig thinking on matters which related to the federal government, particularly banking. He was sympathetic to proposals to limit the President to one term in office. His most creative work was his persistent urging that the federal government should help the states through grants of land it held. Understandably, the federal government was less than enthusiastic.

Foreign Affairs

The state legislature had almost nothing to do with foreign affairs. Even at the national level interest was not intense. His most significant act in this field occurred when in his first term he voted against a paragraph in a resolution which denounced France in some inflammatory language.

Interest

Lincoln strongly supported moves to restrict interest rates. In his third term he sponsored an amendment that made interest in excess of 12 per cent illegal. But when some of his colleagues wanted to impose unrealistically low interest rates on the State Bank, not because they were for low interest but because they wanted to kill the State Bank, he opposed them.

Liquor

Next to the slavery protest signed by Lincoln and Dan Stone, no part of Lincoln's legislative career has received so much attention as his voting on liquor legislation. Much of what has been written, however, by both the "wets" and the "drys" represents the writers' rather than Lincoln's views.

He himself did not drink, and he would have liked to see others follow his example. But he did not believe governmental action was the way to achieve temperance. It is not true that he was "consistently" on the side of the "liberal elements," as one of the best writers in the field states, but it is almost true.[9] During his last term, when an all-out prohibition amendment was introduced, Lincoln made the motion to kill it, and the motion carried 75–8. In his third term he voted against a local option amendment, and it failed when there was a 39–39 tie. If Lincoln had supported this proposal, it would have carried.

Of interest also is Lincoln's action in striking the words that authorized members of the Springfield board of trustees, on which he was serving, to license a liquor establishment. Apparently he did not relish assuming that particular burden.

Fourteen years later Prohibition was a hotly fought issue, but he took no part in the fight on either side.

Military

Lincoln showed no leadership in this field, except to provide special tax benefits to veterans of the Revolutionary War. He opposed setting up a committee to change the laws on the militia, avoided voting on a bill to fine soldiers for delinquencies, and probably supported a bill—no record vote was taken—that those serving should have the right to elect their own officers. His military service in the Black Hawk War was not particularly noteworthy. Nor was his military record in the legislature.

Party Issues

Usually Lincoln worked with his Whig colleagues on party issues. There were exceptions, both on issues and in the selection of state officers, but on the whole he was a loyal Whig.

Patronage

While Lincoln generally voted for Whigs to fill vacant offices— and was criticized by his colleagues when he strayed from this practice—he never felt completely happy with this particular responsibility, either as legislator or as President. At the beginning of his last term in the House, he wrote to Stuart, "This affair of

[9] William H. Townsend, *Lincoln and Liquor* (New York, Press of the Pioneers, 1934), 50–51.

appointment to office is very annoying—more so to you than to me, doubtless. I am, as you know, opposed to removals to make places for our friends."[10]

As President, less than a year before his death, he wrote, "There is not a more foolish or demoralizing way of conducting a political rivalry, than these fierce and bitter struggles for patronage."[11]

The Poor

Lincoln had real compassion for those in dire circumstances, and this shows in his record. Whether it was helping secure an institution for the blind and deaf at Jacksonville, or a bill "for the relief of insolvent debtors," or one for the relief "of persons in case of ejectment," he took a hand in solving the problems of the poor he saw every day.

The "Little Bull" bill, which hurt the small farmer and caused the political death of many legislators, did not harm Lincoln. He had voted for people, not for cattle, and came out on the right side politically.

Procedural Matters

Lincoln's contributions in this field were practical and significant. He made the motion that stopped the endless reading of petitions before the whole House and referred them automatically to a committee. He initiated the practice of not amending bills when they came to their third reading (passage state), a change that is still being followed by the Illinois House of Representatives more than a century later. As House sponsor of a Senate bill, he helped to authorize committees to place witnesses under oath.

His voting on the matter of stopping debate shows no particular pattern. He was not a believer in unlimited debate, yet he did not wish to see debate cut off arbitrarily.

Reapportionment

Lincoln favored legislative houses which were not too large—a position easy to support with logic, difficult to muster votes for.

10 *CW*, I, 221.
11 *Ibid.*, VII, 340.

Regarding Officialdom

For men in public office Lincoln set high ethical standards. He himself was "made of better stuff than that of politicians reaching for the spoils of office."[12] This showed in his Illinois legislative service.

He sought to prevent legislators from abusing for personal gain measures such as internal improvements. He supported a resolution prohibiting legislators from seeking positions for themselves filled by the legislative body, a commonly abused practice. He was even a member of a small minority who believed legislators should not place their relatives into such positions. His record on matters of this kind show Lincoln to be a man of noble character and moral courage, for such positions are not kindly received by some colleagues with whom a legislator must work.

Otherwise, his positions on issues relating to the major public offices are not too unusual. He supported the auditing of some offices that were not being audited. He opposed electing the auditor of public accounts. He wavered between electing and appointing clerks. He favored the election of county recorders and surveyors.

Roads

Strangely, Lincoln was not a strong advocate of public roads. Of railroads and canals, yes, but public roads received his support consistently only when they were in his district. He took a negative attitude toward the single major effort made during his four terms to improve public roads. He supported legislation to require all men to work one day a year on their own local roads.

Salaries

Lincoln followed a middle road with regard to salaries for public officials, sometimes favoring, sometimes opposing increases— usually inclining to a more moderate raise than asked for.

Somewhat typical was the action taken on three measures in one day, February 18, 1841. A bill to raise the pay of Supreme Court judges from $1,000 to $1,500 he supported; one to raise the at-

[12] Randall, quoted by Thomas, *Portrait for Posterity,* 279.

torney general from $1,000 to $1,600 he opposed; a measure to raise the salary of the auditor of public accounts he did not vote on, even though he was present.

Sometimes he voted for, sometimes against, pay increases for legislators.

He favored raising pay for jurors from seventy-five cents to one dollar a day.

Taxation

Lincoln was a "high tax" man, supporting most moves for higher taxes. The situation faced by Illinois in consequence of internal improvements and its huge debt almost forced any responsible legislator to vote for higher taxes. There were several instances, however, when he voted against increases in taxation. He was particularly antagonistic to levying special taxes on various business groups and professions.

Voting Procedure

As previously mentioned, Illinois citizens voted "by voice." They walked in and told the clerk and election judge their choices, and they were so recorded. Twice there were proposals to have a secret paper ballot; once Lincoln was sympathetic, and once he was opposed.

Miscellaneous

This chapter has given the reader a brief overview of Lincoln's approach to the issues. Many other matters of less importance could have been touched upon. For example, the Lincoln record included support for bounty on wolf scalps; he supported a bill to prohibit betting on elections; he supported a bill reducing some of the harsher punishments in the state penal system; he opposed letting the citizens of Vandalia—particularly the Jackson supporters—have the hall of the House of Representatives to celebrate the anniversary of the victory at New Orleans in the War of 1812.

Such were the issues in eight important years in the life of Abraham Lincoln.

14

1854: Lincoln Runs, Wins, and Resigns

We are of the opinion that the Whigs will stick to Lincoln to the bitter end, even if it resulted in no choice this session & the consequent postponement of the election. . . . We also think that Bissel will be a candidate and will secretly urge his friends to press his name. In that event it is probable the free-soil or Anti-Nebraska Democrats will cling to him until the last with the hope of bringing the Whigs over to Bissel. If this shall prove to be the position of the parties and the tactics of each, it would seem that, either there would be no election, or that Bissel would be elected, which would probably be equivalent to no election. Either of these events would be better than the election of Lincoln.—STEPHEN A. DOUGLAS, December 18, 1854[1]

DURING THE PERIOD between 1842, Lincoln's last year as a legislator, and 1854, he maintained his interest in politics. He served one term, 1846–1848, in the United States House of Representatives, where he made two unpopular stands—against the Mexican War and for eventual removal of slavery in the District of Columbia. His political future did not look bright.

But things were happening, changing the picture.

In 1851, Harriet Beecher Stowe's *Uncle Tom's Cabin* was published, first in a magazine, then in book form. It helped to add to the numbers of militant antislavery citizens, as did the increasing number of New England area residents moving in.

[1] To Charles Lanphier, IHL.

Then in 1854, under the leadership of Douglas, the Missouri Compromise was repealed by the passage of the Kansas-Nebraska Act. The Missouri Compromise had been passed under the guidance and sponsorship of Henry Clay of Kentucky. It provided that Missouri was to be a slave state, but after that, new states to the north and west would be free. This was considered by most Northerners to be a sort of "gentleman's agreement." Douglas was trying to work out compromises satisfactory to all both in the North and in the South—and helpful in making Douglas President. Douglas introduced the Nebraska Bill on January 4, 1854. By the time the measure was amended and passed in May, it contained provisions for dividing Nebraska territory into the territories of Kansas and Nebraska—and the repeal of the Missouri Compromise.

This meant that slavery was now an open question in the states which could be organized north and west of Missouri; it previously had been settled that they were to be free states.

Douglas's argument in behalf of his legislation was that this gave each state the authority to make up its own mind. He argued that if a majority of the people wanted slavery, they should have it; if a majority did not want slavery, they should not have it. He wanted to "leave the people thereof perfectly free to form and regulate their domestic institutions in their own way."[2]

But there was tremendous public reaction to this. As one newspaper editor recalled: "When the Nebraska Bill passed there was an explosion in every Northern state."[3] The opposition was caused by the slavery issue, by sectional issues, and by people who were disgusted with Congress "breaking its word."

The public was not alone in being aroused.

Lincoln wrote of himself, "In 1854, his profession had almost superseded the thought of politics in his mind, when the repeal of the Missouri Compromise aroused him as he had never been before."[4] Another time he wrote, "I was losing interest in politics, when the repeal of the Missouri Compromise aroused me again."[5]

[2] Stephen A. Douglas, *Constitutional and Party Questions*, ed. by J. Madison Cutts (New York, Appleton, 1866), 86.

[3] Horace White, *Abraham Lincoln in 1854* (Illinois State Historical Society, 1908), 6.

[4] *CW*, IV, 67.   [5] *Ibid.*, III, 512.

Lincoln soon found himself making speeches against the repeal of the Missouri Compromise, first in the small communities of Winchester and Carrollton. But when Douglas returned from Washington, Lincoln took him on in public debate in some of the larger cities in the state.

It was in this speech, delivered several times during the campaign, that Lincoln gave a "broad and resounding statement" on the issue of slavery. Here for the first time he really made a relatively complete analysis of the problem facing the nation.

A newspaper reporter recalled:

> I have heard the whole of that speech. It was a warmish day in early October, and Mr. Lincoln was in his shirt sleeves when he stepped on the platform. I observed that, although awkward, he was not in the least embarrassed. He began in a slow and hesitating manner, but without any mistakes of language, dates, or facts. . . . I have heard celebrated orators who could start thunders of applause without changing any man's opinion. Mr. Lincoln's eloquence was of the higher type, which produced conviction in others because of the convictions of the speaker himself. . . . Mr. Lincoln did not use a scrap of paper.[6]

Friends persuaded Lincoln to run for the Illinois House of Representatives to further his views on this important issue of slavery in the new states. Getting him to run was not easy, and Lincoln's wife did not like the decision. He did not think of becoming a candidate for the United States Senate at the time, for the state constitution prohibited a House member from being a United States senatorial candidate. Just as important was the consideration that in 1853—two years earlier—when the legislature voted on the United States senatorship, the Whigs were outvoted 75–19. Lincoln was realistic enough not to expect these odds to change enough for the Whigs to win.

But he did want to hit the congressional action in repealing the Missouri Compromise. His plan was to elect enough Whigs, Free Soilers, and Democrats who were opposed to the Nebraska Bill to form a majority, which would then "instruct Douglas to vote for

[6] White, *Abraham Lincoln in 1854*, 10–11.

the repeal of the Nebraska Bill."[7] Douglas would have to do it or make the legislators very angry at him, for he had originally run for the United States Senate with the pledge that he would obey the instructions of the legislature in voting on measures in Washington.

Lincoln's aim was to get the Nebraska Bill repealed and the Missouri Compromise back on the books. He also allowed his name to go on the ballot "because it was supposed my doing so would help Yates," a local anti-Nebraska candidate for Congress.[8] The official canvas showed these results:

Abraham Lincoln	2,143
Stephen T. Logan	2,092
Joseph Ledler	1,456
John Alsbury	1,331

Lincoln and Logan were easy winners. Equally important, the Anti-Nebraska people had a majority in the legislature. Many more Whigs were elected than expected, and there was enough party uncertainty about some of the men elected so that it looked as if Lincoln had a chance to win the office of United States Senator. He started talking to friends and writing letters.

The responses were so favorable that he wrote on November 25 to the county clerk, "I hereby decline to accept the office of Representative in the General Assembly to which I am reported to have been elected. . . . I therefore desire that you notify the Governor of this vacancy, in order that legal steps be taken to fill the same."[9]

To become a United States senator, Lincoln had to resign from the legislature, because of the state constitution.

When the time came for voting, he found the legislature divided as follows: thirty-eight Whigs, but one a Nebraska Whig; eighteen Anti-Nebraska Democrats; forty Democrats; one Abolitionist, (the brother of Elijah P. Lovejoy); plus two unknown. If Lincoln could get the Anti-Nebraska Democrats in his corner, plus the Whigs, he could make it.

Getting the Whig support was his first problem, as he wrote to a friend, "Besides the ten or a dozen on our side, who are willing

[7] *CW*, II, 233.
[8] *Ibid.*, II, 289.
[9] *Ibid.*, II, 287–88.

to be known as candidates, I think there are fifty secretly watching for a chance."[10]

The incumbent United States Senator was James Shields, Lincoln's old legislative colleague and foe.

Stephen T. Logan nominated Lincoln. On the first ballot Lincoln received forty-five votes, Shields forty-one, and another former legislative colleague and an Anti-Nebraska Democrat, Lyman Trumbull, five. A few votes were scattered, and one man was absent. A majority—fifty—was needed for election.

Shields got the Democrats who sympathized with the Nebraska Act; Lincoln the Whigs and some Anti-Nebraska Democrats; Trumbull the Anti-Nebraska Democrats who would vote neither for a Nebraska man nor for a Whig. At one point or another forty-seven men voted for Lincoln, but that was not enough.

After nine ballots it was clear that the election might go as a compromise to the Democratic Governor Joel Matteson, who leaned toward the Nebraska men but was trying to avoid the battle as much as possible. Rather than elect a Democrat who at best straddled the fence, Lincoln threw his support to Lyman Trumbull, an Anti-Nebraska Democrat. Trumbull won on the tenth ballot. Logan, who had nominated Lincoln, wept openly on the floor.

Lincoln summed up what happened:

> The election is over, the Session is ended, and I am *not* Senator. I have to content myself with the honor of having been the first choice of a large majority of the fifty-one members who finally made the election. My larger number of friends had to surrender to Trumbull's smaller number, in order to prevent the election of Matteson, which would have been a Douglas victory. . . . A less good humored man than I, perhaps would not have consented to it—and it would not have been done without my consent. I could not, however, let the whole political result go to ruin, on a point merely personal to myself.[11]

[10] *Ibid.*, II, 303.
[11] *Ibid.*, II, 306–307.

15

What Did It All Mean?

It is fair to say . . . that his [Lincoln's] service as a legislator convinced him that politics was his ruling passion, and that he was well endowed to participate in the political circus. Above all, his horizons were greatly expanded in both political and speculative matters, he developed an even greater self confidence, and he had many of his rougher edges smoothed down. His legislative experience saw him grow from the awkward, slightly precocious, eager young man into a mature, competent, precise, and superbly humane individual, ready for further service and infinitely greater responsibilities —CLYDE WALTON, Illinois State Historian[1]

WHAT REAL significance did Lincoln's four terms in the Illinois House of Representatives have?

The biographer has to attach considerable significance to the simple fact that this was the first public office Abraham Lincoln held, and it was the public office he held longer than any other. But Lincoln's service in the Illinois House of Representatives meant much more to him and his countrymen than its duration would indicate.

Lincoln learned practical politics and found he enjoyed it.

When Lincoln entered the Illinois House of Representatives in 1834, he knew little about the complexities of practical politics. When he left the House of Representatives eight years later, he

[1] "Abraham Lincoln, Illinois Legislator," in *Lincoln for the Ages*, ed. by Ralph Newman (New York, Doubleday, 1960), 78.

had acquired not only a broad knowledge of the many issues on which a legislator must vote, but also an effective working knowledge of how the political world runs.

It is equally significant that, although he had his moments of melancholy, he liked political life as much as anything he had done. From the first campaign of 1832 until the assassin's bullet felled him, politics was "in his blood."

Lincoln became known politically.

When Lincoln entered the Illinois House of Representatives, he was an unknown quantity in the state. When he left eight years later, he had established a state-wide reputation—to some extent among the public, but principally among those who follow political life closely. He entered the Illinois General Assembly as an unknown individual and emerged eight years later as one of the acknowledged leaders of the state's Whigs.

As important as anything, Lincoln learned that he could stand shoulder to shoulder with the top men of the state.

The lean awkward youth of twenty-five who entered the Illinois House of Representatives keenly sensed his educational limitations. His leadership abilities had not been tested but for the brief period of the Black Hawk War where his service as a captain was not exceptional.

Four terms in the Illinois House gave Lincoln confidence in himself. He dealt with issues that confronted the top men of the state and could not help observing that he handled these issues as well as any of them. He served with men who had been in the United States Senate, and with those who were being considered for that post. Sitting near him in the House was Cyrus Edwards, who had narrowly missed being elected governor. Lincoln met and came to know intimately the top officials of the state.

By the end of his second term he found himself on an equal footing with the best of them. When nominated for speaker in his third term, he accepted the nomination with confidence.

Lincoln's legislative service more than anything else gave an easily depressed young legislator the confidence that he could serve his state and nation as capably as could anyone else.

Lincoln learned how wrong public opinion can be.

Illinois public opinion perhaps was never more insistent and more unanimous than in 1836 and 1837 when the issue of internal improvements was before the people. The most distinguished legislative body Illinois ever had was moved by the pressure of public sentiment to pass a foolish piece of legislation that burdened the state with a debt under which it labored for a generation. For Lincoln, whose biggest personal transaction had been the small debt of the Lincoln and Berry store, the immensity of the state debt must have been appalling. Though he voted for it, Lincoln—*afterwards*—saw clearly that the people were wrong, that public opinion should not have been followed blindly. He saw the same lesson in other issues also, but never more sharply than on internal improvements.

Six years after Lincoln left the Illinois House of Representatives, he served in the United States House of Representatives for one term. During his federal legislative service, he courageously opposed United States intervention in Mexican affairs. This time he went against public opinion, although he knew his stand against the Mexican War would be used against him, as it was in the political campaign of 1858 a decade later. Perhaps he would not have had the confidence to defy public opinion had he not learned through bitter experience that sometimes it must be resisted.

Experience taught him both the power of public opinion and how wrong it can be at times. Both lessons he carried with him to the presidency.

Lincoln was unmistakably an honest legislator.

In historical circles and in the legislative halls of Illinois it is sometimes contended Lincoln's legislative ethics were none too high. An examination of the record shows just the opposite. While many legislators were taking advantage of legislation to fill their pockets in ways that were legal yet definitely unethical, Lincoln refused to stoop to such practices, although as one of the leaders he had many opportunities.

It was common for legislators, for example, to arrange to have their names inserted as officers in corporations formed by the legislature. This was completely legal but ethically questionable, and Lincoln never did it.

A few published reports have connected Lincoln's vote for internal improvements with some legal fees from the Illinois Central Railroad. This is incorrect. His work for the railroad came many years after he had served in the legislature. The Illinois Central Railroad did not secure its charter until 1851, ten years after Lincoln had left the House.

The only "conflict of interest" in the record of Lincoln's legal work came in 1840. While still a member of the legislature, he received fifty dollars for sitting several days with the Board of Public Works to examine some claims. Because this is the only such case, and because other legislators reaped much larger financial harvests, it seems fair to assume that in this case, too, Lincoln performed the service to be of help to the state rather than for his own financial gain. Significant also is the fact that the bill for Lincoln's services was in another man's handwriting, not Lincoln's.

Was he an outstanding legislator?

He was an above-average legislator, but if you were to pick *one* legislator for a distinguished service award for each session, at no time would the award have gone to Lincoln. If you had been a spectator trying to determine which legislator might become the leader of the nation, it is not likely you would have chosen Lincoln.

Only when a moral issue like slavery came up did any hint of Lincoln's future greatness appear.

In his first term there were many legislators, including Stuart, more outstanding than Lincoln. In his second term there were several who showed more leadership, including first-term member Douglas. Lincoln's third term was his most effective, but even in this term there were four men with more impressive records. His final term was marred by "the fatal first," but even if that emotionally upsetting experience had not occurred, it is doubtful that Lincoln would have outshone Baker, Hardin, and Lyman Trumbull, a promising newcomer.

In his second term, if an observer had chosen the twelve top legislators, Lincoln might have been among them. In his third term, if an observer had chosen the six most prominent legislators, Lincoln probably would have been one of the six. In his final term his rank was somewhat lower.

No legislator was more honest. Perhaps none was more popular with his colleagues. But others were more creative, and others had more background to meet the problems the legislature faced. Lincoln was gaining knowledge for future service.

Allan Nevins writes, "Men who have Lincoln's generosity of spirit are rare, and men who combine it with his hardheaded practical sagacity are rarer still."[2]

Part of the "hardheaded practical sagacity" was the product of four terms in the Illinois legislature, facing the problems of government with rough-hewn colleagues on the frontier of the United States.

Lincoln's contribution to state government was not particularly significant. In his service in the legislature the state contributed much more to him than he contributed to Illinois. But he repaid that debt a thousand-fold.

He built with what he had and got, and what he received from the Illinois House of Representatives was right for the times and right for the man. The experience was his first step toward the Presidency; it was a big step and a long step.

After President Lincoln's sudden and tragic death, his body was brought to Illinois and lay in state in the Illinois House of Representatives on May 4, 1865. Here he had started his great work. It was fitting that he should be returned here when it ended.

[2] Allan Nevins, "Sandburg as Historian," *ISHSJ*, Winter, 1952.

16

Some Postscripts

I am still [mortified]. More from the fact that I placed a too high estimate on my relations with you, and did not know my position. . . . I did suppose I had a right to a small share of the spoils, but let it pass. . . . But my friend Lincoln they are cheating you. Do you know that you have not as yet appointed a single man from Illinois that was originally your friend. . . . [You] crowd out your friends and put in soreheads and grumblers. . . . Hoping still you may have a successful administration.—Letter to Lincoln from his old legislative colleague, Jesse K. Dubois, written in 1861.[1]

MANY OF THE MEN and issues Lincoln faced in the eight years of his Illinois legislative career, he confronted in later years. His relations with these men and issues furnish significant sidelights.

A complete follow-through would itself require a book longer than this one. This chapter will sketch briefly some of the men and events. Douglas, already portrayed in another chapter, is not studied here.

One of the men with whom Lincoln found it difficult to get along was James Shields. Dark-haired and scrupulously neat, Shields served with Lincoln in the House and was state auditor when Lincoln served his final term in the House. Shields and Lincoln were not "good friends," although Shield's wife in later years so reported.[2]

[1] April 6, 1861, RTL.

[2] *New York Times*, August 15, 1928, an interview with the ninety-three-year-old widow of Shields.

Gustave Koerner, a law partner of Shields and close friend of Lincoln, describes Shields as an honest public official but "impulsive . . . of medium height, very broad-shouldered, and with rather long arms . . . his eyes grey and very sparkling. . . . He was exceedingly vain and very ambitious, and, like most ambitious men, on occasions, quite egotistical."[3]

In 1842 disagreement between Shields and Lincoln became so acute a duel between the two men almost took place on an island in the Mississippi near the city of Alton. The Democrats, who held the state administration in 1842, announced that they would not accept payment of state taxes in state bank notes. This was a logical position to take; the bank notes had little value. But it gave the Whigs a chance to attack the Democrats for "further devaluing" the state bank notes. Lincoln wrote a letter to the *Sangamo Journal*, as did Mary Todd and a friend of hers. These letters criticized political decisions made by the administration and made sport of Shields.

It cannot be said, as some have claimed, that the entire blame for intemperate remarks rests on the two ladies. Lincoln stated in his letter that Shields was "requiring [collectors] . . . to perjure themselves"; that he was "a fool as well as a liar"; that "if I was deaf and blind I could tell him by the smell"; and that at a recent social affair he had made "a conceity dunce of himself."[1]

Shields was furious. He demanded of the editor, Simeon Francis, to tell him who had written the letters, particularly the one signed "Rebecca," since pseudonyms had been used. Francis gave Shields Lincoln's name, but not the names of the two ladies. Shields then challenged Lincoln to a duel.

Lincoln assured Shields: "I had no intention of injuring your personal or private character or standing as a man or gentleman."[5] He said it was written "wholly for political effect."

But if this letter, which Lincoln agreed could be published, did not satisfy Shields, Lincoln was willing to fight a duel according to the following terms:

3 *Memoirs of Gustave Koerner*, Vol. I, 414–18.

4 *SgJ*, September 2, 1842.

5 *CW*, I, 301.

1st. Weapons—Cavalry broad swords of the largest size, precisely equal in all respects. . . .

2nd. Position—a plank ten feet long, & from nine to twelve inches broad to be firmly fixed on edge, on the ground, as the line between us which neither is to pass his foot over upon forfeit of his life. . . .

3rd. Time—one Thursday evening at five o'clock if you can get it so; but in no case to be at greater distance of time than Friday evening at five o'clock.

4th. Place—Within three miles of Alton on the opposite of the river.[6]

The terms were such that if the duel took place, Lincoln could hardly lose. Lincoln was a tall man, Shields a short and athletic man. Fighting with swords, rather than the usual pistols, gave the tall man a distinct advantage. The line of demarcation, the board, made it certain that the confrontation would be head-on and gave added insurance that a tall man would win.

Sometime after this affair Lincoln was asked by a friend why he had chosen broadswords; Lincoln replied, "To tell you the truth . . . I did not want to kill Shields, and felt sure I could disarm him, have had about a month to learn the broadsword exercise; and furthermore, I didn't want . . . [him] to kill me, which I rather think he would have done if we had selected pistols."[7]

Exactly who was responsible for calling off the Lincoln-Shields duel at the last minute is not clear. Mary Todd gave John J. Hardin the credit. The *Illinois State Journal* stated eighteen years later that Hardin persuaded both to cancel the duel "by his arguments addressed to their common sense."[8] A reporter for the *Alton Telegraph* on the scene said that Dr. T. M. Hope of Alton—who had been involved in the Lovejoy incident—was with Shields and argued vehemently with Shields not to go through with it. The reporter credited Hope with stopping it. A report in the *Sangamo Journal* of October 3, 1842, written by Shields's second, John G. Whiteside, also gives Dr. Hope the credit.

[6] *Ibid.*

[7] Linder, *Reminiscences*, 66–67.

[8] *Illinois State Journal*, April 27, 1860, quoted in the *ISHSJ*, Summer, 1953.

Hardin evidently took possession of the swords of both men. More than a year after the near-duel Lincoln wrote to Hardin, "I wish you would measure one of the largest of those swords, we took to Alton, and write me the length of it, from tip of the point to tip of the hilt, in feet and inches, I have a dispute about the length."[9]

Both Lincoln and Shields were present, and both at first refused to budge. The *Telegraph* reporter said the issue finally was resolved without either man formally backing down. In writing, Shields asked Lincoln whether he had written the poem in the *Sangamo Journal* (the one written by Mary Todd and her good friend Julia Jayne, later the wife of Lyman Trumbull). Lincoln replied he had not. This provided the "honorable exit."

Shields later became the first and only United States senator to have served from three states: Illinois, Missouri, and Minnesota. He also was governor of the Oregon Territory. During the Mexican War Shields became a hero, and the people of Illinois wanted to make him their United States senator. They elected him, but Shields, a native of Ireland, caused a problem in Washington:

> When Shields took his seat in the Senate, a question arose as to his right to sit as a Senator of the United States. The Constitution required a period of nine years' citizenship as a prerequisite. Shields had come to the United States before he attained legal age, but upon his appointment by the Governor to the place of State Auditor in 1838, it was deemed advisable that he apply for naturalization to remove any doubt of his eligibility. The term of years between the date of taking out of his papers and his election to the Senate of the United States was less than nine years. Rather than cloud the title of his seat in the Senate, he promptly resigned. The Governor of Illinois convened the Legislature in extraordinary session in December, 1847; a full period of nine years had now elapsed. Ex-Senator Breese and General John A. McClernand were again contestants for the seat, as they had been when Shields was first elected, but the Legislature again elected Shields.[10]

This meant that Shields was elected United States Senator twice

9 *CW*, I, 323.
10 Francis O'Shaughnessy, "General James Shields of Illinois," *Transactions of the Illinois State Historical Library*, 1915.

in one year, perhaps the only man in United States history to hold that unusual honor.

Judge Breese, just referred to, was a much more prominent state figure than Shields when the latter was named to the Senate. The election of Shields rather than Breese was considered quite an upset and led to this story making the rounds:

> At the battle of Cerro Gordo, in the war against Mexico, he [Shields] was shot through the lungs, the ball passing out at his back. His nomination over a man so distinguished as Judge Breese was a surprise to many, and was the reward for his gallantry and wound. His political enemies said his recovery was marvelous, and that his wound was miraculously cured, so that no scar could be seen where the bullet entered and passed out of his body. All of which was untrue. The morning after the nomination, Mr. Butterfield, who was as violent a Whig as General Shields was a Democrat, met one of the Judges in the Supreme Court room, who expressed astonishment at the result, but, added the Judge, "It was the war and that Mexican bullet that did the business." "Yes," answered Mr. Butterfield dryly, "and what a wonderful shot that was! The ball went clean through Shields without hurting him or even leaving a scar, and killed Breese a thousand miles away."[11]

The duel Lincoln almost fought with Shields helped lead to a reconciliation between Mary Todd and Lincoln. The wife of Simeon Francis, the editor who had given Lincoln's name to Shields, apparently brought Lincoln and Mary "together at her house without either knowing that the other was to be there."[12] Mary undoubtedly appreciated Lincoln's not disclosing that she and her friend had been at least partially responsible for his plight in the Shields affair. Within a month and a half after this episode they were married.

The relationship between Lincoln and Ninian W. Edwards in later years was strained. Even during their legislative service there were times when Edwards would get angry at Lincoln "and pro-

---

[11] Arnold, *Reminiscences of the Illinois Bar*, 142.

[12] Trumbull to Jesse Weik, April 17, 1895, Herndon-Weik Collection, Library of Congress.

pose to fight it out then and there."[13] But during these legislative years things went much better than they did later. There were some exceptions to this feeling of coolness between the two. In the 1856 campaign, for example, Lincoln carried a book published in 1853, *Life and Speeches of Henry Clay*, and on the flyleaf of the book Lincoln had written, "A. Lincoln—Presented by his friend, N. W. Edwards."[14]

Edwards became the first Illinois superintendent of public instruction. He served as a member of the Illinois House and Senate again in later years, after he failed to get nominated to the House in 1840.

Edwards did not sympathize with the antislavery movement, supported Douglas rather than his brother-in-law, both in 1858 and 1860, but never hesitated to borrow money and seek positions from Lincoln. In 1849, Lincoln sought the position of Land Commissioner of the General Land Office. Edwards wrote a letter to Washington opposing his appointment, after Lincoln had gone out of his way to be kind to Edwards.[15]

In 1851, Edwards switched from Whig to Democrat, and David Davis wrote to his wife, "People laugh at him [Edwards]. He has been persuaded that he can get to Congress on the Locofoco side—which is all stuff. Many persons say that his wife is the Cause on ac[t] of her ambition. Lincoln is his brother-in-law, you know, and has talked to me on the subject, and is deeply mortified."[16]

After causing Lincoln much embarrassment by supporting Douglas in 1858 (which he did again in 1860), Edwards wrote to Lincoln, "Could you accommodate me with a loan of $1500 at ten percent interest. If it were at all necessary, or if you would prefer it, I could have you ample security."[17] After Lincoln lent

[13] Henry C. Whitney, *Lincoln the Citizen* (New York, Current Literature, 1892), 126, quoting Robert Wilson, who served with both Lincoln and Edwards.

[14] R. Gerald McMurty, "Life and Speeches of Clay," *National Republic*, January, 1935.

[15] *CW*, II, 57–59.

[16] David Davis to Mrs. Davis, March 23, 1851, quoted in King, *Lincoln's Manager*, 74.

[17] Edwards to Lincoln, April 20, 1860, RTL.

him the money, Edwards announced his support of Douglas for President.

Once Edwards wrote to Lincoln for some help on a legal point. Lincoln at that time was a candidate for President of the United States and obviously did not have time to do law work for any-one—particularly someone in the enemy camp. But Edwards was unhappy. Edwards wrote to Lincoln that he was not being dealt with fairly, as he always dealt with others, *"especially the members of my own family. . . .* I was not properly treated."[18]

A few months later, after Lincoln had been elected, Edwards wrote to Lincoln that he could not pay the interest on the loan given him. Then to add a little frosting to the cake, he added that he had recently spoken up in behalf of Lincoln, "but some of our relatives took exception to it."[19]

Edwards wrote Lincoln for a job shortly after Lincoln's inauguration as President. The apparent purpose of his letter was for permission to check something out in one of the departments. This request was made in a very vague sort of way, but then he added that he was really in a bad way financially. Lincoln replied with a "My dear Sir" to his brother-in-law and added: "It pains me to hear you speak of being ruined in your pecuniary affairs. I still hope you are injured only and not ruined."[20] He then suggested that Edwards come to Washington to work out arrangements for getting the information he sought. Lincoln chose to ignore temporarily the not-so-subtle plea for the job.

Edwards became more direct in an appeal for a job, and sent word to Browning to intercede for him with the President. Browning replied that he was "not unforgetful of our long friendship, nor unmindful of the many kindnesses I have received at the hands of yourself and Mrs. Edwards."[21]

Before that request got to Lincoln, the President named Edwards captain and commissary of subsistence at Springfield. Responsible was the President's wife, who had written to David Davis

[18] Edwards to Lincoln, August 10, 1860, RTL.

[19] Edwards to Lincoln, December 28, 1860, RTL.

[20] *CW*, IV, 412.

[21] Exchange between Edwards, Browning and Lincoln, August 9 and 10, 1861, RTL.

for help. Davis wrote to the President urging a job for Edwards.[22] A year later Edwards came with another small request, which the President granted.

Six months after that, in May of 1863, the Republican leaders of the Springfield area requested that Edwards be removed from the position he held in Springfield. They charged that he had used his position "to amass personal fortunes and had made countless enemies for the administration."[23] Even worse from the Republican standpoint, he gave a food contract to Joel Matteson, former Democratic governor. This permitted Matteson to deliver food to the troops "in person" and meant Democratic votes and an "outrage against common decency."[24] When Matteson was governor, he had appointed Edwards state superintendent of public instruction, a position he filled until 1857. Matteson's reputation for integrity was not high, and the Edwards business arrangement under the Lincoln administration had Springfield area Republicans furious. Edwards was transferred. Lincoln transferred him for general ineptness rather than dishonesty. While Lincoln was cool towards Edwards, he did not believe that Edwards had "at this time of his life, given up his old habits and turned dishonest." However, in Lincoln's view, Edwards "seemed to think" that if he could keep his "official record dryly correct," he could "provoke my friends and harass me."[25]

In pleading letters, Edwards told Lincoln that the President had no better friend on the face of the earth. Edwards furthermore asserted that "when it was thought in 1840 that you would [not] be nominated for the legislature, [I] publicly stated if anyone was to be left out . . . [I] should be."[26] There is no mention of this at any time in 1840, and no known reference to it other than in this letter; it seems highly improbable. Again to show his loyalty, Edwards informed Lincoln that in the 1860 election, when he made

---

[22] King, *Lincoln's Manager*, 184.

[23] *CW*, VI, 237–38.

[24] Jesse K. Dubois, William Butler, O. M. Hatch to Lincoln, October 21, 1861, RTL.

[25] *CW*, VI, 275–76.

[26] Ninian Edwards to Lincoln, June 18, 1863, RTL.

speeches opposing Lincoln, he always pointed out "that if there was a man living without a fault I believed you were that man."

One of his fellow state representatives described Edwards as a man of "vanity and egotism. . . . His manners and deportment were not calculated to win friends amongst his equals and superiors, and of the latter class there were many."[27]

Edwards was the last survivor of the Long Nine. He died in 1889, twenty-four years after Lincoln.

On the positive side, Edwards as state superintendent of public instruction fathered ideas "which with slight modifications, became the law which created . . . [the Illinois] free school system."[28]

Joel A. Matteson, state senator for three terms, was elected governor in 1852 and retired after one term as a rather popular man. It later developed that there was scandal in his administration on refunding of canal scrip. The case was "remarkable in view of the magnitude and boldness of the fraud."[29]

One of the men with whom Lincoln frequently engaged in debate on the floor of the House was John A. McClernand, later a member of Congress. "Most authors tend to write him down, simply because his consuming ambition and vanity are easier to describe than his better qualities," notes one of his biographers.[30] McClernand was Lincoln's neighbor in Springfield and practiced law near the office of Lincoln and Herndon. Lincoln and McClernand were good friends.

In the national House of Representatives McClernand became the spokesman for the Douglas forces, doing everything he could to gain ground for Douglas's presidential nomination. When the session of 1860 began, McClernand was a candidate for speaker of the House and had widespread support. Senator Jefferson Davis, though not a member of the House, actively worked for him.

In 1862, McClernand enlisted in the Union Army. A few months after the war began, Lincoln recognized his "great energy, and

---

[27] Linder, *Reminiscences*, 279.

[28] Smith, *A Student's History of Illinois*, 412.

[29] *The Great Canal Script Fraud*, 1859, Report of Evidence (Springfield, Daily Journal Steam Press, 1859), 60.

[30] Victor Hicken, "John A. McClernand and the House Speakership Struggle of 1859," *ISHSJ*, Summer, 1960.

industry" and the fact that he had "effected certainly as much as any other Brig. Genl. in organizing forces."[31] Lincoln eventually made him a major general, but he became a controversial figure. General Grant relieved him of his command "for his publication of a congratulatory address calculated to create dissension and ill-feeling in the army. I should have relieved him long ago."[32] The next year Lincoln restored his command.

In 1876, McClernand was president of the national Democratic Convention. That same year he returned to the Illinois House of Representatives and spoke about the days when he and Lincoln had served in the legislature together.

One whose record was marred by an inexcusably poor performance as attorney general in the Lovejoy slaying was Usher F. Linder, a political opponent but personal friend throughout Lincoln's life. Frequently the two co-operated in legal work.

Linder's son Daniel, who had enlisted in the Confederate Army, was taken prisoner of war. Lincoln released him with this order to Stanton: "Please administer the oath of allegiance to him, discharge him, and send him to his father."[33] He signed the letter the day after Christmas.

Quick-tempered Adam W. Snyder was a Democratic state senator whom Lincoln opposed in debate in campaigns and whose policies he opposed in the legislature.

Snyder's son, plain-spoken and colorful Dr. J. F. Snyder, occasionally felt compelled to say something kind about Lincoln—in print. But his personal comments were not so favorable. Here are some examples from penned notes made by Dr. Snyder in the margin of a book, which show the bitterness toward Lincoln that was handed from father to son:

When an early opponent of Lincoln is quoted as describing Lincoln as "Coarse and vulgar," Dr. Snyder comments, "Good!"[34] The book's comparing Lincoln to George Washington Dr. Snyder excoriated as "drivling nonsense."[35] When the author says that

[31] *CW*, IV, 527.
[32] *Ibid.*, VI, 293, quoted from official government records.
[33] *Ibid.*, VII, 95.
[34] Linder, in copy belonging to IHL, 63.
[35] *Ibid.*

in the Shields duel Shields would have killed Lincoln had they fought with pistols, Dr. Snyder wrote, "It would have been a great blessing if he had."[36]

Orville H. Browning, who served in the Illinois Senate and was a close friend of Lincoln, played a key role among Illinois Republicans in the 1860 campaign, and was appointed to a seat in the United States Senate when Douglas died. When a vacancy occurred in the United States Supreme Court, Browning, who had helped Lincoln get the Republican nomination for President, felt he should receive the appointment. Lincoln at first had him in mind, but finally appointed David Davis instead.

This made Browning somewhat bitter, all the more since he regarded himself as superior to Lincoln in ability. Browning was "aristocratic, proper, and somewhat pompous."[37] Gustave Koerner recalled: "I should have liked him better if he had been a little less conscious of his own superiority."[38]

An interesting exchange of correspondence took place in 1861. General Frémont had issued a proclamation in the St. Louis area which, in Lincoln's words, amounted to "dictatorship." Browning supported Frémont. Browning wrote to Lincoln, "Have traitors who are warring upon the constitution and laws, and rejecting all their restraints, any right to invoke their protection? . . . There has been too much tenderness towards traitors and rebels. We must strike them terrible blows, and strike them hard and quick, or the government will go hopelessly to pieces."[39]

Lincoln replied:

> Coming from you, I confess it astonishes me. . . . If a commanding General finds a necessity to seize the farm of a private owner, for a pasture, an encampment, or a fortification, he has the right to do so, and to so hold it, as long as the necessity lasts. . . . But to say the farm no longer belongs to the owner, or his heirs forever . . . is purely political, without the savor of military law about it. . . . The proclamation in the point in question, is simply "dictator-

[36] *Ibid.*, 67.
[37] Thomas, *Portrait for Posterity*, 45.
[38] *Memoirs of Gustave Koerner*, Vol. I, 479.
[39] Browning to Lincoln, September 17, 1861, RTL.

ship." It assumes that the general may do *anything* he pleases. . . . I have no doubt [it] would be more popular with some thoughtless people, than that which has been done! But I cannot assume this reckless position; nor allow others to assume it on my responsibility. You speak of it as being the only means of *saving* the government. On the contrary, it is itself the surrender of the government.[40]

In 1862 when Lincoln's eleven-year-old son William Wallace ("Willie") died, the grief-stricken President immediately "sent his carriage for Senator and Mrs. Orville H. Browning. Mrs. Browning came to comfort Mrs. Lincoln and the Senator was placed in full charge of the funeral service."[41] Mrs. Lincoln, deeply shaken by the death, was not able to attend the services, and Lincoln asked Browning and Senator Trumbull—two former Illinois legislative colleagues—to ride with him in his carriage in the funeral procession. But the relationship between Lincoln and Browning had its chilly days.

There is more bitterness and disappointment than truth in Browning's comment to a friend in 1864 that he felt from the start Lincoln would not do well. "Still, I thought he might get through, as many a boy has got through college, without disgrace and without knowledge; but I fear he is a failure."[42] This he said in a letter in which he expressed uncertainty as to whether he should support Lincoln or McClellan in 1864 and stated that he noted much enthusiasm for the general's nomination and that he was "inclined to think that there are many republicans [who] will secretly support him [McClellan]."

Browning later served as secretary of the interior and attorney general under President Andrew Johnson. When Illinois drafted its 1870 constitution—the one it operates under today—Browning served as chairman of the constitutional convention.

William H. Bissell served in the House with Lincoln for one term. A doctor and lawyer, he later distinguished himself in the

[40] *CW*, IV, 531–33.

[41] Gerald McMurty, "The Funeral of Willie Lincoln," *Lincoln Lore*, January, 1964.

[42] Letter to Sen. Edgar Cowan of Pennsylvania, quoted in Thomas, *Abraham Lincoln*, 443.

Mexican War. Then he occupied a seat in the United States House of Representatives from 1849 to 1855. His most famous action while there was to accept a challenge to a duel with Jefferson Davis in a heated dispute about the relative bravery of Southern and Northern soldiers. At the last minute, friends intervened and stopped the duel. Surprisingly, one of those who helped prevent the duel was James Shields.

In 1856, Bissell was elected governor of Illinois, the first Republican and also the first man with a substantial physical handicap, to hold this office. Both of his legs were paralyzed.

In 1859 he vetoed a reapportionment bill, and Lincoln wrote the veto message. Everything in the veto message except the date and the governor's signature are in Lincoln's handwriting.[43] Bissell died in office in 1860.

James Semple, speaker of the House in the 1836–37 session, was appointed by President Martin Van Buren as minister to Bogota and served as a United States senator from Illinois. His son, Eugene Semple, became governor of the state of Washington.

Fifteen of the Illinois legislative colleagues of Lincoln entered the national House of Representatives. Among these were Robert Smith, whom McClernand wanted Lincoln to name Army paymaster because he was "one of the earliest and most decided opponents of this disunion and rebellious movement."[44] Smith was regarded as "a rattling strong stump orator."[45]

Colonel A. P. Field, former Illinois secretary of state, moved to Louisiana prior to the Civil War. After the war he was elected to Congress from Louisiana, but the radical Republicans in Congress refused to seat him, as they refused to seat many other Southerners.

Augustus C. French served two terms in Springfield with Lincoln and was prominent in public affairs during many of Lincoln's early political years. A man of very limited abilities, he was urged to run for governor to keep him out of a Congressional race, not with any thought that he could be nominated for the governorship. The unexpected happened and he served two terms as governor.

[43] *CW*, III, 364.
[44] McClernand to Lincoln, July 20, 1861, RTL.
[45] Snyder, *Selected Writings*, 172.

Ironically, in spite of his unimpressive performance in office, he won re-election in 1848 by the largest majority in the state's history. French got 67,828 votes; W. L. D. Morrison, the Whig candidate, 5,659; and Charles V. Dyer, Free Soil candidate, 4,692. That gave the mediocre French a victory ratio of approximately twelve to one over his nearest opponent, a feat never duplicated before or since that time. He was also the first Illinois governor to win re-election.

One of the men Lincoln met through his legislative activity was a young heavy-set lawyer, David Davis of Bloomington. The two became good friends. When Davis became a circuit judge, he reportedly showed such a "marked difference ... to Mr. Lincoln that Lincoln threw the rest of us into the shade," according to one lawyer.[46] At the 1860 Republican national convention, Davis was one of the three or four men most responsible for Lincoln's securing the presidential nomination. As President, Lincoln appointed Davis to the United States Supreme Court. When Lincoln died, Davis administered his estate without charge to the widow and her family. Davis later resigned from the United States Supreme Court, became a United States senator, and while in the Senate served as president pro tem of that body.

Youngest member of the 1836–37 session, the only man younger than Lincoln, was Jesse K. Dubois, later state auditor—and more important—one of the key men in securing for him the Republican nomination for the presidency.

A humorous exchange between Lincoln and Dubois occurred when Dubois heard that the quartermaster general was to be replaced. Dubois, believing the unfounded rumor, sent a telegram suggesting General Allen for the post. Lincoln telegraphed back, "What nation do you desire Gen. Allen to be made Quarter-Master-General of? This nation already has a Quarter-Master General."[47]

In 1864, Dubois sought the Republican nomination for governor of Illinois but did not receive it. Lincoln was asked to enter into the Republican battle over which man was to be the nominee, but

[46] Linder, *Reminiscences*, 182–83.
[47] *CW*, VI, 450.

he declined. A son of Dubois, Fred T. Dubois, in 1890 became one of the first United States senators from the new state of Idaho.

Thomas Ford was elected a judge three times while Lincoln was in the legislature, the last time to the Illinois Supreme Court. He was a frequent visitor at legislative sessions, and Lincoln knew Ford well even though they were of different political parties.

The year after Lincoln left the legislature, Ford took over as governor. He bungled matters relative to the Mormons, but he was the first governor to attack the internal improvements debt with courage and vigor.

Personal tragedy haunted much of Ford's life.

George Forquer, his brother-in-law, who had served in the Senate from Sangamon County during Lincoln's first House term, financed Ford's education and secured for him his first judgeship, but Forquer died at an early age.

Ford had a high squeaky voice and could not finish his own inaugural address as governor. He was "so wholly wanting in self-confidence and practical business sense that he was an utter failure as a lawyer."[48] Mrs. Ford died of cancer of the stomach at the age of thirty-eight. Ford died less than a month later of consumption. The older of his two sons met death by hanging in Kansas under circumstances that are not clear. When Lincoln was President, he tried to be of assistance to Ford's son George.

Joseph Gillespie, the man who jumped out the window with Lincoln in the 1840 special session, presided over the Illinois Republican convention in 1860, which started things in motion for the ultimate Lincoln presidential nomination. In 1858 he wrote to Lincoln, "I shall take the stump and do all that lies in my power"; and he did just that.[49] Gillespie became a circuit judge.

By no means did all the men Lincoln worked with end up as heroes. Josiah Lamborn, for example, did not. He was first a member with Lincoln in the House, then attorney general during part of Lincoln's legislative career. He debated Lincoln several times during the 1840 election. A man of ability and notoriety, one of Lamborn's predecessors as attorney general describes him:

[48] J. F. Snyder, "Governor Ford and His Family," *ISHSJ*, July, 1910.
[49] Gillespie to Lincoln, RTL.

He was wholly destitute of principle, and shamelessly took bribes from criminals prosecuted under his administration. I know myself of his having dismissed forty or fifty indictments at the Shelbyville Court, and openly displayed the money he had received from them—the fruit of his maladministration. . . . He grew worse and worse towards the latter end of his life, and finally threw himself entirely away, consorting with gamblers and wasting his substance upon them. He gave himself up to intemperance, to the neglect of wife and child, whom he abandoned, and finally died miserably.[50]

One of the men Lincoln worked with closely was youthful Edward D. Baker, his legislative colleague from Sangamon County. Baker's oratorical abilities appeared likely to carry him much farther politically than the less polished Lincoln.

In 1843 both Lincoln and Baker wanted the Whig nomination for the United States House of Representatives. The Sangamon Whigs voted for Baker rather than Lincoln. They made Lincoln a delegate to the nominating convention, but pledged the entire delegation to Baker. Lincoln found himself in the embarrassing position of being pledged to Baker when he himself was a candidate. The convention took neither Baker nor Lincoln but Hardin. Lincoln at this time was thirty-four years old, Hardin thirty-three, and Baker thirty two. Two years later Baker was the nominee, and then Lincoln was, leading to much talk that a "deal" had been made.

After completing his term in the United States House of Representatives, Baker later became a United States senator from Oregon. Born in England, he could achieve no higher office. Soon the Civil War broke out. He volunteered to serve and was killed at the Battle of Ball's Bluff, October 21, 1861.

Lincoln, who had named one of his sons Edward Baker, was deeply moved when he learned of the death of his longtime friend. Later he wrote several letters in behalf of Baker's son.

Showing the spirit which existed between the two men was a letter Baker sent when Lincoln received the nomination for President:

The reward that fidelity and courage, find in your person will

[50] Linder, *Reminiscences,* 259.

infuse hope in many sinking bosoms, and new energy in many bold hearts. As I write I am reminded of a great many things in your earlier career which . . . you may scarcely remember; I am proud as a personal friend and a party man to feel that among them all there has been nothing which would not confirm my loyalty as a partisan and my confidence as a friend. You will not wonder that in the great distinction you have won and the great usefulness which I believe awaits you, I feel an interest which later friends can hardly know. . . . My whole heart is with you in the great battle.[51]

John J. Hardin quit the Illinois House the same year Lincoln did. He served one term in Congress, and in that term became known as one of the most gifted speakers in the United States House of Representatives. At the outbreak of the Mexican War he volunteered and was killed leading his troops at the battle of Buena Vista. Had his political career not been suddenly eclipsed by death, it could be that Hardin rather than Lincoln would have headed Whig and Republican fortunes in the state.

Although Lincoln and Hardin worked together on many issues and projects, the relationship between the two was never warm. When Hardin took the Congressional nomination in 1843—the nomination that Lincoln wanted—Lincoln did not vote for Hardin in the general election.[52] The Baker-Lincoln relationship, however, was warm and cordial.

One biographer notes of Lincoln, Baker, and Hardin:

> All three were lawyers. All three were in the Illinois militia in the Black Hawk War. They were together in the Illinois Assembly and they were successively to represent the same district in Congress. All three would be candidates for the Senate. All three would meet violent deaths.[53]

After Lincoln became President, he sent a note to Secretary Seward asking him to take care of a "brother-in-law of the late

[51] Baker to Lincoln, August 1, 1860, RTL.

[52] Donald Riddle, *Lincoln Runs for Congress* (New Brunswick, N. J., Rutgers University Press, 1948), 20.

[53] *Ibid.*, 11.

Col. John Hardin."[54] The man was assigned as consul to Panama. On another occasion Lincoln was of assistance to Hardin's widow.

Dr. John Logan, who served in 1836–37 session with Lincoln, was the father of the famous General John A. Logan. Logan took an active role for Douglas and against Lincoln. When the Civil War started, he was at first furious at Douglas for siding with the North and told him, "You have sold out the Democratic party, but by God, you can't deliver it."[55] Eventually, he joined the Union cause and became a military hero. In 1884, Logan was the Republican candidate for Vice-President.

William A. Richardson served in the House with Lincoln, later went on to the national House of Representatives, and finally came to be a United States senator. A Democrat with a huge body and a deep voice, he used both against the Republicans. Richardson handled the controversial Nebraska Bill in the House after Douglas passed it in the Senate in 1854.

Richardson served in Congress when Lincoln gave his annual message December 1, 1862. In it, Lincoln suggested gradual freedom for the slaves and payment to their owners. It made Richardson furious. He said:

> The annual message . . . is remarkable for what it says, and is still more remarkable for what it omits to say. One-half of the twenty-one pages which it covers is devoted to the negro. No page, no sentence, no word, is given to laud or even mention the bravery, the gallantry, the good conduct of our soldiers in the various bloody battles which have been fought. No sorrow is expressed for the lamented dead. No allusion is made to the maimed and wounded. No sympathy is tendered to the sorrowing widow and to the helpless orphan. . . . The Army is being used for the benefit of the negro. This House is being used for his benefit. Every department of the Government is being run for his benefit.[56]

[54] *CW*, IV, 302–303.

[55] George F. Milton, *The Eve of Conflict* (New York, Houghton, Mifflin, 1934), 565.

[56] Speech of Hon. W. A. Richardson of Illinois on the President's Message, delivered in the House of Representatives, December 8, 1862, University of Chicago Library.

At one time Richardson and Lincoln served in the national House together and worked together well. Lincoln wrote to Mary, "Mrs. Richardson is still here; and what is more, has a baby—so Richardson says, and he ought to know."[57]

During the war Lincoln named Richardson a Brigadier General.

Lyman Trumbull went on to become a United States senator and one of the nation's strong leaders. His relationship with Lincoln was good and the two worked together closely on the national scene. After Trumbull became United States senator in 1855 because of the additional votes Lincoln gave to him, Trumbull worked hard for Lincoln in 1858 against Douglas. In the 1858 debate at Charleston, the question of Trumbull's honesty came up, and Lincoln testified, "In all the years I have known Lyman Trumbull, [never] have I known him to fail in his word or tell a falsehood, large or small."[58]

In 1860, Trumbull was toying with the idea of becoming a candidate himself. He felt Lincoln could not win. Lincoln apparently heard that Trumbull's support was something less than wholehearted and wrote him:

> A word now for your own special benefit. You better write no letters which can possibly be distorted into opposition, or quasi opposition to me. There are men on the constant watch for such things out of which to prejudice my peculiar friends against you. While I have no more suspicion of you, than I have of my best friend living, I am kept in constant struggle against suggestions of this sort. I have hesitated some to write this paragraph, lest you should suspect I do it for my own benefit, and not for yours; but on reflection I conclude you will not suspect me.[59]

The heavy correspondence Lincoln had with Trumbull in the years of the Presidency show that Trumbull was one of the men Lincoln relied on most heavily. Trumbull had a touch of vanity, did not hesitate to ask for favors, but also made a substantial record in the United States Senate. He contributed much to basic

[57] *CW*, I, 495.
[58] *Ibid.*, III, 182.
[59] *Ibid.*, IV, 46.

constitutional and policy questions the nation faced. He showed his stature in the attempted impeachment of Andrew Johnson. Opposed though he was to the Johnson administration, he refused to vote for impeachment and eloquently defended his courageous stand.

There was much talk in 1872 that he might be the liberal Republican candidate for President. Instead, Horace Greeley was chosen. In assessing the rank of prominent men Illinois has given to the nation, Trumbull would have to be placed near the top.

Much has been written about Douglas's interest in Mary Todd, but nothing about Trumbull's. Actually, other than an occasional dance with Mary Todd, Douglas probably took no particular interest in her. Statements to the contrary are of doubtful validity.

But Mary did have her eye on the unmarried Trumbull when he was in Springfield as a legislator. In June, 1841—six months after the "fatal first"—she wrote to her recently engaged friend Mercy Levering about Trumbull, "Now that your fortune is made, I feel much disposed in your absence to lay in my claims, as he is talented & agreeable & sometimes countenances me."[60]

She found herself in the social company of three young state representatives in Springfield who later were seriously considered for the presidency: Douglas, Trumbull, and Lincoln.

Isaac P. Walker, the longbearded man with whom Lincoln served in the House and debated in the 1840 campaign, went from a hater of Abolitionists to becoming an Abolitionist. He moved to Wisconsin and became a United States Senator from Wisconsin.

Lincoln was fond of his House colleague Archibald Williams of Adams County. In 1854, when Williams ran for Congress, Lincoln made speeches in his behalf, but Williams lost. As president, Lincoln named Williams a federal judge.

John T. Stuart's law partnership with Lincoln was dissolved shortly after Lincoln's last session in Springfield. From then on their paths parted frequently. Stuart was proslavery, and Lincoln was antislavery. By 1858 they had drifted apart; Stuart supported Douglas against Lincoln.

In 1860, Stuart ran as a Constitutional Union man on the Bell

[60] Copy at IHL.

ticket for governor. He received less than 1 per cent of the votes cast for his opponent and barely 1 per cent of the votes the second man got.

The only request Stuart made by letter to Lincoln was that David Davis might be appointed to the United States Circuit Court for the territory which included Illinois. Stuart wrote, "I take the liberty of saying to you that his appointment to that office would give me personally more pleasure than the appointment of any other living man." Stuart added that it would please "you old personal friends."[61] Davis did not get this appointment, but later was named to the United States Supreme Court.

In 1862, Stuart ran for Congress and won. He served one term.

After Lincoln was inaugurated, Stuart wrote to him, "My personal attachment and respect for you which I have maintained for thirty years is as sincere now as it ever was, notwithstanding our differences in politics and I hope every success for you—and for our common country."[62]

Even though in 1862 Stuart ran for Congress as a Democrat, he had this to say about Lincoln: "Difference in political opinion since 1856 has in no wise diminished my respect for the man, or the unbounded confidence I have ever had in his personal integrity. . . . If my voice could reach his ear I would be glad to say to him . . . history will erect monuments for you by the side of Washington."[63]

In 1863, when relatives of Stuart wanted to reclaim a plantation they had in Arkansas, Lincoln ordered the plantation returned to them "as long as said Mr. and Mrs. Craig shall demean themselves as peaceful, loyal citizens of the United States."[64]

A touching aspect of the story of these two men is that Stuart became chairman of the executive committee of the National Lincoln Monument Association, and upon his shoulders rested much of the responsibility for erecting a suitable monument to Lincoln in Springfield.

Richard N. Cullom, who served in both the House and the Senate

[61] Stuart to Lincoln, January 24, 1862, RTL.
[62] Stuart to Lincoln, April 3, 1861, RTL.
[63] C. C. Brown, "Major John T. Stuart," *Transactions of the Illinois State Historical Society*, 1902.
[64] *CW*, VII, 83.

in Lincoln's legislative years, became known for his son's activities rather than for his own. His son, Shelby Moore Cullom, held the position of United States senator longer than any other Illinois resident. In 1888 he was seriously considered for the Republican nomination for President and was again a prospective nominee in 1892.

Serving two terms with Lincoln was Mark Aldrich of Hancock County. He was one of the men indicted for the murder of Joseph Smith, the Mormon leader, but none of them was ever found guilty by the courts.

Nine of Lincoln's Illinois legislative colleagues became major party nominees for governor of Illinois: William A. Richardson, William H. Bissell, Robert R. McLaughlin, Lyman Trumbull, E. B. Webb, Joel A. Matteson, August C. French, Thomas M. Kilpatrick, and Cyrus Edwards. French, Matteson, and Bissell were the only successful nominees. In addition, William L. D. Ewing served a short time in the post through succession.

Of the Long Nine, Ninian W. Edwards has already been mentioned, and none of the others distinguished himself particularly:

Robert Wilson became a probate judge and was appointed an Army paymaster by President Lincoln.

Archer G. Herndon became known more for his mercantile business and for his son William, Lincoln's law partner, than for his own limited political activities. In 1854, Lincoln wrote a DeWitt County Grand Jury report indicting Archer G. Herndon for selling whiskey illegally.

Daniel Stone became a circuit judge in the northern part of Illinois and eventually moved to Ohio, where he also occupied the bench. He died in New Jersey.

William F. Elkin held no further major office, other than an appointment from Lincoln in 1861 as Register of the Land Office in Springfield. He lived to be eighty-seven years old.

John Dawson served one term in the House after Lincoln retired, was a member of the state constitutional convention in 1847, and died in 1850.

Andrew McCormick took an active interest in local offices. He served two years as mayor of Springfield.

315

Job Fletcher lived seven years longer than Lincoln, but did not distinguish himself in either state or national politics.

In his later years Newton Cloud, a Democratic House member from Morgan County whom Lincoln liked, became speaker of the House. In 1860, Cloud almost became the Democratic nominee for governor. His funeral in Waverly, Illinois in 1877 was "the largest ever held in this part of the state."[65] A special train was chartered from Jacksonville. Speaker at the funeral was Rev. Peter Akers, founder of two colleges and great-grandfather of an editor of the Chicago Sun-Times.

John Bennett of Petersburg was typical of many of Lincoln's legislative colleagues. He served one term in the House, had no particular liking for the position and did not run again.

However, he occasionally corresponded with Lincoln on political matters and made it a point to save the letters. His experience with the Lincoln letters was not an uncommon one. His great-grandson relates: "The letters received by Mr. Bennett were kept by him in the Masonic Lodge Hall, Petersburg. Mr. Bennett died in 1885 at the age of almost 80. And the lodge brothers grabbed all [the] correspondence."[66]

Lincoln continued to take an interest in what happened in the legislature long after he retired from it. He frequently consulted the legislators and expressed his opinions. An incident in point is related by Judge Franklin Blades: "The first time I met him [Lincoln] was in a caucus of the Republican members of the Illinois House of Representatives, of which I was a member, in the winter of 1857. The meeting was held in Mr. Lincoln's office in Springfield, Illinois."[67] Another time Lincoln wrote to a client, "The Legislature having got out of the way, I at last find time to attend to the business you left me."[68]

James N. Brown served one term in the House from Sangamon County with Lincoln. He became known for his cattle breeding

---

[65] Sara John English, "Hon. Newton Cloud," *ISHSJ*, July, 1930.

[66] Ross C. Pillsbury, Chicago, Ill., September 13, 1960, letter to Paul Simon.

[67] *Abraham Lincoln by Some Men Who Knew Him* (Bloomington, Ill., Pantagraph, 1910), 109.

[68] *CW*, II, 98.

rather than his politics. But the action that raised his stature in history was collaborating with Jonathan B. Turner for the Land Grant Act of 1862 for colleges. In 1861, Brown sent a letter to Lincoln with a request, and Lincoln forwarded it to Seward with the note: "The writer of the letter . . . is one of the best men I know."[69]

Richard M. Young was one of the men Lincoln and the other legislators saw often. In 1837 they elected him to the United States Senate. Later he served as a justice of the Illinois Supreme Court and commissioner of the General Land Office in Washington, D. C. He died in a mental institution in Washington in 1853.

Thomas C. Browne was on the Illinois Supreme Court during all of Lincoln's legislative years, but the year after Lincoln retired, Browne was almost impeached, Lincoln serving as his attorney. Browne was known as a man "who never refused nor offered a drink."[70] One of his colleagues on the Supreme Court wrote later, "If he ever read a law book it was so long ago that he must have forgotten it."[71]

Lincoln's interest in internal improvements prompted him to make his first appearance at a national function. July 5–7, 1847, Lincoln—then a newly elected Congressman—attended a national River and Harbor Convention in Chicago. It was "the largest meeting that ever gathered in America." Its purpose was to protest President Polk's veto of a bill which made appropriations for rivers and harbors around the nation.[72] Lincoln and the others at the convention wanted federal action.

On the second day of the convention, a spokesman for the Polk administration defended the President's veto, and Lincoln replied to him. Horace Greeley reported for the *New York Tribune*: "Hon. Abraham Lincoln, a tall specimen of an Illinoian, just elected to Congress from the only Whig district in the State was called out and spoke briefly and happily in reply to Mr. Field."[73] At this time

[69] *Ibid.*, IV, 540.

[70] Beveridge, *Abraham Lincoln*, I, 177.

[71] Linder, *Reminiscences*, 173, quoting John Dean Caton.

[72] *Lincoln Lore*, July 7, 1947.

[73] *Ibid.*

Lincoln, although elected, had not been to Washington and it was his first bow on the national stage.

When he got to Washington and for the remainder of his life, Lincoln continued to be a strong advocate of internal improvements. One of the few speeches by Lincoln as a Congressman recorded at length in the *Congressional Globe Appendix* was on this subject. But while he advocated federal action, in opposition to those who said this was a job for the states, Lincoln advised proceeding cautiously; he had his Illinois legislative experience in mind. The federal government should do "something and still not do too much. . . . I would not borrow money. I am against an overwhelming, crushing system."[74]

In 1849 he showed his continued interest in this problem in an unusual way. He patented an invention which would enable "a steam boat or any other vessel . . . to pass over bars, or through shallow water, without discharging their cargoes."[75]

As President, he frequently showed interest in internal improvements projects. In his 1862 message to Congress he said, "The military and commercial importance of enlarging the Illinois and Michigan canal, and improving the Illinois River, is presented in the report of Colonel Webster to the Secretary of War. . . . I respectfully ask attention to it."[76]

Lincoln met Richard Yates in New Salem when Yates visited there while a student from college in Jacksonville. Yates saw Lincoln frequently when Lincoln was a legislator. Later Yates became a member of Congress, and in 1860 won election as governor of Illinois. He served in the United States Senate from 1865–71.

While campaigning for governor in 1860, Yates said of Lincoln, "We know he does not look very handsome, and some of the papers say he is positively ugly. Well, if all the ugly men in the United States vote for him, he will surely be elected."[77]

Mentor Graham, the New Salem teacher who had encouraged Lincoln to further his education and in this way helped prepare

[74] *CW*, I, 489.
[75] *Ibid.*, II, 33.
[76] *Ibid.*, V, 526.
[77] Speech of Hon. Richard Yates, Republican candidate for governor, Springfield, June 7, 1860, IHL.

him for his legislative service, in later years became somewhat bitter and moved to South Dakota.

He was a man of limited knowledge and many misspellings; the county school commissioner of Menard County "examined Mentor Graham . . . and had to refuse to give him a certificate of qualification except Fourth Grade."[78]

Lincoln regarded John Calhoun as a more difficult foe in debate than Douglas. He seemed to have every talent, although some politicians in Illinois considered him a little lazy. He was named surveyor-general of Kansas, thanks to the help of Douglas. In a short time he and two other men were running Kansas and doing it in favor of the proslavery forces.

As historian Allan Nevins has said, the Kansas problem "haunted the pillow of all thoughtful Americans."[79] Should the United States become a slave or a free country? Both in the North and South, Kansas was thought to be the pivot on which the nation would turn. In the White House sat James Buchanan, who had the looks of a President but little else. Buchanan was letting the nation drift toward Civil War. He thought he could satisfy the South by letting Kansas move toward slavery.

Calhoun occupied a key position in Kansas, where he had come after being a leading Democrat in Illinois and completing three terms as mayor of Springfield. He meant to keep Kansas open to slavery. He was president of the rigged legislative body that had been "elected" in Kansas. It met in Lecompton, Kansas, and drew up a constitution more proslavery than Georgia's. To get it accepted, he worked with others to falsify voting results in two important elections in a brazen way. In McGee County, Kansas, with fewer than one hundred qualified voters, there were 1,266 proslavery votes cast! In another small cluster of six homes, 1,628 votes were reported. A check showed that most of the names were written by the same person, all taken out of the city directory of Cincinnati.

This caused a national uproar—and not just with the Republicans and Whigs. People in the North, Democrats and Repub-

[78] A. M. Houser, *Lincoln's Education* (New York, Bookman, 1957), 108.

[79] Allan Nevins, *The Emergence of Lincoln* (New York, Charles Scribner's Sons, 1951), 133.

licans, were incensed. Robert Smith, former Illinois House colleague of Calhoun and Lincoln and now a member of Congress, called the Lecompton constitution "obnoxious, not only to the people of Kansas, but to a large majority of the people of the whole country."[80] Douglas had staked his reputation on letting the people of Kansas make their own choice on the direction in which they would go, and now that choice was being denied them. Douglas, "two parts politician and one part statesman," became furious at Calhoun and at Buchanan.[81] The leading Democrat in the North, he openly split with President Buchanan. Buchanan wanted Kansas admitted with Calhoun's proslavery constitution.

When Douglas confronted Calhoun with the evidence of the frauds at the Douglas home in Washington, Calhoun turned pale and left the house. Calhoun's fraud had become a national scandal. But more important than that, Calhoun had been instrumental in splitting the Democratic party into Northern and Southern wings. All of this took place in 1857 and 1858. By the presidential election year of 1860, it was impossible to weld the Democratic party. Douglas became the candidate of the Northern wing, but Calhoun's former assistant surveyor, Abraham Lincoln, was elected President by the new Republican party. Calhoun's support of Buchanan's weak policies made either civil war or division of the country inevitable.

Among Lincoln's fellow legislators who did not turn out well, Calhoun earned the blackest marks. Yet his frauds and inexcusable behavior led to the election of Lincoln.

In September of 1860—in the middle of the presidential campaign—John Hill, son of Samuel Hill of New Salem, wrote the pamphlet *Opposing Principles of Henry Clay and Abraham Lincoln*.[82] He alleged that Lincoln was being inconsistent on the slavery issue, and from Lincoln's legislative record he made statements that distorted the truth. Lincoln took time to give a lengthy reply. What is clear is that John Hill had little regard for facts and

---

[80] "Speech of Hon. R. Smith of Illinois Against the Admission of Kansas into the Union," delivered in the House of Representatives March 20, 1858, IHL.

[81] Nevins, *The Emergence of Lincoln*, 249.

[82] *CW*, IV, 104–108.

tried to use Lincoln's legislative record on slavery against him when it actually was to his credit.

Hill's father, Samuel Hill, was postmaster in New Salem until dissatisfaction with his performance gave the job to Lincoln. It is possible that young Hill inherited from his father a hostile attitude toward Lincoln.

This same John Hill gave currency to the Ann Rutledge story by a story he wrote in the *Menard Axis*, February 15, 1862. Most historians feel Hill got his facts as badly garbled in the latter case as in the former.

Ebenezer Peck, Democratic foe of Lincoln in the House, ended up a Republican and helped Lincoln get the Republican nomination. After Lincoln became President, he named Peck to the United States Court of Claims.

These vignettes could be multiplied. The aim is to give a few glimpses into the lives of some of the men with whom Lincoln served in Springfield and to show how these lives crossed with Lincoln's again and again on the pages of history.

Eight among his colleagues eventually became United States senators, five from Illinois and three from other states; others became cabinet members, high jurists, governors, and state officials.

The story of what happened to these men is one Lincoln followed with interest as it unfolded each day. It is also a story of men and events that directly and indirectly helped shape the fortunes of Abraham Lincoln.

Index

Hogan, John: 92, 143–44, 190
Hope, T. M.: 296
Horse racing: 199
Horse thieves: 166
Hughes, John: 27

Idaho: 308
Illinois and Michigan Canal: 25,
 29, 34, 36, 52, 72, 155, 185–86,
 261–63, 318
Illinois Asylum for the Education
 of the Deaf and Dumb: 160
Illinois Beet Sugar Manufacturing
 Company: 27, 61
Illinois Central Railroad: 292
Illinois College: 31
Illinois Constitution: 134, 228,
 245, 248, 256, 305
Illinois Republican (Springfield):
 68–69, 73, 177
Illinois River: 25, 255, 318
Illinois State Journal: 296
Illinois State Register (Vandalia):
 51, 57, 70, 84, 87, 97–98, 171–
 72, 176–77, 179–80, 184, 192,
 194–95, 201, 207–208, 211–12,
 216, 218, 220–21, 229–30, 242–
 43
Illinois Temperance Herald (Al-
 ton): 165
Illiopolis, Ill.: 60, 93
Indiana: 4, 125, 129, 154
Indians: 8, 15, 19, 32
Insurance, in Mechanics Union:
 199
Interest rates: 6, 8, 41, 52, 67, 113,
 165, 186, 233–35, 241–42, 263,
 279
Internal improvements: 4, 6, 8, 39,
 42, 45, 48–54, 60–62, 65, 69–70,

72, 76–105, 113, 116, 151–56,
 158, 173–78, 182–88, 193, 202,
 210, 223, 225–27, 232–36, 241,
 254, 258–59, 273, 277, 278, 282,
 291, 308, 317–18
Iowa, Ill.: 255
Iowa, state of: 198
Ireland: 224, 297

Jackson, Andrew: 10–12, 16, 21,
 30, 43, 107, 109, 178, 193, 211,
 226, 230, 258, 283
Jackson, William: 167
Jackson County, Ill.: 89
Jacksonville, Ill.: 14, 18, 51, 59–
 60, 90, 92, 96–97, 100, 102, 107,
 114, 126–27, 174–75, 177, 181,
 183, 190, 206, 261, 264, 318
Jacksonville Female Academy: 31
Jacksonville Gazette and News:
 100
Jacksonville Illinoian: 150, 182
Jacksonville Patriot: 91
Jasper County, Ill.: 37
Jefferson County, Ky.: 127
Jefferson, Thomas: 193
Jenkins, Alexander M.: 38, 253
Jo Daviess County, Ill.: 21
Johnson, Andrew: 305, 313
Johnson County, Ill.: 58
Judiciary: 23, 113–14, 134, 140–
 41, 150, 158, 165, 167, 194–95,
 197, 199, 205–206, 225, 247–53,
 276
Justices of the Peace: 25–26, 75,
 165, 179, 266

Kane County, Ill.: 177
Kane, E. K.: 37–38
Kansas: 285–88, 308, 319–20